METHLEY 2000

Published by James H Melvin

Cover illustration

ROBERT WATERTON ESQUIRE

Lord of Waterton, Doubledyke & Saxilby, Co. Lincs.,
Methley, Woodhall & Healaugh, Co. Yorks., Merchedene, Co. Lancs.,
Walwick Grange, Co. Northumberland., Plompton, Co. Warwick.
High Sherrif of Lincoln (1410)
High Steward of the Duchy of Lancaster
Master of the King's Horse & Armour & Master of the King's Running Hounds
Constable of the Castles of Pontefract, Tickhill & Donnington
Steward, Master Forrester & Bailiff of the Lordship of Hatfield;
Steward of the Manor Courts and Wapentakes in the Lordship of Sowrbysshire;
Steward & Master Forrester of Spofforth & Hayley, Co. Yorks.

Published in the year 2000

Printed and bound in Great Britain by FM Repro. Ltd, Roberttown,
West Yorkshire.

ISBN: 0 9539464 0 1

CONTENTS

ACKNOWLEDGEMENTS:

I am very grateful to the following for the use of maps, photographs and other information.

Donald H.C. Briggs (A Merchant, a Banker and the Coal Trade)
Russ Fletcher (heraldry)
Mrs J.E.K. Frogley (A Church Processional Chant)
George E. Kirk (Methley and Mickletown Churches)
E.R. Manley (Meet the Miner)
Henry Moore Foundation (photograph)
Ordnance Survey Department (maps)
R.J.B. Mining (open-cast coal mining)
Thoresby Society (History of Methley)
David Waterton-Anderson (genealogy of the Waterton family)

FOREWORD

Memory is perhaps one of the most fundamental attributes that Man possesses. Of the many benefits it undoubtedly brings, our skills, experience and knowledge are facilitated directly by our ability to store information. When it comes to the more social and pleasurable side of our lives, we draw much from recalling the happy, intriguing and interesting things we have experienced or learnt over our allotted span. Since 'Homo Sapiens' first walked upon this Earth, the process of passing on our experiences, knowledge and memories, continues to create a unique and very special bond between the generations. It is of course, immensely gratifying to witness the uptake of interest by younger generations of what one has held dear and precious in one's own lifetime. The process through which Jim Melvin has gone to produce this book, fits squarely into this mould. The recording of significant information that would otherwise fade as generation succeeds generation, is tremendously important and provides not only a sense of pride in our heritage, but also helps to stimulate our sense of belonging and the value of tradition. There is every potential that this work will be a catalyst for the minds and hearts of many who will open its pages.

Everingham

David A.R. Waterton-Anderson
4th Baron Everingham of Laxton

Carlton-juxta-Snaith
September 2000

14th & 15th century descents of
WATERTON OF WATERTON & METHLEY

WILLIAM de WATERTON Lord of the Manor of Waterton, Co. Lincs. Not of full age in 1315. Paid for one archer to go beyond the seas, 24th May 1346. Served King Edward III in the Scottish wars, he was a member with John & Ralph, his brothers, of the garrison of Berwick upon Tweed, 20th Apl. 1340
= ELIZABETH, dau. of Roger Newmarche (Novo Mercarto) of Womersley, Co. Yorks. & Brecon, Wales.

JOHN de WATERTON Lord of the Manor of Waterton. Esquire of the Body to Henry Bolingbroke, Duke of Hereford. nat: (c1340) Swore to support the "Five Lords Appellant" 20th March 1388.
= JOAN, dau. of Thomas Methley of Methley, Co. Yorks.

CATHERINE, wife to Thomas Egerton.

SIR HUGH WATERTON Lord of the Manor of Wroot, Co. Notts. Receiver of the revenues from the Manor of Minchinhampton, Co. Gloucs. Knighted 1396. Attorney to John of Gaunt, Duke of Lancaster. Member of the Privy Council to Henry IV, 1st Mar 1404. Constable of Queensborough Castle, Isle of Sheppey. Constable of Windsor Castle 5th Feb 1405. ob: Jul 1409.
= ELIANOR, dau. of Robert de Mowbray.
= KATHERINE, dau. of Alexander Walden (widow of John Bromewich).

ROBERT WATERTON Lord of Waterton, Isle of Axholme, Co. Lincs., & Methley, Co. Yorks. nat: (c1365) Esquire of the body to Henry Bolingbroke, Duke of Hereford (Henry IV), with whom he went on Crusade to the Holy Land. Constable of the castles of Pontefract (1399-1425), Tickhill & Castle Donnington. High Steward of the Duchy of Lancaster, Master of the King's Horse & Armour & Master of the Running Hounds. Jailer to James I King of Scots & Scots Nobles & many French Nobles from Agincourt. ob: 1424/5 (will dated: 10th Jan 1424/5) bur: Waterton Chapel, Methley.
= CECILY, dau. of Sir Robert Fleming of Woodhall, Methley, Co. Yorks. Niece of Bishop Fleming, founder of Lincoln Coll. Oxford. nat: (c1375)

ELEANOR, wife to Sir Robert Bapthorpe of Bapthorpe & Osgodby, Co. Yorks. Had one bovate of land in Waterton on marrying in 1409.

JOHN WATERTON, Esq. of the Body to King Henry V. Constable of the castle of Windsor 28th Jan 1414. Banner Bearer & Master of the King's Horse & Armour at the battle of Agincourt 1415 (mentioned in the King's will).
= ELEANOR, dau. of John 9th Lord Clifford (by his wife Elizabeth, dau. of Henry Percy - Harry Hotspur).

THOMAS WATERTON Held one knight's fee at Uggeshall, Suffolk, of John Nevill 1388. Present at the battle of Agincourt, 1415, with his brother John and a retinue of 8 men-at-arms & 24 foot archers.

JOHN WATERTON ob: s.p.v.p.

BLANCHE, wife to Sir Robert Challons

ELIZABETH, wife to John ap Harry of Poston, co. Hereford

KATHERINE ob: s.p.

Children of John Waterton and Eleanor:

JEROME WATERTON ob: s.p.v.p.

JOHN WATERTON ob: s.p.v.p.

MUNDANA, wife to Thomas Metham of Metham, Co. Yorks. viv: 1430-32 (Heraldic glass in Metham chapel, Howden Minster: Metham impaling Waterton)

SIR ROBERT WATERTON, Lord of the Manors of Everingham & Birkin, Co. Yorks. & Laxton, Co. Notts. (jure uxor) nat: (c1385) ob: 1425 (Inq. p.m. Wakefield 11th June 1425) bur: Waterton Chapel, Methley.
= JOAN, dau. of William & co-heir of her brother, Robert de Everingham, 3rd. Baron Everingham of Laxton. (cr: 1309) nat: (c1370) [widow of Sir William Ellis of Kiddal, Co. Yorks. by whom she had one son - Robert Ellis] ob: (ante 1422)
= DAME MARGARET CLARRELL, K.G., dau. of Thomas Clarrell of Aldwark, Co. Yorks. [widow of John FitzWilliam of Sprotborough, Co. Yorks. & subsequently married Sir William Gascoigne of Gawthorpe, co. Yorks.] Wed Robert Waterton in 1422. 'Dame of the Garter.'

SIR ROBERT WATERTON, Lord of the Manors of Waterton &, Doubledyke, co. Lincs., Methley, Everingham, Birkin, Barley, Haighton & Potterton, co. Yorks. & Laxton, co. Notts. nat: 1408/9. Knighted 1434. High Sheriff of Yorks. 1441. ob: 13th Dec 1476. (Inq. p.m: Wentbridge 26th Apl 1477 found seized of nine Manors and many other land holdings in Yorks., Lincs., Notts. & Northants.)
= JANE dau. of John Meeres of Kirton-in- Holland, Co. Lincs.
= BEATRICE, dau. of Thomas, 8th Lord Clifford (by his wife Joan, dau. of Thomas, Lord Dacre) & niece of Maude, Countess of Cambridge (wife of Richard Plantagenet, Earl of Cambridge) ob: s.p. 11th Mar. 1480/1

JANE (or Cecelia) WATERTON sister & heiress in her issue, of her brother. nat: (c1400) marr: 15th Aug 1417 at St Oswald's, Methley. ob: (post 1434) bur: Waterton Chapel, Methley.
= LIONEL, 6th LORD WELLES, K.G. (son of Ives or Eon de Welles by Maude, dau of Ralph, 3rd Lord Greystoke). nat: 1406. Knighted 1426. Lieut. of Ireland 1437-1442. Summoned to Parl. as a Baron from 1432. 'Knight of the Garter' 14th May 1457. Wed Margaret Beachamp 20th Apl 1447. Slain at the battle of Towton, Palm Sunday 29th Mar 1461. bur: Waterton Chapel, Methley.
= MARGARET, dau. of Sir John Beauchamp of Bletso (widow of (1) Sir Oliver St John & (2) John Beaufort, Duke of Somerset, by whom she was mother to Margaret Countess of Richmond - mother to King Henry VII) nat (c1410) ob: 3rd June 1482.

SIR THOMAS WATERTON Lord of the Manor of Woodhall Stanley, Co. Yorks. (which had been gifted by Lord Viscount Welles) nat: (c1440) ob: 28th Feb. 1502/3
= MARGARET, dau. of Sir John Savage of Clifton, Co. Chester. (by his wife Katherine, dau. of Sir Thomas, 1st Baron Stanley & sister of the 1st Earl of Derby). ob: 1st May 1488.

RICHARD, LORD WILLOUGHBY & WELLES nat: c.1428/30 Beheaded 12th Mar. 1469/70 at the battle of 'Loose Coat Field,' Stamford.
= JOAN, dau. & heir of Robert, 6th Lord Willoughby d'Eresby.

ELEANOR, wife to (1) Lord Hoo & Hastings; (2) James Laurence.

CECILY, wife to Sir Robert Willoughby (son of Sir Thomas Willoughby of Parham).

MARGARET, wife to (1) Sir Thomas Dymoke (beheaded 1469/70); (2) Robert Radcliffe.

KATHERINE, wife to (1) Sir Thomas de la Laund of Horbling, Co. Lincs.; (2) Robert Tempest.

JOHN, VISCOUNT WELLES, K.G. mar: Lady Cecily Plantagenet, dau. of King Edward IV.

A BRIEF HISTORY OF THE PARISH OF METHLEY

The name is found with various spellings, e.g. Medelai, Medley, Medelay, Metheley, etc. and, as at present, Methley.

The word Methley appears to be derived from the Old English Middelan leagh – the middle lea or meadow land. It is not difficult to imagine how Methley, lying as it does between the Aire and the Calder rivers, obtained its name.

The history of Methley before the Norman conquest can only be a matter of conjecture but we know something of the district of which it forms a part. In Romano-British times it formed part of the kingdom of the Brigantes. It contained several important Roman settlements among them Legeolium (Castleford).

The earliest mentioned building in Methley is the Parish Church dedicated to St. Oswald (King Oswald) who, in 635 succeeded to the throne of Northumbria. There is no record of the date at which the village first possessed a church but it would appear to have been between the death of Oswald in 642 when he was killed in battle against Penda, King of Mercia, and the coming of the Normans in 1066.

With the coming of the Normans we find ourselves on firmer ground. The Domesday record of Methley reads as follows:

> In Medelai Osulf and Cnut had 8 carucates of land for geld, where 5 ploughs can be. Ilbert has 17 villeins and 5 bordars there with 5 ploughs. Pasturable woodland 1 league in length and 1 in breadth. A church is there and a priest. In King Edward's time it was worth 60s., now 40s.

The carucate, the land of a plough, varied in different districts according to the nature of the soil, but seems roughly to have corresponded to the hide, which contained about one hundred and twenty acres, so that the arable land in Methley in 1087 amounted to something like nine hundred and sixty acres.

Five ploughs meant five yolk of eight oxen, which does not appear to be a very large allowance for the acreage. It must be borne in mind, however, that land was only cropped twice in three years – one year it was in wheat, one in oats, barley, beans, peas or tares, and one in fallow.

We know little more of Methley in Norman times beyond the fact that the territorial Saxon owners were ejected by King William and their property given to Ilbert de Lacy, one of his own followers. Ilbert de Lacy appears to have made Pontefract his headquarters and it was he who built the castle at Pontefract.

In 1313 and again in 1323 we read of royal pardons extended to John de Methley, who probably held the manor under the de Laceys. The pardon in each case was for following Thomas, Earl of Lancaster, who was in rebellion against the king. At some time the de Laceys appear to have passed on their manor of Methley to the hospital of St. Nicholas at Pontefract – whether by sale or by gift is not known. During the 14th century John de Waterton of Lincolnshire married a lady of the de Methley family. In 1408-9 the Master of the Hospital of St Nicholas at Pontefract released to John Waterton all his rights to Woodhall in Methley and in the year 1410 Thomas Towton, then Master of the Hospital of St Nicholas at Pontefract, exchanged the manor of Methley with Robert Waterton for the advowson of Gosberkirk (now called Gosberton) in Lincolnshire.

Robert Waterton, who was married to Cicely, the daughter and heir of Robert Fleming of Woodhall, Methley, and now the new Lord of the Manor of Methley, was a man of great importance and his name frequently appears in documents of this time. Shakespeare makes mention of him in his play Richard II. Robert Waterton died in 1425 and was succeeded by his son, Robert Waterton, aged sixteen years, who later married Beatrix, the daughter of

Thomas, Sixth Lord Clifford. This Sir Robert died in December 1476 and left no legitimate offspring. His estate was divided between the representatives of the four daughters of his sister, Cecilia.

Cecilia Waterton had married Lionel, Lord Welles, who was killed at the Battle of Towton on Palm Sunday, 1461. She had one son, Richard, who was beheaded in 1469. She also had four daughters, one of whom was Margaret, who married Sir Thomas Dymoke who was executed 1469-70 for suspicion of supporting Lord Welles and the Lancastrians. They had one son Robert.

In 1488 an act of partition was drawn up dividing the Waterton property and Sir Robert Dymoke was awarded the manors of Methley and Woodhall in Methley. Sir Robert died 13th April 1544 and was buried at Scrivelsby. He left a son and heir, Edward.

In 1590 a descendant of the Dymoke family, Sir Edward Dymoke, who was king's Champion at the coronation of James I, disposed of the manor of Methley for £2,060 to John Savile, Baron of the Exchequer to Queen Elizabeth I and founder of the present Lord of the Manor of Methley. Sir John Savile, a descendant of the Savile family, was installed as Knight of the Bath, on 23 June 1749, created Baron Pollington of Longford, Ireland on 8 November 1753, and created Earl of Mexborough of Lifford, Co. Donegal on 11 February 1766.

The King's Champion

At the crowning of a king of England, the king's Champion must ride into Westminster Hall when the king sits at his banquet, and then, clad in full harness and bestriding a charger of the best, must challenge all men in defence of the king's right, with iron glove thrice cast upon the pavement.

The first king's Champion was **Marmion of Scrivelsby**, a family that long provided the hereditary Champions at English coronations. It came in with **William I** (the Conqueror), but became extinct under **Edward I**. It was revived when Sir John Dymoke (d.1381) by his marriage (c.1350) with the heiress of the Marmions acquired the Lincolnshire manor of Scrivelsby, and became king's Champion at **Richard II**'s coronation. They had a son John Dymoke (d. 1422) who was king's Champion at the coronations of **Henry IV** and **Henry V**. The succession continued through to Sir Thomas Dymoke who married Margaret Welles, daughter of Lionel Lord Welles. They had a son Robert Dymoke. (This Thomas Dymoke was beheaded in 1469 on suspicion of supporting Lord Welles in the Lancastrian cause.)

We now have to refer to the Waterton family pedigree. Sir Robert Waterton died in 1476 without male heir and in 1488 an act of partition was drawn up dividing the Waterton property between the representatives of the four daughters of his sister Cecilia. One of these daughters was Margaret the wife of the executed Thomas Dymoke, and it is their son Robert Dymoke who was awarded the manors of Methley and Woodhall. This Robert Dymoke (d. 1544) was Champion at the coronation of **Richard III**, **Henry VII** and **Henry VIII**. Edward Dymoke (d.1567) was Champion for **Edward VI**, **Queen Mary** and **Elizabeth I**.

The function of the king's Champion was last exercised at **George IV**'s coronation by Henry Dymoke (1801-65), but Dymokes bore the standard of England at the coronations of **Edward VII**, **George V**, **George VI**, and **Queen Elizabeth II.**

SOME OTHER NOTABLE PERSONS OF METHLEY

Sir Martin Frobisher (c.1535-1594)

English sailor born at Altofts, near Wakefield, Yorkshire. At the age of 11 he went to London and in 1554, he went to sea, sailing for some years as a pirate until he came to the notice of Queen Elizabeth I and was appointed a flag officer in the Royal Navy. In 1576 with the 'Gabriel' and the 'Michael' and a complement of 35 men, he set off in search of a Northwest Passage to Cathay. The Michael was abandoned, but Frobisher, almost lost off the coast of Greenland, reached Labrador and discovered and named Frobisher Bay.

In 1578 on arrival at Frobisher Bay on a subsequent expedition Sir Martin commanded his chaplain to conduct a service of prayer and thanksgiving using the service of Holy Communion according to the rites of the Anglican Church, a significant fact in church history as the Reformation was still taking place in England and the Book of Common Prayer used at the service was only a few years old. This was the first time the new Anglican service of Holy Communion was used in North America, and in 1978 the Archbishop of Canterbury flew to Frobisher Bay to lead the commemorative service on the four hundredth anniversary of the first Communion service there. Sir Martin failed to find a Northwest Passage to Cathay but in addition to discovering Frobisher Bay he also discovered Baffin Island to the west of Hudson Strait.

In 1585 Sir Martin commanded a vessel in Sir Francis Drake's expedition to the West Indies. In 1588 he commanded 'Triumph' and fought along with Sir Francis Drake and Sir John Hawkins against the Spanish Armada, for which he was knighted. In 1594 he was mortally wounded at the siege of Crozon, near Brest.

Sir Martin married twice, his second wife being Dame Dorothy Widmerpoole, widow of Sir William Widmerpoole and daughter of Lord Wentworth. After Sir Martin's death his widow became the third wife of John Savile, Baron, of Methley in June 1597. She died in January 1601 at Methley and was buried in St Oswald's Chapel between the tombs of Lord Welles and Robert Waterton.

Sir Martin had some connection with Methley in that he lived at the Manor House in Methley and also owned property at Low Common. It is interesting to think that he may have worshipped at St Oswald's Church.

Descendants of Sir Martin still live in this area. Sadie Morley, daughter of Florence Frobisher and Ernest Morley, lives at Methley and Joan Richardson, daughter of Annie Frobisher and Albert Richardson, lives at Woodlesford.

Edward Shippen, Mayor of Philadelphia

William Shippen was Overseer of the Poor at Methley in 1642, and Overseer of the Highways in 1656, and some facts of interest with regard to him and his family still remain. In 1626 William Shippen married Mary Nunes (or Nunns), who died in 1672, having had six children. Of these Robert aged 33, Anne aged one month, and Dorothy aged three years, all died at Methley. Their daughter Mary married William Chapman of Normanton in 1663. William, the fifth child, went up to University College, Oxford, as a servitor in 1653, possibly on the foundation of Otho Hunt, and subsequently became Fellow of his College and Proctor of the University. He was preferred successively to the livings of Prestbury, Kirkheaton, Aldford and Stockport where he died in 1693. (His father had also died there in 1681.)

Edward, the youngest child (b. 1639) emigrated to Boston in 1668, where he became a Quaker and was twice publicly whipped for attending the Friends' Meeting. He removed to Philadelphia where in 1695 he was elected Speaker of the Assembly, and in October 1701 was named by William Penn in the Charter of Philadelphia as the first mayor of the city. After filling many honourable offices and bearing no inconsiderable part in the building up of the young colony, he died a very wealthy man at Philadelphia on October 2nd, 1712. He was long remembered as possessing the biggest person, the biggest house and the biggest coach. Edward's home near the north-west corner of Spruce and Second Street was called The Great House or The Governor's House.

Edward married three times and had eleven children, one of whom, Joseph, became the grandfather of (another) Edward Shippen (1728-1806).

This grandson, Edward Shippen, attended school in Philadelphia and later went to London, read law and was called to the English bar in 1750. In 1753 he married Margaret Francis, they had nine children one of whom, Margaret, married Benedict Arnold who fought on the American side in the Revolution (1775-1803) but who defected to the English side in 1780 and became a general. Edward Shippen became Chief Justice of Pennsylvania in 1799, he died in 1806.

It is not known what happened to the The Great House of Edward Shippen but a Shippen residence was built in about 1750 by William Shippen on land granted in 1744 to Joseph and William Shippen. This house at 240 South Fourth Street has been extensively renovated and in 1989 it was opened to provide office accommodation for the Diocese of Pennsylvania.

David Dunderdale

David Dunderdale of Methley established a pottery at Castleford about 1790 for the manufacture of the finer kinds of pottery, especially Queen's Ware and black Egyptian. Mr Dunderdale took into partnership a Mr Plowes, and in 1803 the firm was D. Dunderdale & Co. The works were closed in 1820. David Dunderdale lived at Dunford House, Methley, and was Churchwarden and Overseer of the Poor from 1790 to 1814. He was a First-Lieutenant in the Pontefract Volunteers of 1798-9, of which the Hon. Henry Savile was Major, and the Hon. Charles Savile and John, Earl of Mexborough, were Captains. It is said that David Dunderdale suffered heavy losses during the French War from his goods being captured at sea. He died at Trafalgar Street, Leeds, May 6th 1824, aged 53. There is in the Parish Church at Methley a copper plate with an inscription to the memory of Christopher, aged one year, and Isabella, aged sixteen years, the children of David Dunderdale. The reverse of this plate has been engraved for printing transfers for dishes, etc., presumably at Castleford Pottery.

The Embleton Family

The name Embleton is well known in the village. An estate of houses at Embleton Road, Watergate bears the name.

Thomas William Embleton was the son of Thomas Embleton of Newcastle-upon-Tyne and was born in that city on October 4th 1809. He was educated at Witton-le-Wear Grammar School and afterwards at the University of Edinburgh. His apprenticeship as a mining engineer was served at Gosforth and other collieries under his uncle, Mr George Hill, of Kenton, near Newcastle-upon-Tyne. In 1830, at the age of 21 years, he succeeded Mr Blenkinsop in the management of the Brandling Collieries at Middleton, near Leeds, a position which he retained until 1865. In 1866 he took charge of the extensive collieries belonging to Messrs J. & J. Charlesworth, and retired in 1888. During his connection with that firm he was responsible for the sinking of several new shafts to various seams, among others the Dodworth Silkstone Colliery, Barnsley, and the Albany pits, Rawmarsh. He was consulting engineer for Lord Mexborough for a number of years, and for Mr George Lane Fox, Bramham, near Leeds, and also for the Wharncliffe Silkstone Colliery, near Barnsley, during which time he sank a number of pits and introduced a new system of haulage. In addition to holding these appointments he was a partner in, and had the control and supervision and the sinking of the Monkbretton Colliery, which at that time was the most north-easterly winning of the celebrated Barnsley seam of coal. He was a member of the North of England Institute of Mining and Mechanical Engineers from September 6th 1855 and contributed many papers, one of which was Notes on the Oaks Colliery Explosion on 12th December 1866 and on the Subsequent Explosions.

Earlier T.W. Embleton married Caroline Anne 1812-1875, daughter of Mr Thomas Easton, coal owner of Gateshead, County Durham, and they had nine children, all born at Middleton, Leeds. His children were Caroline Anne 1837-1887, Isobel Adelaide 1839-?, Emma 1840-1903, Louisa Gertrude 1842-1916, Thomas William 1843-1921, Denis Maude 1846-1909, James 1848-1868, Emily Maude 1851-1873, Henry Cawood 1855-1930. The family is first shown in the 1871 census as living at the Cedars, Church Side. It would appear that they moved from Middleton to the Cedars in 1868 after the Rector of Methley moved from the Cedars to the newly built Rectory at Church Side in 1867. All the family, with the exception of Isobel Adelaide, are buried in Methley Churchyard. It is not known where Isobel Adelaide died or where she is buried.

The experience and skill of Mr Thomas William Embleton rendered his assistance at colliery explosions most valuable, nowhere more so than at the disastrous explosion at the Oaks Colliery, near Barnsley on December 12th 1866, where, with Mr Woodhouse and other eminent mining engineers, he had control of the recovery of the colliery. The care with which this was done is evidenced by the paper which he contributed to the Midland Institute of Mining, Civil, and Mechanical Engineers.

Notes on the Oaks Colliery Explosion, on the 12th December, 1866, and on the Subsequent Explosions. By T.W. Embleton

"The first explosion took place at 1.15 pm on Wednesday, 12th December and was indicated to the neighbourhood by a loud report and by a dense volume of black smoke and dust issuing from the shafts.

The winding engine was slightly injured and the cage in No. 2 shaft was blown away and one of the couplings snapped. At No. 1 shaft the cage was broken and disconnected from the rope. Smoke from the down-cast shafts continued for about five minutes and then suddenly ceased, and fresh air began to descend the shafts. When this was observed the rope from No. 2 was taken off the drum, and the rope of No. 1 shaft was wound to the top and examined and found to be injured. The broken cage was taken off and replaced by a new one, and at about two pm Mr Dymond, accompanied by Mr D Tewart, the Underviewer, and Mr C Siddons, one of the deputies, descended and found many men lying at the bottom of the pit, all much burnt. They were drawn to bank as soon as possible and every exertion was made to recover the remainder of the men. Searches were vigorously prosecuted during the whole of Wednesday afternoon and night by Mr Dymond, Mr Potter, Mr Brown, Mr Parkin Jeffcock, Mr Smith, Mr Platts, Mr Maddison, Mr Minto, and other viewers and deputies, aided by seventy or eighty volunteers. They succeeded by 5 pm in recovering thirty men and lads, and before morning the number was increased to eighty, of whom only nineteen were found alive.

Mr Parkin Jeffcock reached the colliery shortly after ten o'clock on the evening of Wednesday, and after having examined the colliery plan in the office, he sent for Mr Minto. From him and Mr Dymond he learnt all they were able to detail respecting the accident and the measures which had been adopted to recover the bodies and reinstate the mine.

Mr Jeffcock, with Mr Minto and Mr Smith (Lundhill), went down the shaft and met Mr Brown, Mr Potter, Mr Cooper, Mr Platts, and others, who were about to ascend, and after a consultation as to the state of the mine, these gentlemen came to the surface. Mr Jeffcock had now been in the mine for several hours, and Mr Dymond, Mr Potter, Mr Brown, Mr Smith (Monkwearmouth), and Mr Minto were about to descend to relieve Mr Jeffcock and others, but Mr Jeffcock sent up word to have the temperature of the air in the upcast shaft ascertained. This was being done, and one of the party was in the act of lowering a thermometer when the force of another explosion from this shaft drove them one over the other to some distance. This explosion took place about nine o'clock am on Thursday, 13th December. The cage at No. l pit was blown into the head gear, where it remained broken.

Mr Jeffcock, Mr Smith (Lundhill), Mr Tewart, and 25 other men (volunteers) were down the pit at the time of this explosion and were killed.

No change was noticed at the shafts till about 7.40 pm when a dense smoke was seen to issue from No. 2 shaft, succeeded by a violent blast of wind; then smoke, accompanied by flames, and afterwards by showers of sparks, as from burning wood. This discharge continued for hours. The furnace shaft and No. 1 pit became downcasts after this explosion.

On Friday morning, the 14th, about 4.30, those who were placed at the pits to give notice of any change, heard the signal bell ring. They shouted down the shaft, but got no reply. A bottle of brandy and water was then lowered to those supposed to be at the bottom of the shaft No. 1, and the bottle was found to have been detached from the rope, and hopes were entertained that some of those below would be got out alive.

The gin rope was taken off the upcast shaft and wound on the drum of the saw mill engine, and the steam was got up and a pulley placed temporarily over No. 1 shaft. By this time the viewers who had remained at Barnsley were summoned, and had arrived at the colliery. It was then agreed that as all was in readiness, an attempt should be made to rescue those who had given the signal. Messrs. Mammat and T.W Embleton junior (mining engineers), volunteered to make the hazardous attempt to bring up those who were below. They found some difficulty in reaching the bottom of the shaft and securing their lights, owing to the large feeders of water falling down the shaft in consequence of the dams being choked up with the dirt thrown up by the explosions. They succeeded in finding one man alive, Samuel Brown, whom they brought safely to the surface; no one else could be heard or seen, and the sanguine hopes before entertained were sadly put an end to.

They observed a large mass of burning material near the top of the incline, probably the timber work there, and the corves of coals in the siding, evidently the cause of the showers of sparks before noticed. These had been ignited probably by the second explosion.

On the same day a further consultation was held, and as there was not the slightest probability that any one remained alive in the pit, it was resolved that the shafts be sealed up."

There were seventeen explosions at the colliery, the last at 3.20 am Tuesday, 18th December. The disaster took the lives of 361 men and boys, including rescuers, 23 of whom were volunteers from other collieries.

Some years later when J. E. Mammatt, the colliery viewer of the Oaks was giving evidence before the Royal Commission of Accidents in Mines (1871-81), Sir George Elliot recalled the occasion:

> I believe you were at the Oaks when I was there with Mr Woodhouse. I remember you performed a very daring deed in going down with young Mr Embleton, for which I thought you ought to have been rewarded with the Victoria Cross.

As mentioned earlier their descent was perilous in the extreme for, as Embleton later described, the explosion had blocked the pump dams and huge feeders of water poured down the shaft as uncontrolled as waterfalls. Only with the greatest of difficulties could they keep a light burning at all.

The Oaks disaster remained Britain's worst mining disaster until 1913 when an explosion at Senghenydd, Glamorgan took the lives of 439 miners.

DEATH OF H C EMBLETON aged 76 at his home 'Nest House', Felling-on-Tyne, on 7 February 1930

"Mr Embleton was one of the best known mining engineers in England. In 1895 he was one of the founders of the Leeds Choral Union. He used to play the organ at Leeds Parish Church; he could also play the piano, cello and harp.

After the Leeds Centenary Celebrations in 1926 he received the freedom of the City. The French Government conferred on him the Diploma of Officier de L'Instruction Publique. He was also a Fellow of the Royal Geographical Society. In Autumn of 1928 he presented his collection of Leeds Old Pottery to the Leeds Art Gallery, possibly the finest collection in the world of that particular craft. He was a great believer in the Entente Cordiale and as an expression of that he took the entire Leeds Choral Union and the London Symphony Orchestra to France about 3 years ago. They gave a number of important concerts and he paid all expenses which amounted to £7,000.

In 1924 the members of the Choral Union showed their appreciation by presenting him with a bust of himself in white marble which is now housed in Temple Newsam.

When Mr Embleton laid the foundation stone for the new chancel at Methley he said he had lived opposite the church (at the Cedars, Churchside) for a good many years and looking from his bedroom window he had in mind that the old restoration was not in accordance with the beauty of the remainder of the church and he hoped to be able to do something to make it in accordance with what it originally was.

The sporting world knew Mr Embleton through the F.A. 'Embleton Cup'. Mr Embleton died a bachelor.

During the 1914-18 war he maintained a convalescent hospital for wounded soldiers and his care continued for them after they left the place. He was one of a family of nine children and the last survivor.

Mr Embleton was actively engaged in the pursuits of private hobbies right up to being taken ill. He had always been interested in the development of coal mines and the cultivation of music. His father was Mr Thomas William Embleton, a mining engineer, who died more than 30 years ago.

Interment took place in Methley on Monday, when extraordinary interest was taken by the public in general. The church was not big enough to hold all the people who desired to hear the service. The coffin had been brought by road from Felling-on-Tyne that morning after a special service at St Chad's, Gateshead, where Mr Embleton attended when in residence at his Durham home. The coffin was carried from the 'Cedars' opposite, followed by Dr Dennis Embleton, his wife and daughter, of London. The coffin was met at the church gates by the Bishop of Knaresborough and Rector of Methley Dr L Smith, the Reverend T Hadfield, Assistant Curate, The Reverend H W Ellwood, Vicar of St Chad's, Gateshead, The Lord Mayor of Leeds, Mr M G Morrison, and Sir Edward Airey, President, Sir Henry Coward and members of the Leeds Choral Union. A memorial service was also held at Leeds Parish Church."

(The obituary notice was taken from the 'Castleford & Pontefract Express' dated 14 February 1930).

EDUCATION

Up to 1870 education for the children of working class parents was provided solely by private individuals, although after 1833 the State gave some assistance in the form of financial grants. From the Middle Ages wealthy landowners and other persons sometimes made provision in their wills for the establishment and endowment of schools for children living on their estates, and many such schools were founded.

Between 1750 and 1850 a large number of private schools came into existence and working class parents who were willing to pay a few pence a week could have their children instructed in reading, writing and arithmetic but the majority were more or less Dame schools in which the children learnt little more than to write their names and read a few simple sentences.

At the beginning of the 19th century the monitorial system was devised; briefly the children of the school were divided into sections, each in charge of a monitor. The master taught a lesson to the monitors and they in turn drilled the information into their respective classes.

The Factory Act of 1833 provided for the compulsory education of all children employed in textile factories for two hours each day. If there was not a suitable school the factory inspectors were empowered to procure the establishment of one. Unfortunately the Act contained no financial provision for the building of schools, so some children were taught in the factories and it is related that in one factory they were taught in the boiler house by the fireman who was engaged in stoking the furnace. It was difficult, too, for children working in a factory to attend an outside school for two hours each day, as work began in the factory long before the schools opened and finished long after they had closed.

In 1839 the state made an annual grant of £30,000 each to the Church of England for Promoting the Education of the Poor and to the Nonconformists who had founded the British and Foreign Schools Society for the purpose of building schools.

In 1846 an effort was made to end the monitorial system; wherever possible monitors were replaced by pupil teachers apprenticed for five years and when this was completed they proceeded to a training college by a system of scholarships.

In 1853 these schools were assisted financially by maintenance grants based on average attendance.

In 1861 a royal commission reported in favour of payment by results and government grants in future would depend on the passing of a proficiency test by each scholar in reading, writing and arithmetic at the annual visit of the inspector.

The Elementary Education Act of 1870 established a dual system. The voluntary or church schools were retained but the nonconformists received no aid from the local rates. Every local authority was obliged to set up a school board elected by the rate payers, the primary function of which was to erect schools in all districts where there was no school accommodation or it was inadequate; they could also levy local rate aid and they could also appoint their own officials, teachers and others necessary to the running of a school. Neither was education free, the 1870 act expected parents to contribute to the cost of providing this education. An upper limit of 9d a week per child was imposed but remission of fees for necessitous children was allowed.

Local school boards could also frame by-laws making school attendance compulsory for children over the age of five. In practice compulsory attendance was also impossible to enforce as long as school fees were charged.

Payment of school fees (also known as school pence) caused much hardship to many working class people and in 1890 an act was passed which required all school districts to provide free places for the children of all parents requiring these. This loss of income by the school was compensated in 1891 by a grant of 10 shillings per child per annum. Not all parents took advantage of this and sent their children to other elementary schools, such as church schools.

Elementary school fees were finally abolished in 1918.

I have written this to help the reader to understand some of the extracts from the school log books which should also help to paint a picture showing the way of life for the children in Methley and also some of the hardships faced by their parents in meeting the requirements of the education acts. Poverty and illness seem to cause the most common difficulty but things did improve as time went on from the early highlight of a child's day being a walk through Mr Salt's garden at Clump Cliffe and having tea and buns in Mr Savile's grounds on 27 May 1864 to a sightseeing visit to London on 17 June 1938.

Schools in Methley

Detailed accounts of schools in Methley prior to 1847 are printed in 'The History of Methley' published by the Thoresby Society in 1937 but a brief account taken from a book 'Methley and Mickletown Churches' published in 1955 by George E Kirk, Librarian of the Thoresby Society states as follows:-

"The replies of Rector John Scott to Archbishop Drummond's Visitation of Methley in 1764 are preserved at Bishopthorpe, York. There were 157 families, only dissenter in my parish is a woman of the Church of Rome. There was no licensed meeting house. Some persons calling themselves Methodists assemble generally once a week and the number of such of them as are in this parish is, I believe, about 30. These, however, attend the Service in the Church pretty constantly. Their teachers are very uncertain. Here is a public school in Pinder Green known as the Dame School or Fatty Cake School built in the year 1637 by one of the family of Savile, but not endowed by him. Lord Pollington repairs the fabric and appoints the schoolmaster. The name of the present master is Job Barker. The only revenue belonging to the School is 40s. a year left in 1742 by the late John Roberts of this place payable out of certain lands and the interest of £100 given by 3 different persons (apparently Samuel Tryon, Esq., £20; Eleanor, widow of John Smeaton of Swillington, Gent., 1744 £20; Sarah Leech, d. 1757, £60, for which sums the schoolmaster is obliged to teach ten children to read English and to write. Lady Pollington has instituted another school lately, but it is not endowed, wherein 18 girls are clothed, maintained and lodged and taught what is necessary for servants. Care is taken in both these schools to instruct the children in the principles of the Christian Religion, according to the Church of England and they are duly brought to Church"

Lord Mexborough paid the yearly sum of £50 to the Schoolmaster of Pinder Green School from 1855 until the death of the Schoolmaster in 1881, from which time the school was discontinued and used by Lord Mexborough as his private property. From January 1884 to January 1888 the school was rented by the Methley School Board to be used again as a school because of an increase of children needing education. In January 1887 it ceased to be a school and reverted to being a private house.

The situation remained much the same until 1844 when an act of parliament was passed to allow for the conveyance and endowment of sites for schools, consequently in 1847 the Rector of Methley, the Right Honourable and Reverend Philip Yorke Savile entered into an agreement with the Archdeacon of Craven, a trustee of the Bishop of Ripon, to grant and convey to the Archdeacon a triangular piece of glebe land belonging to the Rector of Methley, set out from a close called Kirksyke, bounded on the south by the other part of Kirksyke field, on the west by a footpath leading through the said close and on the east by the Turnpike road leading from Pontefract to Leeds.

The school to be built on the site was to be used for the education of adults or children only of the labouring, manufacturing and other poor classes in the parish of Methley and also as a residence for the schoolmaster and schoolmistress and for no other purpose. Control of the school, funds, endowments and the appointments of schoolmaster/mistress and their assistants to be vested in a committee consisting of the Rector, Curate, and four other persons nominated and appointed by the Rector. These four persons had to own property in the village and also to subscribe in the current year the sum of twenty shillings, at the least, to the said school; they also had to be persons in communion with the Church of England. The schoolmaster/mistress had to be members of the established Church and the Rector shall have the superintendence of the moral and religious instruction of the scholars, and the said school shall always be in union with and upon the principles and in furtherance of the ends

The Dame School, Pinder Green

and designs of the Incorporated National Society for promoting the education of the poor in the principles of the established church.

An agreement to proceed with the provision of this school was signed on 5th June 1847 by the Honourable and Reverend Philip Yorke Savile, Rector of Methley, and confirmed by Order in Council dated 10th August 1847.

Research at the Archives and the University College of Ripon and York, at York shows that a Church Schools Enquiry 1846/47 gives the following information:-

"METHLEY:

Two schools, one Sunday and one Day school.

Both schools are under the National Society for the Education of the Poor.

There are 45 boys and 128 girls in both Sunday and Day schools.

Only 46 boys attend on weekdays only and 40 boys on Sunday only.

Total number 131 boys and 128 girls. The population of Methley was 1,702.

Three male teachers and three female teachers employed but only one male and one female teacher were paid, the others were gratuitously paid." (I presume this to mean they were paid by whatever means locally, i.e. endowment by the Lord of the Manor, the Rector, or others who could afford to do this).

In 1877 the Rector, Philip Yorke Savile, was instrumental in the building of two other schools in Methley – the Mickletown and Scholey Hill Board schools.

Following the building of these schools education in Methley continued until the Butler Education Act of 1944. The act of 1944 established a complete educational ladder from the primary school to the university, through the provision of State scholarships and grants. Poverty is to be no bar to a university career provided that the scholar has the necessary abilities.

The effect on Methley of the 1944 act was that in 1953 a new infant school was opened in Little Church Lane, in 1956 a new comprehensive school (Royds) was opened in Pennington Lane, Oulton, and the Board School at Mickletown, after a period of time as a secondary modern school, reverted to being a junior school. Two casualties of the reorganisation of the schools was the closure in 1962 of the Methley National School, Church Side, which had really become inadequate for use as a school, and in 1963 Scholey Hill Board School was closed and demolished, apart from the school house.

Extracts from Methley National School, Churchside Log Books

(Earlier log books may be in existence, this is the earliest that has been found).

1863

1/4	First entry – 141 children present.
17/4	Many children away planting potatoes.
23/4	5 pm Tea for children's parents. Philip Yorke Savile said he was pleased about progress. Eighteen children recited pieces and sang many of their school songs.
27/4	The school pence changed from 2d to 3d in consequence of the re-introduction of payment by the New Code.
5/5	A big ignorant girl sent to school but she was dismissed for being disagreeable and disobedient.
8/5	Many children absent helping their mothers to clean.
14/5	The children in Class 1 improve in copying from print on paper.
15/5	Only 70 children present.
2/6	A colliers' strike is expected and this will greatly affect attendance.
15/6	Stopped lessons at 11.15 for clothing club.
18/6	Four frocks begun.
23/6	Two frocks begun.
24/6	One frock begun, and 1 shirt.
7/7	The Rector took the scripture lesson with the first class.
8/7	Wednesday – the parents' usual wash day which much affects the upper classes.
10/7	A nest of swallows fledged which had built in the girls' bonnet room.
16/7	The Rector gave the Pupil Teachers the treat of a trip to Connisbro' Castle. ALL THE PITS CLOSED. The strike likely to prove serious.
29/7	A good attendance notwithstanding the colliers' strike.
18/8	A good attendance considering the harvest is beginning
20/8	Harvest holiday 3 weeks.
14/9	School opened, numbers few.
15/9	Owing to the strike Mr Briggs, the coal proprietor, has turned parents and children out of his houses and great destitution has been caused in the village in consequence.
21/9	A tea in the school this pm for the benefit of the Leeds new Infirmary.
25/9	Many children absent with smallpox.
28/9	The children each received a piece of plum cake before going home.

29/9 The strike continues – fair attendances.
5/10 First class busy dressing a doll.
7/10 The Pupil Teachers' question and answering evening.
9/10 Notwithstanding the distress the children who come to school are very clean and tidy.
15/10 More families turned out of their homes.
16/10 The people of Methley continue to be much distressed.
19/10 Began for the winter months to open school at 10 o'clock and dismiss at 3.30 pm.
23/10 Many children absent gathering potatoes.
26/10 A school treat in the village.
10/11 The smallpox has almost disappeared.
12/11 The fine weather takes the children off potato picking.
17/11 The numbers increase as the colliers are setting to work.
25/11 The colliers' strike has greatly affected the attendance of the children at school its effects are still very detrimental.
27/11 Children learned the hymn "Safely Through another Week".
4/12 School closed at 11 am on account of the members of the clothing club receiving their money.
8/12 A.E. Greener, a girl in the 4th class taken ill with smallpox.
11/12 The colliers working much better.
18/12 School closed for a fortnight's holiday.

1864

4/1 School commenced, good attendance.
5/1 The colliers are now returned to regular work.
6/1 The cold most severe.
7/1 The cold seems to paralyse all efforts to work.
10/2 Ash Wednesday, children at Church.
23/2 Many of the older children away helping their mothers to wash.
21/3 A good number of children attending school today who have not been for a long time which much interfered with the order.
23/3 School staff – Sarah Fox, certificated teacher, Jane James, pupil teacher 2nd year, Eliza Chapman (designation unreadable).
14/4 Summary of the Inspector's report on the school:
"The school is in good order, carefully taught and well looked after by its Manager.
A very good specimen of a village school. The infants are taught in a separate room, they are in a cheerful state of discipline and of fair attainment."
19/4 Many children away setting potatoes.
27/5 Children on Saturday walked through Mr Salt's garden at Clumpcliffe, played in the garden and had parkin and milk in the courtyard. Returned and had tea and buns in Mr Savile's grounds. The children separated highly pleased with their afternoon's entertainment.
7/7 Closed school at 3.15 pm to be present at the opening of Rothwell school.
21/7 Two boys punished for cruelty to bees.
1/8 Grace Forrest commenced my duties as School Mistress.
22/8 Being unable to undertake my duties from illness Miss Savile kindly took charge of the school.

1865

23/1 Mrs Holmes presented a number of remnants of materials for clothing to the school to be made into different articles of dress by the children.

20/2 The Reverend Philip Yorke Savile brought some dolls for the girls to dress.

11/4 126 children present – 1st and 2nd class 26 each, 3rd class 20, 4th class 23, infants 57.

1866

16/11 A flood arose in Methley; waters of the river Calder rose till they reached the school yard.

1867

24/9 No school today. All the children met at 1 pm and walked to Methley Park through the hall gardens at Clumpcliffe. Various amusements together with tea and buns. Presents of books and toys were given to each child. The day closed with a distribution of sweets, cake and milk among the children by the generous kindness of Mr and Mrs Salt.

1882

15/12 Weather very bad, only 51 children in school on Monday. The Hon. The Revd. Philip Yorke Savile kindly provided the children with soup for dinners during the week.

1883

15/9 Mental arithmetic worst lesson in school. Each class thorough dunces at it.

7/12 I find a great difficulty in getting the children to school in time. They complain they have a long way to walk.

1885

13/4 Rosetta C Braime commenced her duties as mistress.

18/5 The Hon. and Rev P.Y. Savile and the Rev. W. H. Savile visited the school this am.

9/10 Visit by HMI. Great lack of books in school, 20 children had 12 books between them, 17 children had 9 books between them.

6/11 The new reading books came on Tuesday, each class had 3 sets made up.

1886

16/7 School examination took place on Monday and Tuesday morning, 215 children present. On Friday afternoon the Hon. P.Y. Savile took all the children to Woodlesford by train.

13/8 Mary Taylor pupil teacher qualified as teacher but is leaving the school. Mary F Robinson has been taken as probationer.

20/8 The attendance has been very, very poor this week, the greater part of the children are away pea pulling. Work is so scarce in Methley parents and children are glad to be employed for a few days.

3/9 Teachers and choir on a trip to York.

1/11 Elizabeth Stones commenced her duties as Assistant Mistress.

12/11 Children sent home early on account of the dark afternoon, they could not see to go on with work.

1887

11/3 Miss Straiton commenced her duties as assistant teacher.

25/3 The whooping cough is very bad in Methley, a great many of the children are at home on account of this.

13/5 Classes 1,2 and 3 are doing work on paper instead of slates.

24/6 The children had holiday all day on account of the Queen's Jubilee.

1/7 On Thursday the children had their Jubilee treat, splendid tea provided by J Richardson Esq. medals or china mugs presented to each child.

15/7 School closed all day the Hon. Rev. Philip Yorke Savile took the teachers to Saltaire exhibition.

2/9 Standard VI taught decimals, standard V fractions and standard IV reduction of avoirdupois.

4/11 A great many children sick this week, four families have scarlet fever and one typhoid fever.

23/12 On Monday and Tuesday the children of the school gave an entertainment consisting of songs, recitations, musical drills etc. The proceeds to go towards building a lavatory and classrooms for the infants. The Pinder Green Board School and the managers of this school have taken the infants.

1888

9/1 182 children present this morning, 207 in the afternoon. I find the children from Pinder Green very backward in every subject.

14/3 Only 61 children present on account of the terrific snow storm. It is impossible for infants to come.

18/6 S.R. Braime has finished her apprenticeship as Pupil Teacher in this school and has been appointed by the Rector as an Assistant Teacher.

1889

5/4 Fever very bad in some parts of Methley, two of the infants have died from it.

19/4 The Hon. Rev. P.Y. Savile visited school every day, brought the boys a football and the babies some dolls and other toys.

1/11 Children again left early because it is very dark and some children have a very long way to walk home. Miss Clara Braime has been appointed Sewing Mistress.

1890

3/4 28 Children absent on account of sickness, one little boy A. Dickinson at school last Friday died this morning.

21/7 Choir trip to Bridlington.

1891

1/5 The Rector is very ill, not able to leave home.

5/6 The Rector visited the school.

4/12 School disrupted because of workmen putting up gas fixtures.

1892

28/10 Clara Braime resigned her post as Sewing Mistress.

1893

7/7 Children had holiday on Thursday in honour of the Royal Wedding.

4/9 Opened school today for girls and infants the plan was approved during the holidays. The boys have gone to the Board School and 32 girls have been admitted.

15/9 Very poor attendance, children were kept at home to gather coal for their parents. On Thursday soup was made for all the miners' children in school and on Tuesday 198 had their tea at school. Mrs Hemmingway of Holmesville has taken 10-20 every day at her own house for either dinner or tea. A Miss Stephenson had a sovereign sent to provide food for the children.

6/10 The Rector brings breakfast for 7 or 8 little ones every morning.

27/10 Several children are absent on account of having no boots. The children are beginning to be very poor, some buns were given to the poorest on Friday. The girls in 1st class wrote a letter thanking Mrs Beckworth for sending a sovereign for them a tea.

6/11 Soup provided by the Rector at noon today.

21/12 On Thursday tea was provided by the Rector for all the children, cards were also given and books to those children who had made a full number of attendances.

1894

11/4 Not so good attendance this morning on account of Pontefract races. The Rector came to school at 12 o'clock and took some of the little ones on the road because so many conveyances were passing through.

1896

24/1 Attendance very good this week. On Friday afternoon the children had a treat, a large Christmas tree filled with beautiful presents and lighted, was provided by Miss Baker, Miss Beatrice Savile, Miss Savile and the Hon. and Rev. P.Y. Savile.

31/7 Attendance very poor on account of Measles and Fever, little John Webster died of Fever.

30/11 Staff of Teachers at Methley National School, Rosetta C. Braime Head Teacher, M.E. Robinson Certificated Teacher, M.E. Holmes Assistant Mistress, Annie W. Braime Art. 68, Agneta Newman Art. 68, Ellen Langham 3rd Year Pupil Teacher.

December Temperatures during this month very low, ranging from 41F to 52F.

1897

10/7 Summary of Inspector's Report, Girls School, the temperature in cold weather is too low, Infants School the number of children and classes are too large for the room. The warming of the room needs consideration.

23/7 School closed all day also on Monday 26th July on account of the death of the Hon. and Rev. Philip Yorke Savile Rector and Manager of Methley National School.

1898

4/3 The Rector the Rev. H. Armstrong-Hall visited the school in the afternoon.

20/7 Extract of report by HMI. "The special attention of the Managers is requested to the HM Inspector's remarks as to the insufficient warming of the rooms in cold weather, they are reminded that their attention was called to this point last year. The Managers are requested to inform their Lordships what steps they intend to take in order to remedy this defect."

1899

20/2 The amount of the aid grant is £50: this grant is made for the purpose of 1. Increasing Headmistress salary 2. Effecting repairs 3. Providing equipment.

9/10 Very cold, temperature in school 46F.

1900

8/1 Annie Wells-Braime commenced her duties as Mistress and Alice Everjones as Assistant Mistress.

5/2 Miss Annie Gomersal commenced her duties as Assistant Mistress.

16/5 Still much sickness. Two armoured trains passed through the village and children were taken out to see them.

24/5 Children have holiday today for the "Queen's Birthday" and "Relief of Mafeking".

1901

4/ 2 Attendance very poor, over 30 cases of whooping cough reported.

31/5 Staff at school A.W. Braime, certificated mistress, H.E. Robinson, certificated teacher, and ex pupil teachers A.E. Jones, E.A. Pearson, A.E. Gomersall.

1915

28/ 9 All the children taken out for half an hour to see the King pass on his return from Leeds.

15/11 Miss Campbell from Whitwood Mere Infant School is in charge of Standards I and II during absence of Miss Bellwood.

1916

21/ 2 School to be closed for 3 weeks on account of measles.

10/ 7 The children gave a display of school songs and dances on the Rector's lawn in aid of the children in Belgium. About 120 people attended, £3 was raised.

28/11 Many children absent this morning having stayed in bed late owing to the zeppelin raid.

1917

20/12 A special holiday was given today in honour of the West Riding troops in their recent advance.

1937

26/ 6 30 of the older girls went to Windermere with Miss Gleaves and Miss Robinson, and they climbed Orrest Head. A sail was taken from Ambleside to Bowness. Only one girl had previously seen a mountain and all the others declared that mountains were not at all like they had expected.

1938

17/6 A party of the elder children spent a long day sightseeing in London.

28/9 School closed for 3 days for distribution of gas masks.

1940

2/ 5 When the sirens sounded today the children immediately assembled in the A.R.P shelter, time taken 2 minutes.

14/ 5 Whit Tuesday holiday cancelled because of German invasion of Holland and Belgium.

28/ 8 Attendance low due to air raid last night.

1941

10/11 Dinners supplied from the canteen at Mickletown school.

1943

29/ 1 Engagement of Miss Ellen Gleaves as Head Mistress terminates this day.

1/ 2 Miss Jessie Travis took up her appointment as Head Mistress.

29/10 Miss Campbell terminates her engagement as teacher after 26 years service at this school.

1944

17/ 7 Five evacuees from London admitted to school.

1945

8/ 5 V.E. Day – 2 days holiday.

1946

8/10 Group of children went to Leeds Grand Theatre to see Donald Wolfit's Shakespearian company production of the Merchant of Venice.

14/10 Group of children to Bewerley Park Camp School.

1947

1/4 School leaving age raised to 15.

20/11 Day holiday, wedding of Princess Elizabeth to Lieutenant Philip Mountbatten.

1948

26/4 Day holiday, Silver Wedding of King George VI to Queen Elizabeth.

1950

16/6 School becomes a controlled school.

1951

3/7 School visit to the city of Liverpool.

17/10 Items from report by Ministry of Education. Three classrooms but the entrance to the seniors' room is through other classrooms. No accommodation for staff, no hot water for staff/children. Lit by gas. Toilets are obsolete. Because of poor sanitary conditions all boys transferred to Mickletown School; infants 5-7yrs (31) juniors 8-11yrs (26) seniors 11-14yrs (16).

1952

28/3 Report from West Riding to school re. proposal to install electricity.

2/9 School wired for electricity.

15/9 Senior girls transferred to Mickletown School. Churchside is now a Junior/Infant mixed school.

10/11 Electricity to Parish Hall.

1954

12/7 Mrs May Walker a student from Ripon Training College started teaching practice.

1955

27/7 My engagement as Headmistress ends today because of the reorganisation of all the schools in the village.
This is the last entry in the log book.

The school continued under the Headship of Mrs Pauline Milner until 1962 when the school was closed.

On 31 December 1963 the school building and house was sold by conveyance between the Ripon Diocesan Board of Finance and the Parochial Church Council of St. Oswalds, Methley for £1,000 to be used as a parish hall.

In 1969 the interior of the hall was renovated and a major part of the cost of renovation was met by a gift of £750 from Henry Moore together with £400 from the Diocesan Board of Fianance.

The parish hall was extensively altered in 1985/86 and a large extension was added to the rear to provide a much larger central room. The extension was built with stone that originally formed the steeple of St. Oswald's Church until it was taken down in 1933. The cost of the alterations was approximately £35,000. The labour was provided by the Manpower Services Commission operated by Leeds City Council.

Memories of Methley Churchside National School

When we moved in January 1919 from Normanton to Mill Lane, Methley, my parents decided that as I had previously attended a girls' school I should go to the National School, Church Side (near the parish centre). My brother had attended a boys' school, but there were none in Methley, so until July he was at the Pinfold Lane School.

I found life at the National School very pleasant; lovely surroundings, friendly pupils, helpful teachers. The stone building was an L-shape; the stem of the L held standards 1 and 2 at the end where the front door was, and standards 3 and 4 at the other end. The angle of the L, known as The Classroom, held standards 5, 6, 7 and X-7. I began in 3, moved to 4 (though the two were nearly always taught as one) and ended in 6. The Head Mistress, Miss Robinson, was the niece of 'Ossy' Stead, a Churchwarden and a farmer at Hunt Farm. Miss Robinson belonged to the newer type of teacher – college trained, very smartly dressed (I remember a dress with floating panels that we thought marvellous) and very much on the spot. There was a library with some readable books in it, there were fireplaces, and, if I remember rightly, an oven where we warmed-up stuffed potatoes and pieces of fish for winter dinners. There were no buses then, and only about two cars in all Methley, everyone walked to school.

My best friend was Edna Berry, who lived in Top Fold and who now lives in Toledo, Ohio. She visited Methley a few years ago. Bessie Backhouse, Mavis Ward and Connie Thompson were other friends.

I remember little of the content of the lessons except arithmetic. I left at the age of nine, thoroughly versed in problems involving stocks, shares, and brokerage and in the filling of baths by those peculiar people who forgot to put in the plug. Needlework was informal and sociable. We sang songs and told stories while we sewed. I was familiar, thanks to my sister, with Gilbert and Sullivan, and entertained the class with 'Tit Willow'. P.E. consisted of arm exercises for which we stood between the nailed-down seats of the desks, or in the gangways. There was no hot water and lighting was by oil lamp.

Outside the main door was a wonderful beech tree. I never enter the Parish Centre without admiring it. Sometimes when the weather was warm we took our chairs outside and did lessons under the tree.

Written by Lilian Harrison in 1999.

Extracts from Methley Board Schools – Managers' Minutes Book 1874-1890

1874

24/12 First meeting of the Methley School Board, there were present the Hon. & Rev. Philip Yorke Savile, Messrs John Richardson, Joseph Cass and Thomas Winterburn, Wilkinson Waide absent, was held at the National School, Methley, this being the third Thursday after the School Board elections. The Hon. & Rev. Philip Yorke Savile was appointed Chairman and Mr Richardson Vice Chairman. John North, Solicitor, of Leeds was appointed Clerk of the Board at a salary of £25 p.a.

31/12 A census be taken of all the children aged between 5 and 13 years of the Parish of Methley.

1875

14/1 That Mr Arthur Bartlett, Assistant Overseer, be appointed to take the census and also discharge the duties of School Warden at a salary of £10 p.a. from 1 January 1875.

28/1 That a portion of land in Methley Lane forming the eastern portion or boundary of the estate of the Rev. Watson, now under contract to Lord Mexborough, be negotiated as a school site at Scholey Hill. A portion of land in Pinfold Lane, called Little Oaks, be negotiated as a school site.

25/2 The census furnished be adopted (numbers not shown). Half acre of land at Scholey Hill be secured for the school. Mr Gough of Queen Anne's Gate, London, appointed architect at a salary of £5 per cent on the expenditure of the buildings.

11/3 A school to accommodate 700 children on the Pinfold Lane site is necessary. That a school to accommodate 200 children on the Methley Lane site is necessary.

16/4 Amendments to the resolutions of 11 March 1875 show 370 children on the Pinfold Lane site and 180 on the Methley Lane site.

29/10 Letter to the Board of Education that £6,000 is needed to carry out this Board's requirements for school buildings.

15/10 Cost of building the 2 schools reduced to £5,000 and Mr Gough to be informed.

1876

14/2 Messrs Pallinson's tender of £2,445 for Pinfold Lane School and £1,940 for Scholey Hill School approved. Fee of £175 to Mr Gough for his work approved.

23/2 Offer of Messrs Pallinson in their letter to the Clerk of 22 February 1876 to execute the plans for both schools for £5,050 be accepted. (No reason is given for the increase).

7/4 Clerk to write to the Secretary of H.M. Commissioners for an order to the Public Works to grant the loan and obtain the money from the bank.

22/5 Agreed that contract with Messrs Pallinson be signed.

24/7 Conveyance of land from Lord Mexborough for Scholey Hill School approved.

25/9 Conveyance of Mickletown site approved but the minerals thereunder to be leased.

1877

18/4 Architect handed in certificate showing schools completed. Adverts. for teachers to be placed in the 'Leeds Mercury' and 'Yorkshire Post'. Insurance arranged – Mickletown School £1,750 and Scholey Hill £1,000. Caretakers to be obtained for both schools until the opening at Whitsuntide at a sum not exceeding 6s a week.

3/5 Fifty applications received for appointment as teachers.

9/5 Appointments made – Head of Mickletown School Mr Goodacre, at a salary of £120 p.a., Infant Mistress of Mickletown School Mrs Goodacre, at a salary of £70 p.a., also the occupancy of the school house. Head Mistress of Scholey Hill School Mrs Ashworth, at a salary of £80 p.a., also occupancy of school house. Schools to open 28 May 1877.

22/8 Staff of Mickletown Mixed School, apart from Robert and Elizabeth Goodacre – James Cressey, Assistant Teacher, £52 p.a., Elizabeth Clough, Assistant Teacher, £45 p.a., Sarah Hurst, candidate, £8 p.a., Kate Copeman, candidate, £8 p.a. Caretaker Harriet Asquith 12s a week to cover all payments for materials and extra work.

Mickletown Infants School – Elizabeth Goodacre, Infant Mistress, £70 p.a., Eleanor Senior, Assistant Teacher, £45 p.a., Rosetta Braime, candidate, £8 p.a.

Scholey Hill School – Margaret Ashworth, Head Mistress, £80 p.a., Lucy Robinson, Assistant Teacher, £40 p.a. Caretaker Martha Hartley, 6s per week.

29/9 Average attendance Mickletown Mixed School 206, Mickletown Infants School 115, Scholey Hill School 74.

22/12 Letter from H Briggs dated 6 December 1877 offering to accept £500 compensation for not taking coal from under the school. Solicitors to investigate.

1878

17/4 Mr Joseph Charlesworth of Methley be appointed School Attendance Officer at £25 p.a. following resignation of Mr Bartlett.

26/9 A proposal that an Infants School be provided for 250 children adjoining the present Mickletown School was approved.

1879

3/2 Action at Leeds Assizes over dispute between School Board and architect/builders. School Board lost, costs of £198 and £122 to be paid.

24/2 Mr Carson of Leeds submitted plans for new infant room and addition to school at cost of £1,000. Plans approved.

28/4 Tender of Mr Arthur Atkinson for the new school of £732 be accepted.

30/6 Work on Infant School to start during holidays.

29/9 Salary of Mrs Asquith, Caretaker, be increased to 15s per week but she must take entire charge of the heating apparatus.

27/10 The following accounts be passed to pay the costs in Mr Gough's action:

Solicitor	£135.8.5	
Solicitor's action v Gough and another	£285.12.11	
C L Dreyfus – witness/arch./surveyor	£36.15.0.	
Sam Croft – witness/builder	£10.10.0	
Sam Worsnop – witness/slater	£8.8.0	
William Atkinson – witness/slater	£3.0.0	
Arthur Atkinson – builder/slater	£2.14.0	
James Hibbard – witness/builder	£2.7.0	Total £484.15.0.

Reported by the Clerk to the Board that the new school was completed.

£5 to purchase books and prizes for Mickletown School, and £2.10.0 for Scholey Hill.

1880

3/5 List of school fees owing to Mickletown School submitted and Clerk informed to summon in the County Court to recover arrears in excess of £1.

25/10 Clerk reported proceedings in County Court to recover arrears: one parent appeared and asked the Board not to enforce payment of judgement against her and also to remit school fees against her children. Decided some of the fees to be remitted for 3 months.

29/11 The Hon. and Rev. Philip Yorke Savile resigned as Chairman of the School Board.

13/12 W W Wood elected as Chairman of the Board.

1881

31/1 Applications for remission of school fees, 5 were refused.

28/2 More applications for remission of school fees received. One man with 5 children owed 13.11d, promised payment for 2, he was allowed one free for 3 months. Another with 9 children, fees remitted for 4 children for 2 months, daughter to assist with sewing.

27/6 Mickletown Mixed School – on roll 290, average 224.
Mickletown Infants – on roll 193, average 188.
Scholey Hill – on roll 91, average 74.

21/12 William Powell appointed School Attendance Officer as Mr Charlesworth has resigned.

1882

31/1 Several applications for school caretakers. Mrs Asquith, present Caretaker of Mickletown School, said she could not undertake the work at less than 13.0d. a week.

27/2 Mrs Hartley offered to be caretaker at Scholey Hill for 7.0d. a week. It was approved that Mary Ann Stainthorpe be appointed Caretaker at Mickletown School at a salary of 11.0d. a week and Mrs Hartley, Caretaker at Scholey Hill for 7.0d. a week.

The Census by the School Attendance Officer was presented.

No of Houses	No. of children 3-5yrs		No. of children 5-13yrs		No at private school		No at public school		Total
	Boys	Girls	Boys	Girls	Boys	Girls	Boys	Girls	
426	53	37	216	224	6	17	208	215	2113
270	41	36	114	136	1	0	109	129	1233
123	16	14	46	61	1	2	45	49	616
819	110	87	376	421	8	19	362	393	3962

These figures are copied from the minute book but the totals are obviously incorrect the total 2113 should be 976, 1233 should be 565, 616 should be 234 and 3962 should be 1776 The number of houses agrees with the 1881 census.

24/4 Many applications for remission of school fees and payment of arrears. Some were requested to pay as best they could, some offered as little as 2d a week, some were remitted.

25/9 Mr Robert Smirthwaite appointed Clerk to the School Board at a salary of £25 p.a. following the resignation of Mr John North.
Further accommodation needed at Mickletown School.

1883

26/2 Plans for Mickletown School extension approved.

19/3 The salary of the Clerk to the Board increased to £40 p.a.

16/4 An extract from a letter to the School Board, signed by 16 of the ratepayers of Methley, "The present School Board rate, now nearly 1s in the £ is likely to be very greatly increased by the proposed extensive extensions to Mickletown School. The cost of teaching is at present enormous and we trust you will use every endeavour to prevent, as far as possible, these ever increasing expenses."

20/5 The Clerk instructed to call a meeting in conformity with the Education Act and rule to consider the dismissal of all or any of the staff of Mickletown School.

2/6 Special meeting of the School Board. Mr and Mrs Goodacre be asked to resign their respective appointments at the Mickletown School.

4/6 Adverts. in newspapers for a master for Mickletown Mixed School at a salary of £90 p.a. plus house and for a School Mistress of the infant department of Mickletown School at a salary of £70 p.a.

25/6 Letter from Mr and Mrs Goodacre desiring to withdraw their resignations of their appointments under the Board. A motion was carried unanimously that they be allowed to withdraw their resignations.

28/6 It was carried that Mr W H Palmer be selected as Master of Mickletown School at a salary of £90 p.a. plus house.

18/7 Mr and Mrs Goodacre attended the Board and tendered their resignations of their appointments.

30/7 The Board accepted the resignations of Mr and Mrs Goodacre.
Mr W H Palmer appointed Head Master from the 1st September 1873 with house.
Moved that Miss Clara Emma Teale be appointed Infant Mistress of Mickletown School at salary of £55 p.a. with an advance each year of £5 until £70 p.a. is reached.

16/11 Clerk to write to the Education Department to obtain permission to open Pinder Green School and explaining as to population and school children and obtain sanction for infants to be taught at that school.

26/11 Mr B Fisher's eldest boy be allowed to attend Mickletown School half time at 2d a week.

31/12 Advert. to be placed in 'The Schoolmaster' for a Certificated Mistress at £60 p.a. for Pinder Green School.

1884

4/1 Mrs Anne Stillwell appointed mistress of Pinder Green School at a salary of £75 p.a. (This may have been a temporary appointment.)

14/1 Pinder Green School opened, attendance about 60.

20/1 Mary Western appointed caretaker of Pinder Green School at 7s per week, she finding all cleaning materials.

25/2 Mrs Eden Wormald appointed Head Mistress at Pinder Green School at a salary of £60 p.a.

2/3 Charlotte Ashworth appointed monitress at Pinder Green School at 13.4d. a month.

17/3 Clerk submitted estimate for Methley schools of £500 for half year ended 25 September 1884.

1/9 Mr J Farrar be appointed Attendance Officer to the Board at a salary of £20.

27/9 Salary of Mr Palmer, Head Master of Mickletown School, be increased to £100 p.a.

7/11 Letter from H Briggs & Co. re conveyance of Mickletown site was read to the Board. It was agreed that a case be laid before Mr West for his opinion on the Board's rights and liabilities in respect of coal under the site of Mickletown School.

1885

5/1 Mr Hartley, Caretaker, asked for an increase of salary, no advance was made. Refer to entry dated 7/11/84. Further opinion of Mr West that the Board has been advised that Mr Savile was liable.

26/1 Mr James Whittaker appointed Head Master of Pinder Green School at a salary of £60 p.a. in place of Mrs Wormald who has left.

2/3 Head Master of Pinder Green School, James Whittaker, having resigned, the post be advertised at £60 p.a.

20/3 Mr J Sagar appointed Head Master of Pinder Green School at a salary of £60 p.a. with £10 a year extra until a house is found for him. Letter to the Earl of Mexborough to allow the Board the use of the house attached to the school for occupation by Mr Sagar.

8/5 During the strike the school fees of children not able to pay be remitted.

1887

20/3 Letter to be sent to the Earl of Mexborough asking if His Lordship has for some years given a sum of money in aid of Pinder Green School or if anyone else has given money to the school.

6/6 Letter dated 30th April from Mr Richardson to the Board giving notice to quit Pinder Green School.

19/9 Mr Bowling appointed Clerk to the Board at a salary of £25 p.a.
The Clerk to write to the Earl of Mexborough and failing his withdrawing the notice to quit Pinder Green School would the Earl write to Henry Briggs & Co. asking if the Reading Room at Methley Junction could be used as a temporary school.

17/10 The Earl of Mexborough declined to withdraw the notice to quit but Henry Briggs & Co. were prepared to accommodate the children at the Methley Junction Reading Room. Mr Savile also was willing to receive younger children at the National School which he was about to enlarge.

1888

16/1 Plans for the enlargement of Mickletown School received and approved, and also that the school be heated with hot water pipes.

30/1 James Sagar, Head of Pinder Green School, resigned. The school has been given up and the children have been received at Mickletown and the National Schools.

16/4 Tender of £339.9.9d. received for enlargement of Mickletown School and approved.

27/8 Post of caretaker at Mickletown School and the Board's Attendance Officer, having been combined, Mr Bransby Fisher be appointed to the post at a salary of £65 p.a. Mr Palmer Headmaster of Mickletown School attended and was asked as to a report which Mr Atkinson said was current in the parish that the unfavourable report on Mickletown School was owing to the teachers of the Board and especially Mr Palmer being continually 'bullied' by the members of the present board.

Mr Palmer flatly denied the assertion and wished to say that he had always met with the utmost courtesy from all the members and the clerk, and the report as far as he was concerned was entirely without foundation.

Note: Mr Atkinson was a member of the school board.

24/9 The Chairman Mr W Taylor said that a ridiculous report was current in the Parish that the dismissal of John Farrer, the late Attendance Officer, was due to the influence of Mr Taylor over him. The clerk said this was ridiculous as Mr Farrer was especially asked first if he would undertake the combined offices of Attendance Officer and Caretaker which was rendered necessary by the enlargement of Mickletown School but he declined it. Mr Smith said that he had heard Mr Bowling ask Mr Farrer if he would apply for the job.

The Board then decided that the matter be dropped.

Note: Mr Smith was also a member of the Board.

26/11 The Board heard Mr Palmer's explanation with regard to The Inspector's Report and the management of the school. The Board are not satisfied therewith and that he be informed that the Board will look for a greatly improved report at the next examination as a condition of his continuing his engagement.

1889

28/1 Reference was made to evening school at Mickletown.

29/7 Attention drawn to the fact that there were different rates of school fees, some pay 2d and some 3d per week. It was decided that infants under 5 pay 1d a week, over 5 pay 2d a week, mixed department St.l pay 2d, remaining standards 3d a week.

28/10 Mr W F W Shaw, Certificated Teacher, of Leeds Parish Church Higher Grade School, be appointed Head Teacher of Mickletown School at a salary of £100 p.a. in place of Mr Palmer who has resigned.

(This is the last entry in this minute book, there are no other Board minute books available.)

Extracts from Mickletown Board School Log Book 1941 - 1959

1941

5/5 Air raid during the night.

19/5 Death of G Sidebottom, old boy, killed in action Egypt.

2/7 14th Annual Sports held on cricket field. Military band from A.A. Battery, Methley Park, played. The Romans (Green) won the shield which was presented by Dr Dennis.

25/8 During the holidays Mr Harrison, a teacher, joined H.M Forces.

10/9 Award of Merit by the Royal Society for the Prevention of Accidents to Fred Riby for his work in the National Poster Competition.

22/9 Admitted 4 evacuees from Hull.

10/11 School canteen opened, 286 meals served for this school together with Methley C of E, Scholey Hill, Oulton St. John's and Woodlesford.

21/11 1506 meals provided this week.

1942

12/2 £19.3.10d raised by children for aid to Russia sent to Mr Churchill.

2/3 Close of Warships Week, sale of National Savings Certificates raised £389, also free school gift of £17.10.0d.

6/5 Gardening all afternoon.

22/5 Children collected £10.10.0d. for Overseas Tobacco Fund.

1/7 Annual Sports Day, Greens won the trophy.

29/7 Collection for British Red Cross prisoners of war raised £11.0.0d.

8/10 Rabbit Club formed.

4/11 Application received from local farmers for help in the potato fields.

6/11 Some boys helping the farmers.

1943

29/1 Miss Travis ceased duties at this school on appointment as Head Mistress of Methley Church school.

16/4 Wings for Victory week, school raised £525. The total amount raised by this school in National Savings Certificates reached £2,000. Christopher Jackson, old boy, reported died on active service in India.

29/5 Collection for Overseas Tobacco Fund raised £15.

7/7 Annual Sports Day, Greens awarded trophy.

15/11 Letter of thanks for cigarettes received from the Commanding Officer and men of H.M.S. Phoenicia, Mediterranean station.

19/11 Children contributed £6.5.0d. for present to ship's company of H.M.S. Phoenicia.

1944

20/4 Inspection of gas masks and trial in gas van.

6/6 Invasion of Europe.

12/6 Kenneth Naylor, old boy, killed in Italy.

28/6 Bernard Sidebottom, old boy, killed in action on June 6th in Normandy.

30/6 Ronald Thompson, old boy, killed in action.

5/7 Annual Sports Day, Green House awarded trophy.

1/11 18 boys potato picking.

2/11 24 boys potato picking.

1945

24/4 Form 1 visited Clokie's Pottery.

8/5 School closed for 2 days – V.E. Day.

1946

14/10 26 children to Bewerley Park Camp School for 1 month.

1947

2/9 Mr Gibbins appointed Head Master.

18/11 Mrs Bains, Miss Shaw, Head Master and senior girls visited the Grand Theatre, Leeds to attend a performance of 'A Midsummer Night's Dream'.

1948

8/7 Annual Sports Day, Greens win.

1949

6/7 Annual Sports Day, Greens win.

14/7 100 seniors and staff visited Liverpool and crossed on the ferry; highlight for senior girls was a visit to Jacob's biscuit factory – samples much enjoyed.

10/10 School Dramatic Society formed, Mr Waine and Mr Cross in charge.

14/12 School Dramatic Society presented three 1-act plays. House full for 3 nights. £12 raised for school funds.

1950

11/5 A practical experiment in citizenship. The school acted out the proceedings of a local election. Officials and candidates were chosen, cubicles were used, and even a policeman's helmet and cape loaned from the police station.

30/6 Mrs Hyatt took a group of pupils to London.

3/7 23rd Annual Sports Day, Greens win.

August Mushroom project started, beds were laid in the air raid shelter.

21/10 In view of the importance of rhubarb growing in this area, a part of the school garden was planted with 50 crowns each of many varieties given by Mr Wheatley, a local market gardener.

1951

23/2 Inaugural meeting of P.T.A.

12/3 Tree planting on the Hollings estate. School co-operated with the U.D.C. in the project, the first of its kind in the West Riding. Ornamental trees were planted by children who will look after them. Poultry rearing project commenced. Eggs were purchased and incubators loaned, appliances for feeding and rearing to be constructed in craft lessons.

2/4 The first of the chickens hatched.

9/5 Mrs Hyatt and 44 senior children visited Edinburgh for 2 days.

7/7 Annual Sports Day, Blues won.

4/9 Charles Redding commenced duty as temporary Head Teacher.

June 184 boys and 128 girls attend the school. Staff is Head Master, 4 Masters and 8 Mistresses, all of whom are qualified teachers. 750 meals are prepared in the canteen every day, 240 being served here and are of excellent quality.

2/12 Mr Redding ceased duty as acting Head Teacher.

1952

8/1 Mr Brice commenced duty as Head Teacher.

2/5 Have decided to introduce italic writing in the school.

2/7 Annual Sports Day, Greens win the trophy.

1954

27/7 First issue of school magazine 'The Medelain' was presented today.

1955

5/9 School re-opened as a re-organised Secondary School with children being drawn from Mickletown, Methley, Oulton, Woodlesford and Scholey Hill.

1957

19/12 Annual carol service – excellent singing. Soloists S Deakin and Daphne White sang delightfully.

1958

12/3 4th year met with Lord Pollington to plant 50 American Red Oak trees supplied by the Estate along thc main Leeds road.

1959

30/1 Notice of closure of school received.

24/7 This school finally closed today and ended an era in education. All the children will, in September, attend the Rothwell new school under very modern conditions. Goodbye Mickletown. I myself take up an appointment at South Kirby Secondary Modern school. NOTE: The entry of 24/7 is the last entry in the log book. Mickletown School was not physically closed, it re-opened the following September as Methley Junior School with Miss Travis as Head Mistress.

Scholey Hill Board School

Scholey Hill Board School opened on 28th May 1877 as a Public Elementary Board School, Margaret Ashworth, Certificated Teacher, was Head Mistress. Number of children not shown.

Extracts from School Log Book

1877

2/7 I am without assistance in the school this week. I have given copy books to all in the 1st and 2nd classes, the 3rd class, not being able to write on paper at present, but have made some little progress in reading.

17/7 1st class are doing simple multiplication by 2 figures up to 7, 2nd class doing simple addition as far as hundreds.

24/7 1st class did a little writing on paper today which was done fairly for the first time.

26/7 I have put the best scholars in the 4th class to read in the 1st grade reading books.

6/8 The children in the 4th class read in the 1st grade reading book today for the first time.

10/8 The 1st class are now doing simple multiplication of three figures.

13/8 The writing on slates in the Infant School seems to be a little better.

17/9 Re-opened this morning after the summer vacation; very poor attendance partly through illness and partly to children working in the fields.

1878 Summary of H.M. Inspector's Report. "The school is a very commodious one but it seems to me as much too large for the population here as that in Mickletown is too small. Mrs Ashworth seems to be a most diligent, patient and conscientious teacher and under her care there is every likelihood of the children doing well. She has made a good beginning and considering the evident backwordness of those she has to teach the results are credible. The singing and sewing receive due care and attention. The arithmetic supplementary rule must be strictly observed next year."

Teaching staff – Margaret Ashworth, Certificated Teacher, M.A.McGregor, Pupil Teacher.

11/12 So cold the children can hardly write.

1879

10/6 Many of the children have come to school without the school fees owing to bad trade.

11/8 The attendance is not at all good, about half the children gathering fruit, getting in hay, and everything else excepting being made to attend school regularly.

18/12 Prize Day. Prizes given to the children by the Rev. Philip Yorke Savile, Chairman to the School Board.

1880

30/7 Pupil teacher Mary Ann McGregor finished her service at the school.

20/8 As I am still without a teacher I am teaching the whole school.

4/10 Annie Mansley came to school this a.m. to assist me. She is now a monitor and will take Pupil Teacher papers for end of first year.

1882

20/2 Attendance Officer has visited the homes of absent children and reports much sickness.

24/4 At the School Board meeting today the following school fees and arrears were remitted: Until arrears are paid Hemp to pay 3d a week, Naylor to pay 6d a week, Richard Leonard to pay 6d a week, Annie Webster to pay 2d a week. All arrears were remitted for Mary Webster, Sarah Speight and Sarah Anderson.

Report of H.M.I. of Schools in July 1882. "The results of the examination in standard work are very satisfactory, reading continues to be well expressed and the other subjects have improved. The 1st and 2nd standards now form a sound foundation. Class subjects not so good. Children should be taught to think for themselves and reply in their own words, random answering must be checked. The infants are well prepared by the Pupil Teacher, they are in good order, read and write well and recite with nice expression."

Teaching staff Margaret Ashworth, First Certificated Teacher, Annie Mansley, Pupil Teacher 2nd year.

1884

23/6 Out of the 60 infants 12 are present, the remainder ill with measles.

1885

14/4 Received the sanction of the School Board to remit the school fees of those colliers' children who are out on strike.

15/6 School fees seem to be coming in fairly after the colliers' strike.

1888

July School Report by H.M.I. (part extract). "The forms and gallery should have comfortable backs and the children's feet should rest on the ground when seated on forms."

1889

July Comment by H.M.I. "Conduct of the infant boys in the playground is very improper, the Board should provide a urinal for them."

1893

1/2 Received notice from Clerk of School Board that the salary of the Assistant Mistress Charlotte Ashworth is increased to £10 per annum from 1 February 1893.

1907

18/2 Report by H.M.I. "The proposed addition to the staff and the transfer of Std. 1 to the infant room will permit better grouping of the classes and should have good effect. The infant class temporarily in charge of a new supplementary teacher continues to be the weakest part of the school. Reading and number are particularly backward and the children are slow in speech and movements generally. The lower group in the mixed school is also in charge of a new teacher who gives distinct promise of better things. The Head Mistress works with great energy which is reflected in the briskness of the older children, much of the work in this class deserves praise. The book work, writing, summing and drawing is very neat and oral answering is prompt and intelligent."

17/6 Poor attendance this day owing to the anniversary of the United Methodist Free Church and the Miners' Demonstration Day.

13/9 Received schedule of grants for year ended 30 June 1907.

	Actual Average Attendance	Average Attendance for Grant	Rate per School	
Mixed School	76	76	22s	£83.12.0d
Infants		43	17s	£36.11.0d
Annual Grant Payable				£120.3.0d
Full Grant 119 at 10 shillings				£59.10.0d
Deduct Instalment Paid				£40.17.6d
Balance of Grant Payable				£18.12.6d
Annual Grant				£120.3.0d
Net Amount Payable				£138.15.6d

10/10 Daisy Green Std. VI scholar who left school in September has won a scholarship to Wakefield High School.

1908

13/1 Temperature of classroom at 9 a.m. is 35f, infants' room 32f.

22/5 Empire Day. Speeches made by teachers and children and patriotic songs were sung.

9/10 Visit by HMI. Accommodation mixed 147, average attendance 66, infants 80, average attendance 54.

1909

14/3 Visit by H.M.I. "Infants, some of the desks are too high and lack back rests."

23/6 School closed, holiday on the occasion of Messrs Briggs & Co annual trip.

21/7 26 children absent with scarlet fever.

1911

23/3 Forwarded list of garments for year ended this month, 112 sold for £3.14.10d.

22/4 Two days holiday for coronation.

24/4 Miss C Kaye appointed teacher at salary of £45 p.a.

18/12 Pupil aged 8 refused to go into another room, kicked the door and threw a bible at it. Has a very violent temper and is a source of continual annoyance to the whole school.

1912

10/7 Holiday today in honour of the King's visit to Wakefield.

1913

15/4 Miss A Maynard still Head Teacher.

4/11 Two cases of diphtheria in the infants' class, one girl Clarissa Illingworth died at Rothwell Hospital on 7 November 1913.

26/11 School fumigated.

27/11 Nine cases of diphtheria. School closed by order of Dr Wigan, M.o.H.

1915

26/4 58 children absent owing to whooping cough.

27/4 School closed today for 6 weeks by order of Dr Taylor.

1917

21/7 Mr Craven visited the school and gave a lesson on Section 1 of the Board of Education temperance syllabus.

20/12 Special holiday, children assemble to hear a 'Special Order of the Day' and a talk about the war.

1918

8/1 Temperature in school 30f.

1/11 School closed for 2 weeks, flu epidemic, 46 children absent.

1919

26/5 Since July 1918 the school has been closed for 8 weeks owing to flu.

1920

19/11 Commenced the house system this week, have already found it decidedly helpful.

1921

25/4 Owing to the strike the children are being fed at noon by voluntary subscription.

9/6 Elizabeth McMillan Campbell from Mickletown school commenced as acting head teacher due to illness of Miss Maynard.

1922

27/4 Received letter of congratulation from the Education Committee on obtaining the highest % of average attendance in the Division.

29/6 Boy aged 13 years was extremely impertinent and disobedient to Miss Guise. This boy has a bad influence on the other children and would be better in a reformatory.

1923

9/4 Staff at school: A Maynard Head Teacher, S Wilkinson, E Guise, D Robinson.

1925

25/5 Celebrated Empire Day by singing patriotic songs and saluting the Union Jack.

28/7 Ivy Littlewod WRCC Supply Teacher took charge of school during absence of Miss Maynard.

1/10 Received with salary sheet instruction that Miss Maynard's position as Head Teacher terminated on September 9th 1925.

11/11 Miss Guise and Miss Robinson absent with permission to attend the funeral of Miss Maynard.

1926

18/1 Herbert Arundel took up position as Head Teacher.

4/6 Miners' strike, 58 children given dinners under a voluntary subscription scheme.

29/6 Breakfast started being given 3 times a week to necessitous children.

1928

4/5 140 absences due to illness.

1929

18/2 Temperature in school at 9 am 34f.

17/6 19 senior scholars and 3 teachers went by train to Shipley, walked through Shipley Glen and over the moor to Ilkley.

12/7 Half day holiday given by W.R.C.C. because of the highest % of average attendance during April. Highest attendance since 1904 .

30/9 12 children to receive milk under the scheme of W.R.C.C.

1931

5/7 22 children and 2 teachers on trip to Flamborough.

1932

2/7 17 children paid visit to York and visited the Guildhall, the Minster and the Museum Gardens.

1934

1/6 Received notice that Jack Darton had been successful in gaining a prize for his essay 'Why I Should Keep Healthy'.

1936

28/1 School closed for funeral of King George V.

21/10 Report by HMI "In this school there are 56 children who vary from 4-13 years. In the main the vitality and progress of the school is highly commendable".

1937

7/5 Distribution of souvenir spoons for coronation of King George VI.

21/10 School assemble to see the King and Queen pass by.

1938

28/9 School closed for 2 days for distribution of gas masks.

1939

1/9 School opened for inspection of respirators.

18/9 School opened, 1 boy absent because parents refused to send him until adequate provision had been made for his safety in case of air raid.

6/10 Trench for air raid shelter dug in playground.

1/11 Steel shelters delivered to school.

1940

8/3 Gardening takes place of craft work.

24/7 Air raid practice.

19/8 Swimming instruction started for the school.

28/8 23 children absent out of 58 owing to air raid warning lasting to 3 am.

11/12 Visit of school dentist.

1941

29/4 Clerk of Works visited re gas fire for firewatchers.

22/5 Rothwell U.D.C. architect visited re use of part of classroom should communal feeding be necessary in the district.

10/11 School meals started, 17 children stayed to dinner.

1942

6/1 Anti-splinter netting put on windows.

2/2 Potatoes and some seed received for planting in vegetable plot.

21/4 Lecture on hygiene and temperance by Mr Burrell of the Yorkshire Band of Hope Union.

2/11 Mr Charles Alan Mason took charge of school following retirement of Mr Arundel.

1943

5/1 Kathleen Braime took charge of the school as Head Mistress.

10/3 Today, a warm bright spring afternoon, we planted parsnips and broad beans in the war emergency garden.

7/5 Dr Taylor immunised 16 children for the first time today.

10/5 Miss Greenwood commenced today her preparations for the opening of the Nursery School.

21/6 Nursery class opened, 10 children under 5 years admitted.

1944

23/3 Hilda Allatt chosen to represent the school at the presentation of school children to H.R.H. The Princess Royal on the occasion of 'Salute the Soldier Week' at Rothwell.

5/4 To date we have subscribed £32.10s.0d. to 'Salute the Soldier Week'.

26/4 Children's gas masks checked by A.R.P. officer, most were changed for new ones which were then tested by each child passing through the gas van.

24/7 Mrs Banham appointed school caretaker.

29/9 Today we held a short harvest service. During the week we collected fruit, vegetables and flowers which were sent to the wounded soldiers at Pinderfields hospital.

1945

8/5 V.E. Day. We are given 2 days holiday.

1/6 An excellent report on the school by Mr H.Woodhead, H.M.I.

1946

18/12 Lighting during the day is almost impossible because there is no gas pressure.

1947

26/2 Much snow of late. School closed for County Minor. Very heavy blizzard overnight, 2 candidates walking to Mickletown school found Park Lane blocked with drifts 4-5 ft high, they followed a snow plough and reached their exam. places in time.

15/4 Senior class of 26 to Mickletown school this morning to hear an orchestral concert given by the Northern Philharmonic Orchestra

21/7 It has been arranged that the 11+ would be transferred to Whitwood Modern School in September. Scholey Hill School will become a junior and infant school.

2/9 School re-assembled today as Scholey Hill Junior School, juniors 14, infants 14, nursery 16.

20/11 School closed because of the wedding of Princess Elizabeth and Prince Phillip.

1949

28/1 The building of new housing estates such as Woodrow is causing a rapid drop in numbers.

10/2 The nursery class to close from 28/2/49.

28/2 This is now a 2-teacher school with a roll of 37.

19/5 Took 18 junior children to the Star Cinema in Castleford to see 'Scott of the Antarctic'.

2/9 Ten delicate children from Welbeck Street, Castleford to be brought to the school from 5/9/49.

31/10 A crate containing an easy chair for the staff room was delivered by British Rail. On unpacking the chair was found to be broken.

9/11 Lighting in school has been most inadequate and detrimental to children for many years. I have made many complaints. Gas pressure so low today that craft lessons abandoned through poor light.

11/11 Mary Weaver of Welbeck Street missed the school bus, but she walked to school arriving at 9.40 and received her mark.

1950

1/1 Price of school dinners is now 2/6d weekly.

25/4 Mrs E Grainger to be new caretaker from 1/5/50 as Mrs F Banham is to cease duties as caretaker.

18/12 Electric wiring of school and school house finished today, but it may be 2 months before it can be connected to the main supply by the Y.E.B.

1951

20/7 Electrical installations completed.

4/9 School opened, 25 children on roll.

2/10 Irene A. Thomas took charge this a.m., Miss Braime absent with leave for l term to attend Leeds University.

1952

8/1 I, Irene Alexandra Thomas, took charge of the school as Head Mistress.

1953

21/5 School closed for coronation, all children received a coronation mug from the W.R.C.C.

11/6 Report by H.M.I. of school inspection dated 1/5/53 received, "This admirable, joyous school is a good example of what can be accomplished when gifted teachers understand the ways of young children and possess the necessary knowledge and artistry to give them a full education".

1955

27/7 Today I cease my duties as Head Mistress.

5/9 I, Irene Fallam, took charge of the school, children on roll 19.

1956

26/6 School visit to Whitby.

1958

30/3 A party of children to St. Oswald's Church to take part in the Palm Sunday service.

1959

13/5 Miss Lawson, H.M.I. had lunch at the school to see if the meal was hot, we had salad.

1/9 19 children on the roll.

17/11 Miss Metcalfe Smith, Leeds University Lecturer, and Professor Ketcham, U.S.A. visited the school to observe our teaching methods.

1960

2/1 Park Lane and Watergate flooded. Mrs Clark, teacher, carried through the floods by Corporation van to Oulton, Stanley, and then to Scholey Hill.

29/3 Mr Mmurumah, an Education Officer from Japan visited the school.

6/9 Number on roll 19.

1962

31/1 2 boys left to emigrate to Australia.

27/7 Today I ceased duties as Head Mistress.

4/9 Miss Dennison, W.R.C.C. supply staff, took charge, 12 children on roll.

5/10 Nurse Tonks inspected the children.

6/11 Parents invited to attend a meeting and discuss the future of the school.

1963

4/3 Official information that school will close on 1/8/63.

1/8/1963 School closed.

THE LOCAL DEEP COAL MINING INDUSTRY

Coal occurs in a great number of seams but there are about seven major seams which vary in thickness from 3 ft. to 5 ft. The measures are faulted on a south-west/north-east axis by a major fault – the Methley Junction fault, which follows the 125 ft. contour on the northern side of Altofts, and another fault, the Loscoe fault running parallel with the Methley Junction fault about a mile and a half to the south. The measures on the southern side of the Methley Junction fault are downfaulted by about 300 ft. and those on the southern side of the Loscoe fault are up by about 60 ft. The faults have proved valuable in working the seams.

The technical innovations of the eighteenth century increased the demand for coal, as did the mechanisation of the Lancashire cotton industry, followed by the Yorkshire woollen industry. Coal was already being exported to Goole and Hull on the canal system, and until the 1820s coal for York was imported by sea from Tyneside. The hinterland of this city, the North and East Ridings, was now a market. There was also great demand in the south of England.

The earliest record of mining coal in the parish was 1346; coal pits were worked in various locations and are named Garden Pit, Mulberry Pit, White Hall Pit, Ings Pit, Parlour Pit, Engine and Bye Pit. Coal had been worked at Altofts in the fourteenth century but as the demand for coal grew locally and elsewhere and the shallower mines further to the west of the exposed coal field became exhausted fresh fields were sought in the deeper coal measures lying to the east. As the demand was for large quantities of coal, good transportation facilities were essential. The completion of the railways in 1840 brought these facilities and the rich coal seams underneath the agricultural land in this area lay ready for opening up.

Although this account is intended to show the effects of coal mining on the village of Methley, I think it is important to give some idea of the extent and complexity of the coal mining industry in the adjoining villages because they all had to work together. Men from Methley no doubt worked at pits outside Methley and the reverse was true, all were inter-dependent upon each other, but I am mainly concerned with the Whitwood collieries of Henry Briggs & Sons because they had mines in Methley.

The following writing shows the influence of the Briggs family in the coal mining industry of this area.

Briggs – A Yorkshire Family History

The following notes are taken from a book entitled 'A Merchant, a Banker and the Coal Trade – 1693-1971' and compiled by Donald Henry Currer Briggs.

"The head of the family was John Briggs of Hull, born in 1693, who at that time was associated with the banking world and the development of the coal trade in the West Riding of Yorkshire. John Briggs was a merchant in the export trade of Hull, he was particularly connected with woollens and textiles produced in the active industrial areas centred around Wakefield, Halifax and Leeds, all places connected to the port by water transport, either river or canal.

In 1726 on June 22nd John Briggs married Sarah Buttry in York Minster. Their eldest son, also called John, was born on March 23rd 1727; he died on March 19th 1782. He is described as a citizen of Hull and Hessel and he married Mary Rawden of Bilborough, near York.

No record has been found giving the name of the eldest son of John and Mary Briggs, who possibly died in infancy, but their second son Rawdon, was born on October 23rd 1758 in Hull. He married Ann Currer, of Clapham, on October 10th 1791. They lived at Ward's End, Halifax, until she died on August 2nd 1802 and they had three sons and three daughters; the sons were namely Rawdon (junior), born August 17th 1792, William, born May 30th 1795, and Henry, born August 10th 1797. It seems probable that Rawdon (senior) was originally sent to Halifax by his father, John (junior), to learn a trade and to promote the export of wool and cloth by ship through Hull and had also become a partner with his brother-in-law, William Currer of Halifax in a firm known as Currer, Briggs and Co., producing woollen yarn and carpets.

Henry Briggs, third son of Rawdon (senior) and Ann Currer, born at Ward's End, Halifax in 1797, married Marianne Milnes, younger daughter of the late James Milnes of Flockton Manor on June 3rd 1824. They had two sons, Henry Currer, born 2nd March 1829, and Archibald, born 16th January 1833. At the time of his marriage Henry was still associated, as he had been since 1816, with the firm of Currer, Briggs and Co. of Luddendenfoot, near Halifax, as also was his cousin, Henry Currer. In 1826 Henry left the Halifax business and joined his brother-in-law, William Stansfeld, husband of Marianne's elder sister, Margaret and together they developed New Flockton Colliery. Before this time James Milnes and his father Richard, who had been described as a timber merchant, had built a wooden railway from Flockton to Horbury to provide an outlet by waterway for the timber: this railway was relaid with iron rails in 1825 to provide the necessary transport for coal from the colliery. The New Flockton Colliery finally closed in 1893 after a prolonged strike. In 1839 Henry Briggs retired from this partnership and in the following year, 1840, he became associated with Charles Morton of Normanton in the development of Newton Pit, near Allerton Bywater; this venture was not successful. Morton then obtained a lease from Lord Mexborough dated December 1st 1841, to which Henry Briggs was a party, this lease allowed them to work various seams of coal in the Whitwood area on the south side of the River Calder. The first pit sunk was called Fairies Hill, followed by Ratten Row, then Speedwell and Common pits. In 1844 Charles Morton was appointed as one of the first Inspectors of Mines, on a part-time basis, but when he was appointed District Inspector on 21st November 1850 for the area covering Yorkshire, Derbyshire, Nottingham, Leicester and Warwick he left the partnership.

In 1854 Henry Currer Briggs married Catherine Shepherd, daughter of Edward Shepherd, Governor of Wakefield Gaol and assisted in the management of a jute mill owned by his father-in-law at Thornes, Wakefield. William Briggs (banker) and James Fletcher Tonge (corn miller) agreed to purchase all the freehold, copyhold, buildings, lands, etc., property of Benjamin Burnley, now deceased, also all the leasehold minebeds on seams of coal called the Lofthouse or Haigh Moor coal, the Warrenhouse coal and Stanley Main under the estate of the Earl of Mexborough hereinafter called the 'Junction Colliery'. A new partnership deed was drawn up with Henry Briggs, Henry Currer Briggs, William Briggs and James Fletcher Tonge as co-partners. From 1860 onwards the deeper and larger pits were sunk, comprising Whitwood Haigh Moor, Good Hope, and Dom Pedro.

Between 1860 and 1865 there was considerable unrest amongst the colliers as the trade unions were becoming more active organisations, and many stoppages of work took place at intervals. This caused considerable loss of output, and after a particularly long and acrimonious strike of 13 weeks in 1863 the following letter was received by Henry Briggs on October 13th 1863 at Outwood Hall:

> 'Mr Briggs,
> I will tell you what I think about you about this struggle. You are getting an ould man and besides you are a tyrant – ould B…r now Sirs what do you think to that bit – we have stopped 13 weeks All ready, but I have myself sw to take your life and your son also. But you shalt not live 13 days. Depend on it my nife is sharp But my Bullits is shorer than the nife and if I can under the time I will by God – if it be at noon today wen I see you shall have the arra if it be in your

Charrit. Like ould Abe Now reade that and pray to God to forgive your sins to be reddy'.

After this Henry Briggs and his son decided to promote a scheme of co-operative management under which both customers, officials and workmen could share in the profitability of the undertaking. The scheme provided for the division of the profits after proper provision for depreciation, etc. and after setting aside a sum to remunerate the invested capital, to be shared equally between shareholders and employees, as a bonus percentage on the money invested in shares, or for non-shareholders as a similar percentage on wages earned during the year. There was no obligation for workmen or officials to put their share of bonus back to buy shares, but many did so, and therefore they received not only the current bonus on earnings, but also the dividend on shares bought out of past bonuses; in addition it was provided that the employees should elect two members to the board of directors, provided that no strikes took place and that all disputes in the event of dissatisfaction should be settled by arbitration. This scheme proved highly satisfactory for many years and upwards of £40,000 in bonus was divided amongst the work people and more than 300 became shareholders.

From 1865 to 1868 the chairman of the company was Mr Henry Briggs followed by Henry Currer Briggs from 1868 to 1881. From 1865 rapid expansion of the company took place with the sinking of the Whitwood Silkstone pit with a downcast shaft of 18 ft diameter and an upcast shaft of 20 ft diameter and with a prospective output of 1000-1200 tons per day, later with the use of modern machinery the shaft has drawn 3,300 tons in a single shift of eight hours. In 1876 the output of the company was 598,000 tons per annum and by 1881, when Henry Currer Briggs died, the output had reached 660,000 tons per annum.

Henry Briggs was a confirmed Liberal and believed in deciding his own code of conduct; one not easily deterred from his objectives. He was a most conscientious Unitarian and spent much of his spare time in promoting the education of the young. He was noted as a keen and regular Sunday School teacher at Westgate Chapel, Wakefield and on many occasions acted as a Lay Preacher.

Henry Currer Briggs, who succeeded his father as chairman of the company in 1881, had been managing director of the company from 1865 to 1868, and then handed over that office to his brother Archibald Briggs who held it until his death in 1876. It was for this reason that he joined the Dundee firm of Thompson, Shepherd and Briggs, jute spinners, and lived in Dundee until 1869 when he moved down into Saltburn following the death of his father. Whilst in this district he became interested in the Carlton Iron Company, the Merrybent Railway and Apedale Lead Mines, and also the Bratsberg Copper Company in Norway. These various activities covered coal, iron, lime, lead, silver and copper production. He was a strict Unitarian and helped in founding a chapel in Dundee on 12th March 1870 and one in Stockton-on-Tees on 18th November 1872.

Following the sudden death of Henry Currer Briggs on October 20th 1881 whilst on a visit to Norway, Mr Richard Tonge became chairman and Arthur Currer Briggs, eldest son of Henry Currer Briggs, became managing director and in 1893 he became chairman.

In 1883 Arthur Currer Briggs married Helen Jones and they lived at Red Bank, Newton Park, Leeds. They had one daughter and two sons, Reginald Martin Currer Briggs, born 1891, and Donald Henry Currer Briggs, born 1893.

At this time it became necessary to find a profitable means of dealing with the considerable output of small coal arising from the breakage of coal in transport for which no reasonable market existed; in fact large quantities were available on the open market at no more than 6d per ton and as it ranked as a waste product, it was frequently used as railway ballast being no more than ¾ inch in size. It was therefore decided to join with Messrs

Demster Bros. of Elland, makers of gas production plants to build a carbonising plant on the old Good Hope pit site, which had now been cleared. Here they manufactured coke, benzol, sulphate of ammonia and gas to light the district. This venture, started in 1883, proved highly successful and much coke was shipped to Scandinavia, whilst German dye works took most of the benzol. This was known as the Whitwood Chemical Company Limited.

From 1865 to 1886 the profit sharing scheme on co-operative management lines persisted; there were seventeen workmen shareholders who served on the board. Early in 1886 much outside pressure was brought to bear on the workmen as the Miners' Union made progress in the district, and after a short but partial stoppage the workmen directors resigned requesting that the union in future should deal with any disputes; this proved the death blow to the attempt to substitute the arbitration principle for the 'strike'. Thus ended the period during which workmen directors were elected by the general meeting of the company's employees.

In 1895 to 1899 considerable progress was made by the company and the Snydale pit was bought from Rhodes and Dalby to take the place of Streethouse pit which had been closed down. It came into production that year and the company produced over one million tons for the first time in 1900, but there was a considerable reduction in output following the South African War, when production was down to 800,000 tons per annum until 1906 when the Newmarket Colliery Company owned by the Hargreaves family was bought.

On August 31st 1906 a second severe blow fell upon the company. It was on the day of the annual general meeting of that year that Arthur Currer Briggs died suddenly of a heart attack and Mr W G Jackson was appointed to fill the chairmanship. During his time as chairman Arthur Currer Briggs became an Alderman and J.P. and also Lord Mayor of the City of Leeds. In 1904, after he had been a member of the council of the Yorkshire College (later the University of Leeds) for eleven years, he raised a fund to build the Mining Department.

By 1908 over 1,000,000 tons of output were reached again, until 1910 when Dom Pedro finished, but its place was then taken by the New Water Haigh Colliery at Woodlesford. From this date the output rose gradually and from 1914 to 1919 the average annual output was 1,380,000 tons. In 1907 Mr Jackson added to the board Mr Walter Hargreaves and in 1919 he appointed Walter Hargreaves as managing director, who in the meantime had moved from Loscoe Grange to Aberford, and for the last 5 years to Bowcliffe Hall, Bramham.

Following the end of the First World War there were strikes due to conflicts between the profitability of the coal mines and wages paid, apparently the industry was losing a million pounds a week. These difficulties were resolved and in 1923 the company reached its peak with an output of 1,725,000 tons. .Mr Hargreaves had earlier been a student at the Yorkshire College and was instrumental in obtaining funds of £20,000 with assistance from the Yorkshire Coal Owners' Association and the Miners' Welfare Fund to build a new mining department at the University of Leeds in 1920.

The company was overtaken by the long strike of 1926, again caused by dispute between profits versus operating costs. The Coal Mines Act of 1930 introduced regulations on output and prices and by 1939 output again rose to 1,600,000 tons a year. In 1934 both Reginald Martin Currer Briggs and Donald Henry Currer Briggs became joint managing directors and in 1940 the Chemical Company ceased due to its main market in Scandinavia being occupied by the enemy.

The Coal Industry Nationalisation Act became law in 1946 when the company and its subsidiaries ceased to operate."

The Methley pits continued producing coal for the National Coal Board until the latter half of the 20th Century. Methley Junction pit closed 1958-59, Newmarket pit closed in September 1983, and Savile pit closed in 1984.

The total amount of coal drawn from all the Briggs collieries up to nationalisation in 1946 was 72,274,000 tonnes.

Summary

1845	Possible date of sinking Methley Junction Colliery shaft.
1867	Good Hope pits completed, sixty-two cottages and new infants' school built, 975 workmen became entitled to bonus of 4½ percent to 12 percent on gross earnings.
1868	Workmen's co-operative system working well and 41 additional shares were taken up by employees.
1869	Gas Works and Iron Foundry established. Industrial partnership system so satisfactory that workmen entitled to elect representative on Board.
1871	Loscoe Brick Company formed.
1872	Dom Pedro pit sunk to Stanley Main. New sidings at Whitwood and Methley.
1873	Whitwell Main Colliery purchased from Ellison and Broadbent for £55,000.
1874	Yorkshire Coal and Steamship Company Ltd established. Commencement of depression – reaction from inflation of last few years – Franco-Prussian war. Savile pit begun.
1875	Following four weeks' strike Directors can no longer recommend a continuance of the system of industrial partnership owing to altered relations between the company and the workmen. The payment of a bonus on wages earned by employees discontinued. Employees now members of the Miners' Union and act under instructions of the union. Whitwood Silkstone pit begun.
1876	Unexampled stagnation of trade. Savile pit completed.
1877	Severe trade depression continued.
1878	Exceptional depression.
1879	Exceptional depression.
1880	No improvement.
1881	No improvement.
1882	Depression continued; no dividend paid.
1883	Depression continued.
1884	Depression continued; no dividend paid.
1885	No improvement in trade; two months strike, no dividend paid; loss on year of £2,732.
1886	End of ten years depression. Last workman director appointed.
1887	Good Hope pit worked out. Henry Briggs, Son & Co. joined in formation of Whitwood Chemical Company on site of Good Hope pit.
1890	Dividend 13% free of tax.
1893	Export trade cut out by Scotland, South Wales and North of England, where much lower rates of wages paid . Gas and steam coal prices show serious reduction.
1894	Miners' strike in the Midlands came to the rescue of Yorkshire trade.
1895	Yorkshire Coal & Steamship Co. sold following death of Mr Meek of Goole, Manager for 21 years. Four months strike in Scotland.
1987	Snydale Collieries purchased from Rhodes & Dalby.
1898	Company agreed with 3,430 out of 3,453 men employed to adopt the scheme of mutual insurance in lieu of the provisions of the Workmen's Compensation Act.
1901	Considered closing two pits owing to duty of one shilling per ton on export coal.
1907	Newmarket Haigh Moor Colliery purchased from W. Hargreaves.
1908	Sinking of Water Haigh Colliery commenced to develop the Beeston seam under the Calverley Royalty at Oulton.

1910	Full burden of Eight Hours Act felt, involving large capital outlay to minimise its disadvantages.
1915	1,100 men on active service.
1923	Company took control of collieries of Robert Holliday & Sons Ltd., East Ardsley, Wakefield.
1937	Company acquired control of Micklefield Coal & Lime Company's Collieries at Peckfield, near Castleford.
1940	Briggs Collieries Limited formed, capital £1,200,000.
1943	Main line railway waggons sold. Inauguration of contributory pensions scheme for officials and staff of Briggs Collieries Ltd.
1944	Sale of gas works to United Kingdom Gas Corporation.
1945	Commencement of production of briquetts by the Whitwood Chemical Co., Ltd. for the Ministry of Fuel and Power.
1946	Company was nationalised.

NOTE: In the years following 1900, 4,000 workmen employed, by 1914, 5,000 and 1923, 7,000.

Additional information.

1945 Names and productive capacities of collieries

Whitwood Silkstone	**2,500**	**tons per day**
Whitwood Haigh Moor	450	tons per day
Savile	600	tons per day
Methley Junction	Used for riding men	
Dom Pedro	Used for riding men	
Water Haigh	2,000	tons per day
Snydale	750	tons per day
Peckfield	1,200	tons per day
East Ardsley	500	tons per day
Shawcross	800	tons per day

COLLIERY YEAR BOOK AND COAL TRADES DIRECTORY

TABLE 10. – AVERAGE EARNINGS PER WEEK (OR SHIFT) OF THE VARIOUS CLASSES OF COLLIERY WORKERS IN 1886, 1914, 1918 AND 1923.

[Based upon the Board of Trade "Return of Rates of Wages in the Mines and Quarries of the United Kingdom" (1891) *; and upon information supplied to the Coal Industry Commission* (1919), *and to the Royal Commission on the Coal Industry* (1925.)*]*

Class of Worker	1886 (Oct.)		1914 (June)		1918 (Nov.)		1923 (Sept.)	
	(a) Average Weekly Earnings							
Men : Below-ground.	s.	d.	s	d	s	d	s	d
Deputies, Firemen and Examiners	28	10	43	9	85	5	84	5
Contractors and their helpers	Particulars not available						66	9
Coal-getters : Piece-workers	24	6	38	0	78	11	70	5
" Day-Wage	20	4	30	1	63	10	54	4
Fillers, Wagon-loaders, etc. (at the Coal-face)	22	1	}29	1	62	5	53	1
Putters, Hauliers and Trammers	19	8	}					
Timbermen, Stonemen, Brushers and Rippers	23	0	34	11	70	3	66	3
Other Workers	20	2	28	11	59	8	52	2
Men : Above-ground								
Enginemen : Winding	}23	10	{47	0	90	4	}75	}3
" Other	}		{35	11	72	10	}	
Stokers and Boilermen	19	6	31	6	69	8	58	11
Pit-head men	20	2	27	9	60	9	}46	6
Screen-men	18	4	23	6	52	9	}	
Tradesmen including Mechanics, Joiners, Blacksmiths, etc.	23	9	32	9	65	3	59	1
Other Workers	19	0	25	10	55	3	49	6
Average for Men	22	11	33	6	69	7	61	11
Lads and Boys.								
Below-ground	11	0	16	8	34	0	29	4
Above-ground	9	7	11	9	27	9	23	11
Women	8	2	}9	0	31	3	18	10
Girls	5	7	}					
Average for all classes of Workers	21	1	30	7	62	3	54	11

Class of Worker	1886 (Oct.)		1914 (June)		1918 (Nov.)		1923 (Sept.)	
	(b) Average Earnings per Shift							
Men : Below-ground.	s.	d.	s	d	s	d	s	d
Deputies, Firemen and Examiners			7	8¼	14	6	13	7¼
Contractors and their helpers			?	?	?	?	13	8¼
Coal-getters : Piece-workers			8	10	17	0	14	5
" Day-Wage			7	0	13	5¼	10	8½
Fillers, Wagon-loaders, etc. (at the Coal-face)			}6	5½	12	9	10	5
Putters, Hauliers and Trammers								
Timbermen, Stonemen, Brushers and Rippers			7	6	14	4½	12	5½
Other Workers			5	9½	11	5	9	7
Men : Above-ground.								
Enginemen : Winding			{7	1¾	13	3½	}11	0¼
" Other			{5	7¼	10	11	}	
Stokers and Boilermen			4	11¼	10	8¼	8	11¼
Pit-head men			5	1¾	10	9½	}8	2¼
Screen-men			4	9¼	10	0	}	
Tradesmen including Mechanics, Joiners, Blacksmiths, etc.			5	7½	11	1¼	9	5¼
Other Workers			4	9¾	9	9¾	8	3¾
Average for Men			7	1	13	8¾	11	8½
Lads and Boys.								
Below-ground			3	7	7	4	5	9
Above-ground			2	5½	5	4¾	4	4¾
Women			}					
Girls			}1	11½	5	11¾	3	9½
Average for all classes of Workers			6	5¾	12	5¼	10	5

NOTE.-In 1914 and 1918 the wage-rates for men relate to workers over 21 years of age, except where the rate for adults applies to workers of a lower age. In September, 1923 the wage-rates for adults appear to relate more exclusively to persons of 21 years of age and above.

Coinage

£	s	d			DECIMAL
		½	=	Half penny	One fifth of a new penny
		1	=	One penny	Two fifths of a new penny
	1	0	=	One shilling (or 12 pence)	Five new pence
	2	0	=	One florin (24 pence)	Ten new pence
	10	0	=	Ten shillings	Fifty new pence
1	0	0	=	One pound (or 240 pence)	One hundred new pence

Welfare and Housing

Henry Briggs and Company in connection with the District Welfare Committee took part in a convalescent scheme to assist workmen to recuperate after accident or illness, and the local hospital (Castleford) received support from the company and workmen on an agreed basis.

Welfare Centres were built in connection with all the collieries owned by the company. At Whitwood grounds were laid out for cricket, tennis and bowls and a hall was built for dances, lectures and other functions. The hall was erected to the memory of the late Mr Arthur Currer Briggs, who was chairman of the company from 1893-1906. Similar schemes were in existence at Methley, Woodlesford, Snydale, East Ardsley, Crawshaw & Warburton's and Micklefield Collieries and some of the sports pavilions are complete with baths and tea making arrangements. Pit-head baths were erected at Waterhaigh Colliery and at the pits of Crawshaw & Warburton's Ltd.

'The Co-Operator' dated 1867

'The Co-Operator', a fortnightly record of co-operative progress by working men, edited by Henry Pitman of Manchester, dated 1st October 1867, No. 121, price 1d.

"The Second Annual Commemorative tea party took place on Saturday, September 21st and was given for the work force of the five pits. It took place in a large new waggon shed built at the Whitwood Colliery – decorated with flowers, flags, Chinese lanterns, mottoes, trophies, etc. the trophies being industrial implements such as picks, Davy lamps, shovels, and a section of a seam of coal nearly seven feet thick. Seven tea tables in the room, at which nearly 1,800 people feasted, between 4 pm and 7 pm, enlivened by the Leeds Model Band and closing with a fireworks display. Apart from the Chairman of the Company who attended, there was also the Reverend Philip Yorke Savile, Rector of Methley.

The Reverend Philip Yorke Savile spoke at this tea and said that the sight of this harmonious meeting of masters and men was most agreeable. It carried him back to the days of Boaz when he said to his workmen 'The Lord be with thee', and they said to him 'The Lord bless thee'. Philip Yorke Savile then went on to say that having been born within two miles of this spot and lived in the neighbourhood above half a century he felt a deep interest in their welfare and rejoiced at their prosperity. The Reverend Gent. also expressed a hope that as gas was being introduced to Methley Junction works it might be extended to the schools and colliers' houses. It would also be very welcome at his own house, and also especially to those who had to work on the night shift. He would be happy to reciprocate the boon by granting the use of a suitable field as a recreation ground, which was so much wanted by the hard working population.

The Chairman's Address. He said that the company had prospered. In 1866 the bonus given in proportion to wages was £1,800; this year, 1867, it was half as much again, £2,700. The Chairman proceeded to speak about the improvement observable amongst the colliery population. When he was a young man there was cock fighting, bull baiting and gambling. He feared there was a little gambling yet but he hoped it would soon disappear as had these barbarous sports. They had built a school years ago. The Chairman hoped that the bonus of £2,700, which was a large sum to distribute to a small community, would be spent in a useful way to promote the comfort and improvement – social and intellectual – of the operatives." End of extract.

NOTE: The bonus was being awarded because it was the second year of working under the co-operative system at Whitwood and Methley Junction Collieries.

A Visit to the Methley Junction and Savile Collieries in 1877, extracted from the 'Halifax Guardian' 1877

"On my second visit to the collieries of this firm, I was more than ever impressed, not only with their magnitude, but with the advantageous position they occupy with regard to facilities for the carriage of coal, both by rail, river and road. By Great Northern train via Holbeck, I reached Methley Junction at an early hour in the morning, and was there met by Mr Stones, the manager of the colliery there. This pit is situate close to the railway, and has direct communication with the Midland, North Eastern, Great Northern, and Lancashire and Yorkshire Railways, and also with the river Calder, and thus with all the system of internal navigation in the kingdom. This Methley mine, I understand, was purchased by Messrs Briggs before the limited company was formed, it being originally the property of Mr Burnley.

Before going near the pit, we walked down a tramway to the banks of the river Calder, and saw some dozen boats 'laying-on', or waiting to be loaded. The process of doing this is very simple. The waggons are let down by rope, and each one is then separately hauled on to a platform (not very different to those used at the execution of criminals), which is lowered into the hold of the boat. Each of these barges takes a load of 50 to 60 tons, and are removed either by horses or a steam tug to their destination, whether that may be inland, or to some of the ports on the coast. The only disadvantage of this river communication is that in case of floods, the work of loading cannot be proceeded with; but I will show further on how this difficulty has been guarded against at another and newer colliery belonging to the company. At Methley Colliery, or close to it, there are also extensive sidings in connection with all the railway companies above mentioned. Returning to the colliery, I looked at the six boilers, each of nominal 30 horse power, and which were worked at a pressure of 45 lb.

Nor is it a small amount of steam that is required from these boilers; for in addition to the pair of powerful horizontal engines used to work the drawing of coal, there are several others about the premises, and a pair underground, all supplied with motive power from the same source. The engine house is a spacious building, and the engine tenter a solitary individual during working hours; nor would it be wise that he should have company to distract his attention from the important duties he has to attend to, upon which the lives of many people depend. He has to thoroughly comprehend the exact number of strokes required by the engine to lift the cage from the bottom to the top, as one more than the proper number would be of very serious consequence, if not to the men, to the working plant; and hence the notice on all engine-house doors – 'no admittance'.

Passing from the engine room, the next places visited were the shafts. At Methley, as at most other places, there are two in number. One is used for drawing the coal, whilst the second one, in addition to being a means of ventilation, is so constructed that in case of accident it can be used for drawing out the men, for pumping, and even, if necessary, for hauling coal. The ventilation of this mine is effected by a large fan, worked by an engine of 30-horse power, made by the Grange Iron Company, Limited, Durham, in 1872. This engine is in duplicate. It is remarkable for the easiness with which it works, and makes scarcely more noise than a lever watch. Close to the top of the shaft, around which are all the necessary screens for sorting the coal, are the workshops, including saw mill, carpenters' and blacksmiths' shops, stores, etc., so that slight repairs can be done on the premises, whilst the heavy work is all done at the central depot at Whitwood. At the top of the premises is a winding engine, worked with friction gear, by which coals are let down to the wharf and the various sidings on the railways, by which they are intended to be sent away, and as the output at Methley is about 500 tons per day, it can readily be imagined that this engine has not an idle time.

We next proceeded down the shaft, and found the state of things at the bottom much the same as at those pits previously described. The large gallery is lighted up with gas, and the scene is one of business. Close to the bottom of the shaft is a pumping engine, which sends water to the surface. Usually pumping engines are at the top, and lift the water; but in this case, by what I think is a better and more economical plan, the engine is at the bottom, and the water is forced to the top. Of course, the engine is a powerful one, as the weight of the water lifted increases by 1lb. to the yard all the way up the 150 yards shaft. The cylinder is one of 18 inches, and there is a 6¼ inch ram, and by these means the water is forced to the bank, after which it runs to the reservoir, and from thence supplies the boilers and anything else about the premises needing it. The deputies' office, also near the bottom of the shaft, is smaller than the one at Dom Pedro, but is furnished with exactly the same kind of books and material.

Passing from here we entered the stables in which there were 60 horses, every one of which looked healthy, and, what is more strange, clean and sleek in their skins. The stables are well ventilated, thoroughly whitewashed and clean, and in quite as good condition as any one would wish to see in stables above ground. Having on many occasions heard it asserted that horses which have been underground for a few years became blind, I made enquiry, and was told that such was the case in many instances; but it was by no means the rule. In this mine I saw many blind horses, but it was marvellous with what sagacity they worked, seeming to know every turn and bend in the roads they travelled with unerring instinct. There are some very small ponies down here, several of which can go into places where even one of the corves cannot be forced. All these animals are well fed and kindly treated, but it is singular what a propensity they have to lightness of heel, which no doubt arises from the good-natured teasing of their boy drivers.

Adjoining the stable is the blacksmith's shop, a very large apartment, where not only the horses' shoes are made and fitted; but in which all the picks, etc. used in coal-getting, are sharpened and repaired. The furnace in this department needs no manual labour to blow the coal into a glow. By a simple arrangement it is connected with the ventilation from the top, and can be put into a roar in less than a minute. The smith's shop is kept very orderly, and the walls are whitewashed, which gives it a pleasant and cheerful appearance – so much so that a person ushered into it, without knowing that he was underground, would associate it at once with the famous 'village smithy', celebrated in song, with the absence of the 'spreading chestnut tree', and even the latter could be imagined to exist in the lofty roof overhead.

The next room is the tool house, fitted up all over with racks for the tools of the men, which are left at night to be sharpened and repaired, and delivered out to them next morning when they resume work. In immediate proximity to this is an engine-room, where a pair of powerful horizontal engines do the work of more horses than the mine could contain. They draw coal from three different quarters by means of a drum on which there is coiled 1,200 yards of steel rope, whilst in order to connect waggons to this, horses have to bring them from a distance of over 600 yards beyond. These engines are regularly and continuously in use, and bring to the eye of the pit 80 waggons at each pull, each waggon containing about 8 cwt. of coal.

Another large apartment is the lamp cabin, where all the safety lamps are deposited at night, cleaned, filled with oil, and distributed next morning. Some years ago all lamps of this kind were locked and opened with an instrument resembling a carriage key; but colliers soon found means of tampering with these, and they became no longer 'safety lamps'. Without lock or key, they are now made so that it is impossible to open them without detection being certain. At the place where they are closed, a small plug of lead, a little over half an inch long, is inserted and then by a machine is squeezed up, and fastens the entrance to the lamp. By the squeezing process, one end of the plug has impressed on it a crown, whilst the other is impressed with the words 'H.Briggs & Co'. This renders it impossible to tamper with the lamp, as, if it comes back with this plug broken, detection of the offence is certain.

All about the foot of the shaft of this mine it has been rendered necessary to erect massive masonry works to support the roof, this being caused by the fact that when the pit was first opened the coal was worked at the least expense, from the immediate neighbourhood of the 'pit's eye', instead of the usual, but more expensive plan, of driving the headings first, and working the coal back.

In the Methley Colliery, where a good specimen of the Haigh Moor coal is wrought, provision is made by which a second pump can be at work in a few minutes, should any accident occur to the first one. The mine has been worked for about a quarter of a century, and finds employment for about 350 men and boys, 230 of these being coal getters.

Coming again to the surface of the earth, we look through the village of Methley, where there are numerous cottages for the colliers, a large reading room, Primitive Methodist and other chapels, a board school of very neat design, and other institutions. It is needless to say that there are numerous public houses and that these have a fair share of patronage.

Passing from Methley Junction pit we went to the one most recently opened by Messrs. H.Briggs, Son & Co. Limited, and which in a short time will prove a most prolific source of coal supply. Before noticing the Savile Colliery at all, as a locomotive was ready in the siding, we mounted it, and were speedily run up to the junction of the company's sidings with those of the railway company. Messrs Briggs have here two long sidings on the main line of the Midland Railway. In addition to these a most useful connection has been made with the canal, which runs at a short distance from the mine, and which affords a very short route to Leeds. To facilitate the loading of coal at this point, which, taking the canal route, is nearer by eight miles to Leeds than the Methley Junction Colliery, the company has constructed a basin, or properly speaking, a dock, which is 75 feet wide, 175 feet long and 10 feet 6 inches deep, the water line being 8 feet 6 inches. This has a four foot brick wall all round, and there is a drawbridge dividing it from the canal.

The coal from the mine is brought down in hopper-bottomed trucks, by a locomotive. Each waggon is lowered by a platform, until it is nearly level with the bottom of the boat, when the bottom of the truck is opened, and the coals are dropped gently into the hold of the boat.

Close to the basin there is a stable for hauling horses, and also accommodation for boatmen and their assistants. The whole of this work – the making of the basin and its adjuncts – has been accomplished since last August, the machinery is of such a simple character that a child can work it, and it will enable the company to put on a boat a very large proportion of the output of the Savile Colliery, without the trouble arising from variations in the level of the water, such as occur at shipping staithes on the open rivers.

It is not quite twelve months since coal was first worked in the Savile pit, but although the whole of the main roads are not yet complete, it promises to be one of the most productive belonging to the company. The drawing shaft is 140 yards deep and 14 feet diameter. In consequence of the quantity of water found during the sinking, nearly one half of the depth of the shaft is 'tubbed' or lined with iron. On arriving at the bottom of the shaft, those who have been in the mines before described have a feeling of disappointment at the absence of light, the fact being that gas has not yet been laid on at the Savile pit, and, therefore, by the more dim rays of oil lamps, it is some time before the proportions of the galleries and roadways can be discerned. Having obtained lamps, however, in the office, which is being fitted up exactly similar to that at Dom Pedro, we came out again to the porch, which is of immense proportions, being 55½ yards long, 19 feet wide, and 17 feet high. From this porch two main roads have been driven. One of these leads in the direction of Methley Junction colliery, with which it is intended to open an underground communication. The seam of Haigh Moor coal at Savile pit is an excellent one. It is 5 feet in thickness, 3 feet 6 inches of which is best coal, having under it 18 inches of good seconds coal, there being but a very slight band of dirt between the two. There is a good and sound roof over the coal. At present there are no horses in the Savile pit; but ample provision is being made for them by the construction of very spacious and lofty stables. In the meantime the coal is brought to the eye of the pit by lads.

There is a second shaft, of equal dimensions to the first, for the purposes of ventilation. Whilst at the bottom of this, and speaking with Mr Stones, the Manager, and two other gentlemen, I heard voices seemingly above us. I asked if there were men working nearby, but was told that the voices I heard were our own, repeated by an echo. I then tried the experiment of speaking when the rest were quiet, and found that this was so, and that the echo would repeat almost a whisper.

Ascending the shaft, I noticed that the top platform and screens are not yet roofed in, but that in all other respects the arrangements are completed. The engine room (which by the way is like everything about the place, beautifully clean) is a very large one , and the woodwork in it, including a high wainscotting around it, is of varnished pitch pine. The engines are a pair of nominally 35-horsepower each, but of course their power is not limited to that. They were made by Davy Brothers, Limited, of Sheffield, and are similar in construction to those at Dom Pedro, nothing having been spared to secure their solidity and strength. Motive power is supplied to them by four very large boilers, made, as most of the other boilers belonging to the company have been, by Messrs. Horsfield, of Dewsbury.

This pit is also ventilated by a fan which is worked by an engine that runs almost as silently as a watch. As invariably the case with fan engines, this is constructed in duplicate; and in case one engine should become disabled, the other can be attached in a quarter of an hour, so simple and ingenious have the makers, Messrs Easton and Tattersall of Leeds – made the connecting apparatus. The fan itself is 36 ft. diameter and 10 ft.wide. It is calculated to make sixty revolutions per minute; but, of course, at present this velocity is not needed. The fan is situated near the top of the upcast shaft, to which it has communication by two air passages, each 32 ft. high and 3 ft.wide. As the foul air is extracted from the mine it is passed up a chimney. As there are not yet more than forty coal getters at work in the pit, there is not much foul air, and therefore we descended into these air passages, and by the aid of a safety lamp only, which is permitted here, saw the immense proportions and the substantial character of the work in and about the fan; and had the opportunity of noticing how silently the latter did its work.

Near the colliery are the usual workshops and stores, saw mill, etc., all new, and erected in a most substantial manner. Lengthy sidings are being laid down, and everything prepared in a manner which shows that those who have thus invested so large an amount of capital in preliminary works, know, for a certainty, that there is an immense field of coal to be won.

Messrs Briggs & Co. Limited, are also shipowners; and under the name of the Yorkshire Coal & Steam Shipping Co. have, out of their general capital, £60,000 invested in steamers. They have four of these vessels, all fine and powerful boats. They are named the Altona, the Marianne Briggs, the Dinnington, and the Whitwood. The first two are each of 700 tons burden, and the latter two are 500 and 400 tons respectively. Two of these vessels ply regularly between Goole and Hamburg, and the other two between the same port and Rouen; carrying coal principally on the outward voyage, and general cargo on the return. The Hamburg boats also carry passengers. The Company has offices at Goole, Hamburg and Rouen, and does a very considerable amount of business".

Coal Mining and its Dangers

Violent death on a small and large scale was a frequent visitor to the coal mines of Britain caused, for example, by crushing, roof falls, flooding, explosions of fire damp/coal dust, entombment, suffocation by afterdamp, and breakage of machinery.

The coal measures of this country deposited between 350-270 million years ago are formed from the decayed remains of tropical forests and vegetation. These decayed remains formed peat which when buried and subject to pressure and chemical changes turned into coal. The change produces a marsh gas called methane, also called firedamp, which is trapped in the coal. It is a colourless, odourless flammable gas which becomes highly explosive when mixed with air and ignited. The combustion of a methane mixture and coal dust in a colliery leaves behind various gases, one commonly called 'afterdamp' will contain a sufficient percentage of carbon monoxide to be quite lethal. In Britain's worst mining disaster ever, that at Senghenydd, Wales on 14th October, 1913 all but a tiny minority of the 439 victims died of carbon monoxide poisoning. It will be seen that rescue operations however speedily done, often came too late to save very many who might have survived the actual blast.

Attempts to work the gaseous coal seams in the Barnsley area resulted in a number of catastrophic explosions. Between 1847 and 1866 at least 750 local men and boys were killed in this way.

Another disaster occurred at the Combs Colliery at Thornhill, Dewsbury on 4th July 1893 when 139 men and boys were killed. This incident shows that £36,000 was raised nationally by appeal and how the appeal money was shared out.

7s.6d. per week to each widow during widowhood
3s.6d. per week for 1 child under 15 years in a family
6s.6d. per week for 2 children under 15 years in a family
8s.6d. per week for 3 children under 15 years in a family
10s.6d. per week for 4 children under 15 years in a family
12s.6d. per week for 5 children under 15 years in a family.

In the case of children left without father or mother a widows allowance of 7s.6d. per week for payment for them to be looked after until the youngest child reached 15 years of age.

Forty pounds in respect of each boy killed, either in bulk or weekly instalments to their parents or other relatives who had custody of the boys.

The following example shows the ages of children working in mines. An accident occurred at Huskard Colliery, near Silkstone, Barnsley on 4th July, 1838 when 26 children were drowned when torrential rain flooded the pit. The dead included 7 boys under the age of 10 years, and girls one aged 8, one aged 9, two aged 10, two aged 11, two aged 13, two aged 15, and one aged 17. The public were appalled and following an outcry Anthony Ashley Cooper (afterwards 7th Earl of Shaftesbury) was instrumental in bringing about the Mine Regulation Act of 1842 which prohibited boys under 10 years and females from working underground. In 1860 the minimum age was raised to 12 years.

Mining Explosion at Methley – Six Lives Lost

"An explosion of fire damp occurred yesterday, Thursday, December 9th 1875, at the East side of the workings of the Methley Junction Colliery belonging to Messrs. Henry Briggs, Son & Co. Six men and boys were killed including 1 Deputy. Their names are:

Alfred Hanson, Deputy, married with 7 children
James Hussin, married with 2 children
Thomas Thompson, married with 5 children
James Inman, boy
Samuel Stirlan, married with 6 children
Thomas Smithhurst, married.

It is understood that about 300 descended the pit and it is a cause of great thankfulness that the bulk escaped.

All was well until about half past eleven in the forenoon, when the appearance of a dense column of smoke from the mouth of the main shaft told plainly of some disaster.

The workmen were quickly drawn out and an exploring party came upon the dead body of one of the men in a part of the workings about a mile from the shaft and the other 5 about 40 yards further on.

It is supposed that the explosion occurred in a bank which had been newly started and was caused by a fall of the roof liberating a blur of gas. The mine is worked with naked lights.

The men who were killed were working between 60 and 100 yards further on than the bank and from their appearance death came upon them with the dreaded after damp".

NOTE: The inquest (Rothwell Times, Friday, December 17th) was concluded on Tuesday last upon the then miners who were killed and resulted in a verdict of accidental death.

(A few days earlier an explosion at a pit in Barnsley resulted in the death of over a hundred people).

Providential Escape

"A singular accident occurred a few days ago at Tinglebridge Colliery, the property of Earl Fitzwilliam, about five miles south of Barnsley. Shortly after the men had commenced working on Tuesday morning, one of the miners fired a shot for the purpose of felling some coal. Soon afterwards the fallen coal ignited. The men attempted to extinguish the fire by 'waffing' their caps and smocks, which had the effect of driving the sulphuretted air to the burning mass, which soon increased the fury of the fire so much that the men considered it dangerous to continue in the pit. They therefore ascended the shaft; and shortly after they arrived at the top the mass burned with such vehemence as soon to blaze and roar like a furnace. They then made a stage at the mouth of the pit, for the purpose of extinguishing the fire, by preventing any air getting to it. This business occupied the men near an hour. While thus employed, the signal-bell rang. This the men thought was occasioned by the material which they were putting down to close the mouth of the pit having fallen against the bell wire, being confident no one was in the pit. They again resumed their labours, and had been at it some time, when the bell again rang. They then looked round the pit hill, and found that one man was not amongst them. Some were positive they had seen him on the hill with the rest of them; others doubted it. It was then agreed that a messenger should be sent to his residence, to see if he was there. The man's residence being a mile and a quarter from the pit, some time elapsed ere the messenger returned, during which time the men stopped putting more material down the shaft. However, the bell rang more violently than before; and, by the advice of the engine tenter, the covering was taken up again and a corve put into the chair, and lowered to the bottom of the shaft; and when drawn up again, it was found to contain the missing man and two boys, who had been buried in the burning pit above an hour, and brought out unhurt. It appears the man and boys, although present when the others were endeavouring to extinguish the fire, thought there was no danger; they therefore went to their work in another part of the mine, and commenced their labours, not knowing but the others had done the same, until they found the air bad. At seven o'clock the pit remained on fire, and will be closed for some time."

This extract is taken from the 'Illustrated London News' dated Sept. 13, 1851.

A Vision of Hell

Henry Moore was comissioned 29 August 1941 to produce some coal mining drawings. He arrived in December 1941 and made drawings at Wheldale Colliery where his father had worked: 30 years later Moor remembers the experience vividly.

"Crawling on hands and knees and reaching the actual coal face was the biggest experience. If one was asked to describe what hell was like, this would do. A dense darkness you could touch, the whirring din of coal cutting machines throwing into the air black dust so thick that the light beams from the miners' lamps could only shine into it a few inches...."

Underground, Wheldale Colliery, Castleford 1941 Photograph reproduced by kind permission of The Henry Moore Foundation

Meet the Miner

"When he had finished describing his present work, the old man went on to speak of his early life in the pit. He was first employed as a 'hurrier'. Sixty years ago, gates were very much narrower and lower than they are today, and there was barely room for the small tubs – 'corves', they used to be called – to pass along them. There was no room for a pony, and boys pushed the corves along with their heads. The roof was so low, that if the 'hurrier' was not careful, he would take the skin off his back.

It cannot be too often insisted upon that, if the miner sometimes behaves rather differently from what a sentimental idealist might expect, there is that in his recent past which makes him a man apart. Imagine such lads – thousands of them in Yorkshire alone, working day after day down there in the dark on hands and knees in rocky tunnels, propelling several hundredweights of coal at a time by the simple means of pushing it along with their heads!! In the same village before the last war there was another even more homeric contest. In those days, lawlessness in mining villages was taken so much for granted that free fights could take place almost without interference. A gang of navvies had been brought up to make a railway extension and the miners regarded them as a heaven-sent occasion for rough fun. One of the navvies was known to be handy with his fists. He was a quiet, decent sort of fellow, not at all disposed to throw his weight about, but a collier who rather fancied himself as a fighter sought him out as he was drinking a glass of beer in a public house and offered to take him on. The navvy refused in quite a friendly way, but the collier would not take no for an answer and started getting awkward. He succeeded in nettling the navvy, who finally exclaimed, 'Reight, tha's asked for it, and tha sall ev it'.

They adjourned to a small level paddock behind the public house, and the whole village turned out and lined the low wall which enclosed it. The fight lasted over an hour and there were no rounds. The navvy was the better boxer; he had more science and his footwork was much superior, for the collier's strength is in his loins and arms rather than in his legs. Still, a collier is very tough, quite devoid of fear and indifferent to pain. As the fight wore on, the navvy assumed the mastery and gave his opponent three blows for his one; but to the last the collier was game. It was only when he was reduced to a scarcely conscious, blinded hulk, that the fight came to an end. When he was at last revived with copious douches of cold water and staggered to his feet, his first words were, 'Ee, that were grand'. And he continued to fight at every favourable opportunity.

Tales of such conflicts are part of a lad's inheritance in mining villages. An old man, dead a few years since, used to tell of two colliers who, some fifty years ago, made a perfectly friendly arrangement for a private fight between themselves in an old quarry, now filled in between the villages of Lofthouse and Thorpe. They did not intend to share their fun with an audience, but met with no witnesses and fought on and off a whole morning with short intervals by mutual consent. They damaged each other so severely that they had both to be taken to hospital, where one had to remain for three months and never completely recovered.

Such large families occur even today, but twos or threes are becoming increasingly common. There is still essentially the same atmosphere. A miner may be a pigeon fancier, and in his yard he will have a loft full of fascinating beings that no child could fail to fall in love with. Such a man will initiate his lads into all the mysteries of this delicate sport. These are no lessons to be taught in public, but secret knowledge to be handed on almost wordlessly over the years of childhood. A picture comes immediately to memory: it was a collier, father of two sons. The day was beautifully still and clear, and the collier was giving a young bird its first lessons. He had some grains of maize in his hand, and, as the bird fluttered round in wide circles, he called to it, not as a man will summon a dog with a certainty of obedience, but whistling persuasive notes, and then uttering cries in a high penetrating tone. And while he stood there in the little paddock practising his art, his two lads squatted motionless, drinking in through eyes and ears the lore of bird control.

The present war has made such a drain on the staff of education offices that few school attendance officers are available for their normal duties; but not long before it began, one called at a miner's dwelling in South Yorkshire and knocked at the door. In rough districts, such officers have found it necesssary to behave roughly and, when no answer came, he pushed open the door. In a double bed, in the downstairs room, were a man and woman, whom the officer took to be father and mother of the truant, supposing the man to be a night shift worker. The officer began to lay down the law to the man about his child's absence, and threatened him with the police court. Presently, the man sat up in bed, and said, 'Hi, mister, this has got nowt to do wi' me. You talk to 'er: I'm t'lodger.'

The most heroic sacrifices are sometimes made and without the least self-pity, for the miner does what he does because he wants to and asks for no man's commiseration. The struggle was often severe before the war. One unemployed miner, with two children at grammar schools already, did not hesitate when a third child won its scholarship. Though the total family income was only 29/6 a week, the boy had to have his chance. No one who has not managed to keep three children well turned out and sufficiently fed to follow a grammar school course on such a sum can ever appreciate what contriving is involved, what rigid self-discipline the parents must impose upon themselves and what skilful economy must be employed in eking out the slender income. The provision of a pair of football boots becomes a major financial operation and the loss of a gym slipper may capsize the family budget for several weeks.

Take another case – one in thousands: a girl of fifteen always beautifully clean and neat, with well-kept clothes and full range of school equipment, told the writer that she would have to leave (school). In reply to his questions, she said it was because her brother was getting married. That seemed an insufficient reason till she explained that her father was an invalid living on compensation received for an accident in the pit. When her brother left home, the family income would be the princely sum of sixteen shillings a week. The brother had been contributing to the family resources and his marriage meant that there was no option; the sister must find a job at once.

No miner, or any other man, could possibly see his children through in such circumstances if the mother was not a woman of great quality. Before such mothers, one can only stand in silent admiration, for they are beyond praise not merely for the excellence of their intentions, but for the sheer genius of their achievement.

That it is the woman who plays the essential part is shown by the way miners' widows can bring up their orphan families. Three lads spring to mind immediately, all of whom distinguished themselves in this war. They were all sons of miners' widows. The first had two sisters, and he and they all passed successfully through the grammar school, although funds made it quite impossible for them to remain past the school certificate stage. The boy has done brilliantly in the R.A.F., and the citation announcing the award of his decoration refers to the work of 'this fine captain'. It tells how he led his team over and over again in raids upon the enemy and how his cool and skilful leadership brought them safely home. His mother was as fine a captain, and she, too, deserved a similar citation, for she brought her team through as great difficulties and with not less skill and devotion.

The other two lads both rose to commissioned rank, but one of them will not come home again. His patrolling aircraft, after a normal signal to its parent ship, just vanished silently into the Atlantic.

The writer went to visit a sick child, the son of a collier, in one of these dwellings, and found him in a double bed in the downstairs room, and at one point during his visit no less than twelve persons of all ages were in the room. It was a surprisingly happy home, though a desperately poor one, for, at the time – it was just before this war – the father had only worked two shifts during the week and money was tight.. This had not prevented his wife from adding an adopted child to the strained household, and the little girl was cheerfully playing before the fire. And then a girl of perhaps eighteen or so appeared from above as trimly dressed and carrying herself as confidently as a society belle. With a cheery salutation to the family, she passed out through the door. How they do it is a mystery, but a miner's daughter can emerge from a tiny room which she must inevitably share with others though it is no bigger than a toolshed, and take the air as well turned out as many a girl who has a bedroom and suite of furniture all to herself.

There are some traditionally tough spots in mining communities where the less conventional families congregate. Some Yorkshire villages have little isolated off-shoots generally called 'lumps', and it can be taken for granted that any such 'lump' is more than usually hot. Such a little collection of houses will cluster round a pub on a knoll and have its own general shop and 'fishery'. The men will only leave it to go to the pit or to make joint excursions to football matches or Blackpool. The women will leave it very seldom, and will then take a day to go with a neighbour or two to do some special shopping in a nearby industrial city. Thus, the atmosphere of the 'lump' follows them wherever they go and its life is the only really compelling interest. The inhabitants know everything about each other. In health or sickness, in feud or friendship, their lives are the property of their neighbours. So much do they feel that anyone not a member of their community is to be suspected that there was an agreed grape-vine signal put into operation by the family at the end of any street who saw a stranger approaching. A poker would be rattled against the fire back, and the signal would be carried forward at amazing speed from house to house till all were warned of the presence of an invader.

Such a community is two small to have a policeman of its own and though major crime is as unknown as elsewhere, minor dereliction, such as raids on farmers' fields for turnips and cabbages, or poaching, fighting and drunkenness, used to be taken for granted and are still not unknown. The families are usually prolific, and children swarm amongst the little houses and are usually deplorably dirty from the black ash with which the yards and alleys are paved.

And what a time the 'lump' has on occasions of special joy or sorrow, such as a marriage or a funeral! Money, never the master in such places, is then not considered at all. The food there is to eat! The neighbours know by ancient custom just what each will do by way of baking, and the tables are stacked with home-made delicacies and above all, ham. To be 'buried with ham' is a mark of conformity with the best traditions: to be buried without ham is to sink into oblivion worse than death.

Miners' wives do not normally go out to work. They have large families and stay at home to look after them and provide them with hot meals as they go to and return from their varying shifts. The pit canteen, where there is one, has done something to ease their lot; but many miners do not use either the canteen or the baths and go straight home 'in their dirt' to the sort of food they prefer – and it must be ready for them.

The head of the house will take his place at the table, and he is waited on like a pasha. His wife will keep an eye on his plate and see that he has what he wants when he wants it. When he has finished, she will side the pots and wash them up while he stretches himself out in the chair and lights his pipe. A suggestion that he should wipe the pots, let alone wash them, would be met with an incredulous stare by both man and wife.

Miners' homes are by no means all alike, but they nearly all have a recognisable quality. They may be unspeakably dirty, or they may be spotlessly clean, but there is always evidence of some interest of a kind that does not count cost. It may be a pedigree fox terrier of a prize-winning strain, or a pigeon loft with its half-dozen aristocratic beauties, or a highly-polished cornet, a harmonium or violin. It may be a good piano or a disproportionately massive set or suite of drawing room furniture. Then there is almost always a smell of home-made bread, a noble fire and a sense of welcome.

Conditions in pits were appalling as can be judged by the report of the Royal Commission of 1840. It referred, amongst other evidence, to an account in the 'Yorkshire Herald' of the flooding of one of the Silkstone collieries. 'When the water burst in, there were in the mine 44 children, of whom 18 escaped and 26 were drowned; of these, 11 were girls, and 9 of the 26 were under 10 years of age.' Not many years ago old miners were still alive who could remember being carried on their father's backs to the pit as tiny children, and never seeing the light of day throughout the whole winter."

Miners' Housing

The opening of the collieries brought about a demand for labour which needed housing. Housing in Methley grew from 366 houses in 1841 to 870 in 1891, so the houses were either built by the colliery proprietors or by others who let them out on lease or rented them direct to the tenants. The only houses I can find that were built by a colliery owner were those at Methley Junction built by Henry Briggs and Company. In 1871 there were 104 houses at Methley Junction housing 290 males of whom 151 worked in the mines. As the census of 1871 shows a total of 600 people were employed in the mines so much housing elsewhere in Methley must have been built by others and rented out but I have no information on this.

The houses at Methley Junction were made of brick which were much smaller in size than today's bricks, with blue slate roof tiles and were built in terraces, Burnley Row had 25 houses but this was very small compared to the 104 terrace houses in Loscoe Grove built by

Henry Briggs, which is now part of the Hopetown Industrial estate at Normanton, no doubt for the miners working at the nearby Dom Pedro colliery. Some of the houses often had large numbers of occupants, as many as nine or ten, many of whom would be lodgers.

A typical miner's house had four rooms, two up and two down. The living room was big enough to take a sideboard, table and one or two chairs and stools. The living room also contained a cast iron range with an oven and an open fire. Every Friday the iron range was polished with black lead and made to gleam: it was the pride and joy of every housewife. The other downstairs room was the scullery with a sink and cold water tap. One corner of the scullery held the set pot in which clothes were boiled: it was square, built of brick and inset into it was a deep metal bowl. To use it a fire was lit in the small grate underneath. The washing of clothes was a laborious task. Boiling water was taken from the set pot and put in a tub with soap and dirty clothing and swirled about with a peggy stick which was something like a three-legged stool with a long handle, the clothes could also be agitated with a poss, a wooden stick with a perforated metal plate on the bottom. Water was squeezed from the clothing by passing it through a mangle, a device with hand turned wooden rollers. Monday generally was washing day and in winter clothes had to be dried on a clothes horse in front of the living room fire, a dreadful day, nowhere to sit and steam everywhere. The ironing of clothes was just as laborious using a flat iron heated on the fire.

Every miner was given an allowance of coal, generally one ton a month, as part of his wages and this was kept in a cellar underneath the kitchen. Roaring fires generated a lot of soot in the chimney and it needed cleaning. One woman was known to buy a penny squib from the local shop. She would then stand in front of a dead fire, light the squib, stand with it in her hand until the very last second and then throw it up the chimney where it exploded sending down loose soot.

Personal washing was done at the kitchen sink and baths were taken in a tin bath in front of the living room fire, but pit baths were later provided for the miners.

Lighting originally was by candle and paraffin lamps, later gas, and later still electricity

The toilets or closets of today were not available for the early miners. They had to use dry earth closets with ash pits at the back and built three or four side by side between the streets. In winter they were very cold and draughty so you would not be too keen to go and have a read or a chat with the person sitting on the next lavatory seat. The contents of the closet and ash pit would be collected from time to time by a worker from the colliery with a horse and cart. With the passage of time modern drainage and sanitation systems were introduced allowing indoor toilets and hot water.

In addition to building houses at Methley Junction an account book of Briggs Methley Junction Colliery shows the cost of a chapel at Methley Junction as £86.5s.5d. but this building is not shown on the ordnance survey map of the time; the only chapel shown is the Methodist Chapel. The company also built the 'Institute' at the end of Front Row; it was commonly called the 'Reading Room' and was to house the Methley Junction Mutual Improvement Society. It included a reading room for newspapers, magazines, etc. which were delivered free courtesy of the company. There was a games room with billiard tables and card tables. It also had a lending library and a bathroom. Political or denominational meetings were not allowed, nor was foul language, drinking, gambling, excessive noise and dogs.

Following the nationalisation of mines in 1946 and the closure of the Methley Junction pit in 1968, many of the houses were bought by the occupants. In about 1985 Methley Junction was proposed to be declared a clearance area and the houses were bought by Leeds City Council. The houses were demolished, apart from the two railway station houses and Garden House, number 265 on the O.S. map, at one time the house of the local police officer, was sold by the Mexborough Estate in 1946 to a local resident. The bricks of these old houses proved to be valuable as they were considered to be rustic; they were dressed and sold to build new houses.

Pit Head Baths

The provision of pit head baths was of tremendous value to the mining community. The miner in his dirty clothing covered in coal dust returns to his small house by himself or with brothers, sons or lodgers. How did they keep clean? Cold water only, this to be heated, tin bath brought out, bathing, getting rid of the water, and what about the dirty clothes?

In 1907 a Royal Commission reported in favour of the establishment of pit head baths but the Coal Mines Act 1911 stopped short of making them compulsory, instead baths should be provided by a majority of the work force voting in favour of them and agreeing to pay half the cost of maintenance. Very little progress was made until the Mining Industry Act of 1920 which established the Miners Welfare Commission for the social wellbeing, recreation and conditions of living of workers in or about coal mining. It started with a levy of 1d on every ton of coal mined. In 1926 a separate fund for the building of pit head baths was established and paid for by a levy of one shilling on every one pound of royalties paid on the production of coal. The value of pit head baths is summed up by one miner who said "It seemed to make our time above ground two hours longer. Before we could wash here, we went home at 3 o'clock in our dirty clothes and perhaps we did not change and wash ourselves until 5 pm. Now, we come up and we are dressed for the evening a quarter of an hour after reaching the surface."

By about 1946 about one third of pits had baths but not Methley Junction pit; Water Haigh pit had baths prior to 1938 and Savile pit 1955/56.

Coal and the Environment

The taking of coal from the earth was not a matter of simply digging it out and burning it, it was a much more complex operation. The coals had to be graded into suitable sizes and cleaned under favourable conditions by efficient machinery with modern washing plants with great care taken to prevent breakage.

Screening Coal, 1878

The process of grading was called screening and I have no doubt that some readers will recall working on the screens mostly as young boys. Sorting out the stone and rubbish from the coal was partly done by hand, it was nail breaking as there were no gloves in those days, filthy and cold, as the screens were high off the ground and fairly open to the elements. When the coal had been screened and washed the fine coal and dust, together with the stone sorted out from the coal, was put into skip hoists and conveyed by aerial ropeways to what would later become vast slag heaps towering over the countryside. Because of spontaneous combustion the coal in the slag heaps later ignited. If you stood on the hill at the top of Methley Junction and looked south towards Normanton it looked as if the entire countryside was engulfed in smouldering fires giving off much sulphur, soot and noxious smells. The whole valley became a filthy poisoned site, chemicals, oil and dust drained into the rivers Aire and Calder; it was a barren wilderness.

When times were hard children and adults would often go picking usable coal from these slag heaps, mostly to keep their own fires burning. The surface of the slag heap was crusty in many places and dangerous to walk upon and it was not unknown for people to fall through the crust and be badly burned.

During the 1960s as the mines became uneconomic and were closed plans were made to reclaim the land and return it to its original state. The burnt out shale from the slag heaps provided the embankment to carry the M62 across the flood plain of the river Calder, all the buildings and apparatus of coal mines were buried beneath the slag heaps which were then contoured, covered with top soil and grass and trees planted. Today sheep graze, golf is played and people use the many leisure walks.

My Collier Grandfather

The long row of terraced cottages, two up and two down, were of brick, once red but now crazed and dirtied and blackened by the incrustations of years of noxious and corrosive soot from multitudinous chimneys. But these cottages were home to many people and, if you were a collier getting the monthly load of almost free coal, they were always warm from the scorching fires banked up on old-fashioned cast iron ranges glistening with the effort of a lifetime's polishing with black lead.

My maternal grandparents lived half-way down the street and as a small boy I loved to visit them, particularly as my school was near to their cottage. I visited them almost every day, and spent most weekends with them.

Grandma, a native of Staffordshire, was a tallish woman, taller than Grandad. A quiet woman, she was always knitting – socks in particular. Four, or perhaps three short steel needles clicked away like a tap dancer's shoes, turning out thick woollen socks with square toes and heels ready for stitching up.

Grandad was a short, stocky man whose hands, face and nose were covered with blue scars, the trade mark of a miner. He was tremendously strong with broad shoulders and muscular arms, the ideal build for a collier who spent his working days mole-like in a low tunnel digging out coal amid explosive dust and creaking pit props at the coal face of the pit.

Grandad worked hard all his life and had very little illness. His hobby was gardening and he took a pride in growing lovely flowers and succulent vegetables – small golden, juicy turnips, long glistening carrots, and fat, sweet green peas – all of which were a temptation to a small boy. Self-denial was difficult but Grandad was perceptive and a couple of slashes with a tobacco-stained pen-knife provided me with some delicious tit-bit on which to chew.

In common with most colliers at that time Grandad wore clogs. I often sat with my grandma waiting for him to come home from the pit and, as no two pairs of clogs sound the same, it was fairly easy to identify him from the other colliers by the fast speed of his pace and the lightness of his tread. On his belt he would be carrying his snap tin and, threaded through the belt, his bannickers, which were a pair of thick cotton drawers, the normal dress for a collier at work. From one extra large pocket sewn inside his relegated Sunday jacket he would take an empty quart bottle which had contained cold tea or water and from another equally large pocket he might take a small sawn off piece of pit prop for use as firewood.

The week was spent in working, with little time for pleasure – that would start at noon on Saturday when a buzzer sounded for 'knocking off' time and the streets would gradually fill with folk rushing home to get ready for the local football or rugby match, dog meeting, shopping expedition, or fishing trip. It might even be a mad rush to the 'bookies'. Often it would not only be pocket money that was gambled away but the rent money and, if the bug was biting hard and the tip a 'cert.', the housekeeping money as well. Grandad, although he worked hard and played hard, never deprived his wife or home, and I do believe he even managed to save a bit; certainly I always got my Saturday penny. Grandad could enjoy himself without spending money. He often told the tale of how once, when on a visit to a fair with his mates, he met a man with a big black bear, the man offering a fiver to anyone who would wrestle the bear for three rounds. Grandad, always ready to flex his muscles, had a go and held his own until the monster started to hug him, whereupon Grandad, fearing for his ribs and thus his next week's pay, submitted. But he had had his fun and that was all that mattered.

One of my greatest pleasures was to go with Grandad to his allotment about half a mile away. On Saturday I would wait at home for him and then off we would go. Sometimes we took a large wheelbarrow, home-made, with wheels that had previously graced two old-fashioned mangles. Grandad would push and I would ride. Occasionally we would stop at the local slaughter house where, by arrangement, the fresh, glistening, discarded offal from the morning's slaughter was shovelled into the barrow, then off we would go again. Grandad was a great believer in 'mucking' the ground and all useful material, including horse manure, would be gathered and used. Our arrival at the allotments – there must have been three or four hundred of them – was the start of a stop/go walk all the way to Grandad's plot. The stops were to enquire about Bill's back, Sam's missus, or the hundred and one items of gossip that made up the social life of the miners. I would listen gravely, always impressed by the courtesy of these tough men one to the other.

The allotment was a long, thin pencil of rich soil, extensively cultivated and covered, according to the growing season, with neat, well-weeded rows of vegetables in various stages of development. At one end there was a long, shallow pit into which the offal was dumped and then covered with earth. Filling the pit was a continuous affair, fresh material was added at one end and good humus was taken out at the other end. This was the secret of his good husbandry. Grandad did not have a garden shed; instead he had an old hansom cab, without wheels and standing on old railway sleepers. This cab could be anything I wanted and it provided me with many hours of fun, when I wasn't fetching water from a stand-pipe about fifty yards away, or weeding, or even planting if the seeds could be planted individually like peas or beans. Rhubarb was commonly grown and used to make wine which fermented in the warm kitchen before being racked and clarified in the cold, damp, whitewashed celler. The wine when bottled was brought out for drinking only on special occasions. Sometimes a noise akin to a weak cough would emanate from the cellar and Grandad would rush down and re-cork a bottle of wine. On rare occasions the cellar would shudder as if a shell had exploded. This time there would be no rush, just a sigh, as if an old friend had passed on.

Sunday mornings saw the Seidlitz powder ritual enacted. The contents of two packets were mixed with water and consumed by Grandad, who swore by them. 'They clean the blood', he would say before disappearing for a time. Later in the morning we would go down to the allotment and bring back whatever vegetables were required for dinner, along with flowers for the house. Grandad would choose a flower to wear in his button-hole when he later went to the Horse & Jockey to pay his 'death and divide' and have his beer. Sometimes I went with him and I would wait in the Jug and Bottle or stand just inside the door and watch the men, many of them smartly dressed in blue serge suit with tie and spotless white shirt and with a gold guard hanging heavily across the waistcoat and a flower in the button-hole. Other men would be unshaven and wearing a striped flannel shirt and a knotted scarf around the neck instead of a collar. The pub was like a hive of bees buzzing with conversation, with the worker bees rushing in to collect the nectar in pint tankards topped by a creamy collar of froth. The air would be heavy and streaky with the black, pungent smoke of 'thick twist' tobacco smouldering and spluttering in a variety of pipes – clay or wood, straight or curved – or the more refined but acrid smoke of Woodbine cigarettes, so much so that my eyes would soon be smarting and I would gladly escape outside for a breath of fresh air.. There was no music, just the buzz of conversation, the chink of pint glasses and the rattling of dominoes. Grandad always introduced me to his friends and there was a seemingly never ending succession of pats on the head and cries of 'My, he's a big un'. Occasionally, if the friend was sufficiently tranquilised by infusions of Joshua Tetley's bitter beer he would hand me a halfpenny and if the infusion was of a stronger nature or the quantity consumed greater I would be the grateful recipient of a penny.

Then it was home to a dinner of Yorkshire Pudding and roast beef, a glance at the 'News of the World' and then Grandad would be off to bed till tea-time leaving Grandma clicking away with her needles and listening to the wireless until she too succumbed to the effect of the warm fire, and the needles were stilled. When Grandma also went for a nap I occasionally had an illicit puff at Grandad's pipe, sometimes with disastrous results. Often I sat making paper spills which Grandad used at a prodigious rate to light his pipe.

Grandma suffered various illnesses for which she was treated in hospital. She underwent much surgical treatment and I was to learn later that this was for the cancer that finally took her some twenty years later.

As I grew older and left school I found other interests and this meant less and less time being spent with my grandparents, but I never lost touch with them. Later I went overseas and bade farewell to Grandma, never to see her again, and on a later visit to England I bade farewell to Grandad, never to see him again.

This account was written in 1968.

The village now looks as though it has been scythed by another reaper. The street in which my grandparents lived has gone – under the teeth of a bulldozer. The pit has gone. The whole area has been flattened and cleared. Nothing is left to remind a passer-by of the community that once lived and died there. The towering, burnt-out slag heap of red shale has gone to provide foundations for roads. Thus it was returned to the earth from which it had been so laboriously and painfully taken.

JHM

Open-Cast Mining

Much of the area in and around Methley has been subject to open-cast mining. Some surface coal working was in operation at the outbreak of World War II and by 1942 there were six sites in the Leeds area. The first of these sites was at Temple Newsam Park and since then open-cast mining has moved south following the river Aire. Presently coal is being removed from the grounds of Methley Park and also at St Aidan's site, which is north of the river Aire between what was the old Lemonroyd lock and the old Caroline swing bridge. For further details of this site see the item entitled 'A Canal is Born'.

Following the flooding of the St Aidan's site and subsequent reconstruction work the site became operational again in February 1998. St Aidan's site has an area of 340 hectares with an excavation depth of 84 metres to remove three seams of coal which range in thickness from 0.73 metres to 1.54 metres.

There are two large walking draglines on the site. One of these machines B-E 1150 B, built in the U.S.A. between 1947/48 was the largest walking machine of this type in the world; it was nicknamed 'Oddball' because it worked on the American 60c/s supply which required special equipment. 'Oddball' has ceased to work and will remain on site to become a visitor attraction after all the coal has been taken. The other dragline working on the site is a Rapier W 2000 with a bucket capacity of 27 cu.metres.

Since the reopening of St Aidan's site in February 1998 the total excavation by June 2000 was 27 million cu.metres of overburden, including 750,000 cu.metres of sand and gravel and 1.52 million tonnes of coal which has been transported by canal to Ferrybridge Power Station.

Approximately 100 workers are employed at the site. Contrast this with the manpower needed for deep coal mining at the collieries of Henry Briggs who, for instance, in 1923 employed 7,000 men to reach a record output of 1,725,000 tons.

The coaling operations at St Aidan's site are anticipated to end on August 2002 and all coaling operations will be completed in August 2003.

When mining is complete the site will be restored to a country park with major emphasis on nature conservation and quiet amenity. The wetlands will provide flood storage capacity to protect downstream towns and villages.

Recently, whilst excavating coal from the site opposite the Caroline bridge, old deep mining tunnels were exposed in the 1 metre thick Barnsley Top Softs seams, the tunnels were about 1 metre high and 70cm wide. They had collapsed but the outlines were obvious and it may be that they originated from the Bowers Row area.

In addition to the taking of coal by open-casting there is also the taking of sand and gravel. Methley stands on the flood plain of the rivers Aire and Calder and under the good agricultural soil are vast quantities of sand and gravel which is graded, sorted and transported by road. It would seem that in view of the vast quantities available and the increasing demand for building material this extraction will continue despite much local oppositionr

Rapier W 2000 at St. Aidan's site

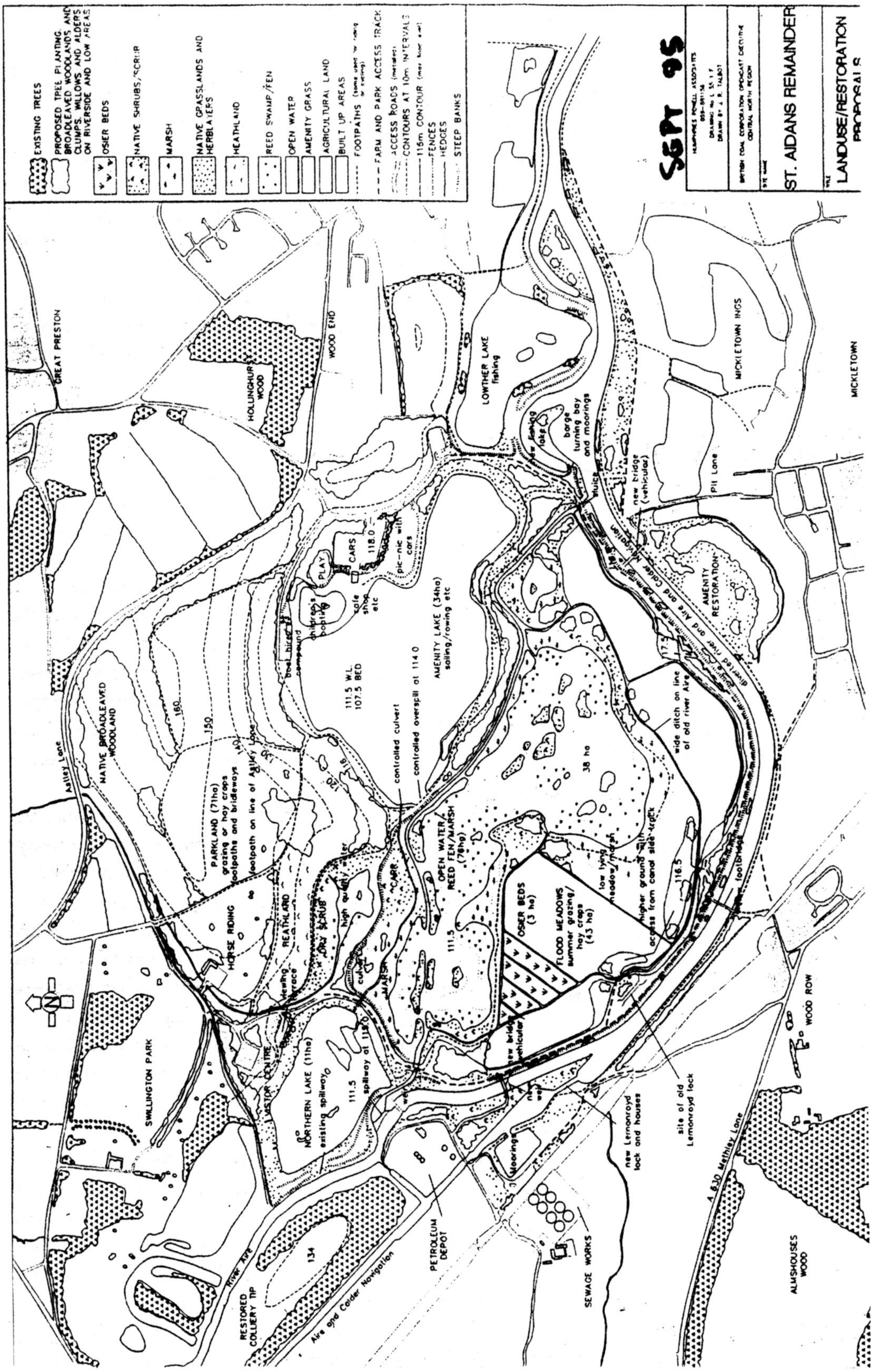

St. Aidan's site in the future.

A CANAL IS BORN

"For well over 200 years in this country we have used inland waterways and canals as a means of shaping and improving our environment. Canals have played a vital role from the Industrial Revolution onwards and helped to change the face of Britain.

The development of the Aire and Calder Navigation began back in the 17th Century with the boom in the cloth trade and remained one of Britain's busiest commercial canals transporting oil, sewage sludge and aggregates and particularly coal along its length.

But in 1988 something happened on the Aire and Calder Navigation that was to provide the British canal system with one of its biggest challenges for a hundred years. In March 1988, following seven years of coal production, the St Aidan's Extension open-cast coal site in West Yorkshire was flooded when the river Aire breached its banks. The site was flooded by 17 million cubic metres of water to a depth of 70 metres over the 1½ kilometres of the workings.

The cause of the breach is not entirely clear. It is believed there is a fault under the river Aire, and a combination of water pressure down that fault and lubrication possibly of deposited clay bands caused a large wedge of the side of the site to fall in.

The situation posed a major threat to the integrity of the Aire and Calder Navigation because the deepening scour of the river bed as the water poured into the breach at high velocity caused rapid erosion of the opposite river bank and a loss of support to the canal embankment. At one stage the river bank was receding at a rate of one metre per hour causing the evacuation of the lock-keepers' cottages. It very quickly became apparent that the coal site could not be saved so all efforts were spent on protecting the embankments. As well as spending £1m on nearby quarries to save the canal embankments, excavators were used upstream to divert the river's energy directly into the mine site. In the event, this two-pronged attack proved successful with the coal site filling in only 3 days. Once the water and the excavation wall became stable questions remained over the integrity of the coal site and, more importantly, the nearby Aire and Calder Navigation.

British Coal open-cast responsibilities were to restore the site satisfactorily, to reconstruct the river, and to protect the commercial waterways. In consultation with British Waterways they commissioned consulting engineers to carry out desk-top studies on a number of schemes designed to safeguard the river and canal, to allow the site to be pumped dry, and for coaling to be recommenced. Several possible recovery schemes were considered, all of which included the diversion of the river to a new course. Most involved the diversion of the canal which runs alongside. As the canal and river were parallel and close to each other alongside the open-cast site the option of combining the river and canal into one single channel was a solution which could satisfy all parties. This option would provide a channel for navigation and river flows, would use established low risk technology, meet ecological and environmental requirements, and be cost effective. The quantity and complexity of the negotiations involved made St Aidan's a unique project.

Leeds City Council granted permission for the scheme, but this was only the first stage. British Coal Open-Cast, British Waterways and the National Rivers Authority all had their own statutory responsibilities so common ground took some time to achieve. But the next stage was potentially the most difficult. Because the construction of the original Aire and Calder Navigation required an act of Parliament, the diversion works also required an act, and this was progressed through a private bill. But because of the many parties involved in consultation on the scheme, negotiations actually took over 2 years before the act of Parliament was finally passed. Much consultation was required with a number of other parties to satisfy concerns about the diversion and reach compromise solutions, but finally the contract for the diversion was awarded and the contractors moved on to site in August 1993. The £17m contract for the river and canal diversion was a 22-month project and would create the first length of new canal for 90 years and allow access to the remaining 2.7m tons of coal.

The construction, a major feat of engineering, required the excavation of around 2.5m cubic metres of soils, alluvial material, colliery spoil and sandstone and mudstone along its 3.5 kilometre length. With the channel excavated a lining was required to prevent leakage and this was provided by a mudstone layer up to 2.4 metres thick. The sloping banks were protected to the one-year flood level by a geotextile filter fabric, a transition stone layer of 150 mm and a final layer of heavy rip wrap. The rip wrap consisted of around a quarter million tons of stone to protect both banks of the 3½ kilometre stretch. The transition and rip wrap had to meet stringent N.R.A. requirements and was brought in from nearby magnesium limestone quarries. To protect future open-cast workings from ground water, mentonite diaphram cut off walls were installed under sections of the new river.

The cross section of the canal will be large enough to allow 60 metre long 550 ton barges to pass, as well as allowing the river flood waters. Besides two Bailey bridges built for plant access to isolated parts of the site, permanent routes across the new channel would be provided. Three new bridges were constructed, the largest being Caroline bridge. Caroline bridge, built to carry road vehicles, has an overall span of 85 metres. A 50 metre clear span between the two piers allows for the safe navigation of barges. The impressive structure has reinforced concrete for the abutments and piers and pre-cast concrete units to protect against erosion from the river flow. The pre-formed steel beams designed to produce an aesthetic curve required a giant mobile crane to place them. Shan House bridge is of similar design but is for pedestrians only. The third bridge is the 25 metre long Lemonroyd bridge which crosses the new Lemonroyd weir. As the new river course was shorter than the original, a new weir was required to adjust the river levels. Lemonroyd weir is 25 metres wide and has a maximum drop in normal water levels of one metre. The weir also incorporates a fish pass. Built at a cost of £1.2m the construction involves 2,300 cu. metres of concrete and 550 tons of sheet piling up to 20 metres in length.

In order that the majority of the new water course could be built in the dry, two temporary channels were constructed to divert the river. One of these took the diverted river through the flooded site. However it was still necessary to build three sections in the wet. Throughout the construction of these sections great care had to be taken to ensure the lining and stone protection was placed at the correct profile.

In May 1994, with the channel well under way, work started on the construction of Lemonroyd lock, upstream canal approach, marina, and downstream moorings.. As the new channel would be at a lower level than the original canal a new lock would be necessary to link the new waterway level to that of the existing canal upstream. The new lock, which replaces two on the old navigation, is 70 metres long, 7 metres wide, with a 4.6 metre drop in water levels. The lock has a capacity of over half a million gallons of water and is large enough to accommodate 24 double-decker buses. It was built at a cost of £1m using both the latest technology and established traditional methods. The lock gates were built off site using age-old techniques. They are made of ekki, a West African hardwood which is very dense and durable. Before installation the gates were stored immersed in water to prevent them from drying out. Whilst the Lemonroyd lock chamber had been constructed using the very latest techniques care was taken to ensure that the final appearance was in keeping with the traditional style of the Aire & Calder Navigation. The new lock is equipped with a fine control cabin with state-of-the-art computer control. Control can also be switched to lock side operation, where the user-friendly gate-side pedestal allows leisure traffic users to operate the sluices and gates safely and easily.

The new mooring basin provides space for over 60 craft and purpose built moorings that have both a water supply and lighting. Both upstream and downstream approaches have been designed so that commercial and leisure traffic are separated. Alongside the basin a new footbridge has been built to provide continuity of the towpath alongside the new waterway. Three replacement lock cottages have also been built, with the first tenants taking possession in November 1995.

Throughout the design and consultation process, environmental concerns were uppermost, with the consulting engineers working closely with the National Rivers Authority. Future fish populations were given a head start with the design of shallow water burns, fish pipes, off-river channels and bed and side variations. Even the rip wrap used in the canal lining construction was specifically chosen because it allows aquatic invertebrates to shelter between the stones, and algae to grow on the stones. The derelict Savile Colliery received a face lift and the new channel bisected the spoil heap and other surface features of the landscape. As part of the excavation came within a few metres of a wetland site of special scientific interest, measures were needed to ensure that water levels were maintained with suitable water from the deep watering well point. Public access to the lower Aire valley has been greatly enhanced by new bridleways along both sides of the water course.

As the design of the new navigation required it crossing the old in two places it was necessary to close the Aire & Calder Navigation to traffic for a period of six weeks. The closure occurred in February and March 1995 and the contractors worked round the clock to build the new sections and ensure disruption to traffic on the navigation was kept to a minimum. Although freight traffic had to be temporarily postponed the six week closure brought a new challenge – how to transport 20 ton pleasure craft through the site. Areas of hard standing were set up at Fleet Lane and the new Caroline staithe, and a giant mobile crane was on standby.

An extendable articulated lorry was used to do the carrying along the unsurfaced roads, with the crane following on behind ready to offload back into the canal. In all, the operation was carried on four times without so much as a broken piece of crockery, a credit to all concerned. It was around this time that ownership of the St Aidan's site passed to RJB Mining, following the return of the coal industry to the private sector.

The period of closure was successful and on the 3rd April 1995 the canal was reopened; the national and local press were invited. The day was well attended and provided the project with excellent coverage in the national media, as well as raising the profile locally. Journalists, photographers and TV crews were able to record the first barge through a new stretch of the canal for 90 years. They also had the opportunity to experience a trip through the new lock and along the new canal. A helicopter was provided so the scale of the project could be appreciated from the air.

With the canal open again to freight, work progressed quickly on all remaining aspects of the development. Special attention was paid to improving the site's appearance and providing erosion protection with around 100,000 trees and shrubs being planted. The landscaping progressed quickly and was sufficiently advanced to stage an official open day.

On the 23rd September 1995 the local community were invited along to celebrate the major engineering achievement. It was a highly enjoyable day for visitors and those responsible for the canal construction. The public was invited to board one of three boat trips to navigate the section after the official opening. The official opening was performed by Pat O'Brien, Director of RJB Mining and Brian Dyce, Chief Executive of British Waterways. It was a day designed to be informative and fun for the whole family with a bouncy castle, face painting and environmental displays. In celebrating what was an historic event, the open day also helped to cement the relationship between the locals and those who had worked on the project.

The next major task would be to safely pump out the void, an operation that will take some 2 years to complete. Geotechnical and environmental monitoring will continue during this period to ensure that the pumping operation has no impact on the environment. Once the pumping operation is complete coaling will resume to retrieve the remaining 2.7m tons of coal. The coal will then be transported along the waterway, via the new Caroline wharf, quickly, cheaply and in an environmentally friendly manner, its destination the nearby power station Ferrybridge 'C'.

The successful completion of this project is a testament to the expertise of all involved. The wholehearted commitment of British Waterways, RJB Mining and the National Rivers Authority has ensured that this major civil engineering scheme has been satisfactorily completed. Once the open cast mining is complete the 900 acre site will become an integral part of a 10 year plan to develop a public amenity and major conservation in the Lower Aire valley".

(Reproduced by kind permission of RJB Mining).

METHLEY CENSUS RETURNS 1841-1891

As part of the work on this book about Methley I thought it would be worthwhile to publish details of the above-mentioned returns which are kept on micro-film at Rothwell Library and which could prove useful in tracing family histories and in showing changes in the life and work in the village during the Nineteenth century.

The censuses were compiled nationally every 10 years from 1801 onwards, but the earlier ones were purely statistical; only a few scraps of the returns prior to 1841 giving individual names remain.

What makes the returns so valuable a source of information is that they list every person present in a household on the night of the census.

The 1841 returns are not so detailed as the later ones, giving only names, ages (the ages of people over 15 are rounded down to the nearest term of 5 years), professions and whether the person was born in Yorkshire or not, but the returns from 1851 onward give names, the relationship of each member of the household to its head, exact ages in years, professions, and town or village of birth.

However, it should be remembered that street and house names were not used with any great frequency or even consistency in the earlier censuses, so the absence of a name in any of the indexes should not be taken to mean that a particular street or household is not included in the returns.

The earliest population figures for Methley are quoted by Yasumoto Minoru, a visiting Japanese professor at Leeds University and the author of a publication 'Industrialisation and Demographic Changes in a Yorkshire Parish'. He chose Methley for his report which is very statistical and the only information that may be of value to the reader is the population figures which were 1234 in 1801, 1385 in 1811, 1492 in 1821, and 1293 in 1831.

I have not shown all the names and occupations of those present at the census because of the numbers involved, only those that show the trend in certain occupations. Some of the entries may seem odd, such as the census return for 1861, Area 13, where the occupant of Methley Hall is shown not as the Earl of Mexborough but as Titus Salt, Manufacturer, of Saltaire, Bradford and his family. (Was the Earl on vacation at the time?) Then there is the return of 1881, Area 8, which shows the occupant of the Rectory as 28 year old miner, Charles Abrams, and his family. (Where was the Rector?)

The figures I quote are correct in the number of dwellings and in the population and are also generally accurate in describing certain occupations and numbers. Not all occupations and numbers are shown, i.e. labourers, domestic servants, housekeepers, etc. Many domestic servants were often daughters kept at home either to help mothers or to keep house for widowed fathers.

It is worth pointing out that the Church Lane mentioned in the returns is now called Little Church Lane. The 1881 and 1891 returns were the first to show street names, particularly at Methley Junction, and it was for this reason that I have shown them in full, together with the fact that 100 years later the original Methley Junction has ceased to be a mining community and has been demolished.

A pledge is made at the time of each census that the personal information in them will be kept confidential for 100 years so copies of the 1901 census will be available to the public in 2002, but the Registrar General is prepared to consider release of the age and place of birth of named persons in the return of 1901 to the persons concerned or their direct descendants.

The returns for 1901 onwards are held at the Office for National Statistics, Segnesworth Road, Titchfield, Fareham, Hants. PO15 5RR, and are not open to public inspection.

PARISH OF METHLEY CENSUS 1841 Ref.HO/107/1269/Area 1

All of the township of Methley which lies to the South-West of the railway from Leeds to York and bounded by the Wakefield road on or towards the West.

Railway Bridge – Luke Uttley 35y Railway Superintendent, with family of four.

Church Side – Thomas Rider 45y, with family of six. Rev. Dawson Lumb 44y, w Pricilla 54y, d Ellen 17y, d Emma Priscilla 16y, d Fanny Priscilla 14y, Mary Cockburn 26y House Servant.

Railway Bridge – George Ackroyd 25y Carpenter, w Catherine 25y and two children.

Church Side – Mrs Harrison 75y independent means, Esther Wilson 40y House Servant and one other House Servant. John Farrar 35y Farmer, w Mary Ann 35y, Elizabeth Farrar 65y, with three children and four servants.

Pinder Green – Edward Dodd 29y School Master, James Lambert 28y School Master, Hannah Cheeseborough 14y Domestic Servant, William Goulding 14y House Servant, all in the same house. Sarah Robinson 45y Farmer, William Robinson 30y, John 25y, Sarah 25y, Thomas 25y, Ann 15y, Fanny 10y, Benjamin 10y, Edward 5y, Mary 5y, Charlotte 5y.

Watergate – William Long 20y Shoemaker, George Shillito 40y Agricultural Labourer, w Ann 40y and their six children. Joseph Dobson 35y Coalshipper, John Greaves 76y Carpenter, William Greaves 34y Shoemaker, Joseph Greaves 25y. John Pickersgill 15y. John Bentley 50y Carpenter, w Elizabeth 55y, s Joseph 20y Shoemaker.

Scholey Hill – Thomas Wilson 20y, w Ann 25y Dressmaker. Robert Scatcher(?) 30y Innkeeper, w Rachael 35y. William Wilson 30y Farmer. John Atkinson 30y, Christopher Atkinson 60y Carpenter. Stephen Elliott 60y Farmer. David Dixon 46y Waterman. Matthew Atkinson 36y Shoemaker. Benjamin Wright 42y, w Sarah 40y and their seven children. Mathew Atkinson 36y Shoemaker.

Lanes – Robert Nelson 45y Farmer. Mary Ann Nettleton 50y Farmer.

West Hall – Benjamin Idle 40y Engine Driver, s William 15y Miner.

Houses 56, Males 140, Females 143, Total Persons 283.

PARISH OF METHLEY CENSUS 1841 Ref.HO/107/1269/Area 2

All that part of Methley which lies to the West of the railway from Leeds to York and bounded by the Wakefield road on or towards the South-East.

Woodrow – Phoebe Hollins 53y independent. John Sissons 45y Publican. John Farrar 20y Joiner. William Patrick 25y Tailor. Thomas Wilson 30y Carpenter. Joseph Braime 40y Carpenter. Charles Patrick 50y Stonemason. William Greaves 70y Boat Builder. Ann Longbotton 80y School Mistress. Joseph Braime 35y Farmer. Moses Howson 35y Printer. William Evans 65y Farmer. John Shillito 30y w Jane 30y. Mary Pullein 60y Gate Keeper.

Methley Park – George Scott 50y Lodge Keeper. Richard Hampshire 60y. John Hall 30y, William Robinson 25y, Julia Sutton 55y, Sarah James 30y, Sarah Howell 20y, Jane Crake 20y, Matilda Hanley 20y all servants of the Earl of Mexborough.

Clumpcliffe – Joseph Robinson 30y Gamekeeper.

West Lane – James Turner 50y Blacksmith. John Nelson 70y Farmer.

Hungate – Edward Atkinson 65y Wheelwright. William Redman 45y Farmer. Henry Dalton 30y Butcher.

Methley Park Gardens – Joseph Spink 30y Butcher.

Scholey Hill – George Mitchell 25y Gamekeeper.

Houses 60, Males 120, Females 126, Total Persons 246.

PARISH OF METHLEY CENSUS 1841 Ref.HO/107/1269/Area 3

All that part of the township of Methley which lies to the South-West of the high road from Allerton Bywater ferries through Micketown to Wakefield having the railway from Leeds to York on the South-West.

Mickletown – Martha Ward 45y Grocer. Benjamin Illingworth 25y Cordwainer. John Ripley 20y Potter. Thomas Bell 25y Tailor. R Thompson 30 y Fellmonger. Mary Bilton 60y Dressmaker, s William Bilton 30y Shoemaker. John White 12y Miner. John Taylor 40y Farmer.

High Green, Mickletown – Abraham Cheeseborough 20y Chandler.

Coney Moor – James Stocks 75y, w Phillis 77y of independent means. Dean Watson 60y, John Watson 50y described as paupers. Thomas Leek 40y Butcher.

Boat Staithe – Giles Denison 45y Farmer.

Mires – William Jennings 30y Gamekeeper.

Dunford House – Thomas Dean 50y, w Jane 50y live with son-in-law Charles Nichols 25y, w Jane 25y, and servants John Warrington 15y, William Smales 15y, Reuben Harrison 15y, Elizabeth Boothery(?) 15y and Mary Harrand 15y.

Green Lane – William Hardcastle 65y Farmer, w Sarah 65y, s Charles 30y Tailor.

Windmill Moor – John Taylor 57y Farmer, w Jane 53y. George Higham 70y Farmer.

Parson Close – William Willis 30y Labourer, w Ann.

Coney Moor – John Shillito 40y Farmer, w Martha.

Mickletown – William North 40y and John Mackay 38y, Surveyors and Road Contractors. John Giles 35y Fellmonger. Samuel Perkin 40y Basket Maker.

Houses 122, Male 290, Female 286, Total Persons 576.

PARISH OF METHLEY CENSUS 1841 Ref.HO/107/1269/Area 4

All that part of the township of Methley which lies to the North of the high road from Allerton Bywater ferry through Mickletown to Wakefield and bounded by the rivers Aire and Calder on towards the North.

Streets not shown, the area covered is classed as **Methley**.

Benjamin Turpin 61y Bricklayer, w Sarah 60y. Christopher Hall 65y Farmer, w Hannah 55y, Daniel Atkinson 70y Cooper. Sarah Heptonstall 45y Farmer. James Waide 35y Farmer, w Mary 35y. John Clarkson 30y Butcher, w Ann 25y. James Taylor 55y Farmer, w Sarah 50y. Joseph Braime 30y Joiner, w Elizabeth 30y, children Edwin 10y, Joseph 8y, George 6y, Barsilla(?) 4y, Frederick 2y. Thomas Wright 25y Tailor, s of David Wright 65y Coal Miner. Benjamin Popplewell 70y Tailor, w Ester 65y. James Spencer 35y Banksman, w Mary 35y. Joseph Pickersgill 40y Engine Worker, w Sarah 40y. John Roberts 35y Bookkeeper, w Mary 35y. Joseph Charlesworth 45y Farmer. Moses Popplewell 35y Tailor. John Nicholson 70y Boat Fitter. George Beevers 50y Shoemaker. John Arundel 65y Colliery Steward. Jane Wilson 25y Straw Bonnet Maker, lived with her father, James 55y Farmer, and mother Sarah 50y Dressmaker, also brother John 20y Butcher. Thomas Brooks 50y Lock Keeper. James Turpin 45y described as a Navigator. Robert Hollins 30y Farmer. Richard Illingworth 30y Shoemaker. John Monath(?) 40y Clerk. John Bland 55y Corn Miller, also John Abbott 50y Corn Miller. Moses Thompson 25y Surgeon Apothecary. John Pullein 40y Inn Keeper also John Fletcher 50y, w Ann 45y. Peter Gill 50y School Master.

Houses 128, Males 282, Females 291, Total Persons 573.

TABLE OF HOUSES, PEOPLE AND OCCUPATIONS FROM THE 1841 CENSUS.

	Houses	Male	Female	Total
Area 1	56	140	143	283
Area 2	60	120	126	246
Area 3	122	290	186	576
Area 4	128	282	291	573
Total	366	832	846	1678

OCCUPATIONS

Banksman	4	Gamekeeper	3
Basketmaker	1	Railway Gate Keeper	2
Blacksmith	4	Grocer	1
Bookmaker-Clerk	2	Hatmaker	1
Boatbuilder	1	Innkeeper/Publican	3
Bricklayer	8	Lockkeeper	2
Brickmaker	3	Mason	6

Butcher 10
Carpenter 26
Chandler 1
Clergyman 1
Coalminer 79
1x10y,1x11y,1x12y
Coalshipper 1
Colliery Steward 1
Cordwainer 1
Cornmiller 2
Engine Driver 1
Engine Tender 7
Farmer 26
Farm Labourer 81
Fellmonger 3

Navigator 1
Organist 1
Potter 1
Printer 2
Railway Superintendent 1
Railway Worker 5
Surgeon 1
Surveyor/Road contractor 2
Schoolmaster 3
Schoolmistress 1
Shoemaker/Repairer 16
Tailor/Dressmaker 14
Waterman 1
Wheelwright 1

PARISH OF METHLEY CENSUS 1851 Ref. HO/107/2329/Area 1A

All that part of Methley which lies to the South-West of the railway from Leeds to York and bounded by the Wakefield road on or towards the North-West including Watergate and the East side of Scholey Hill.

Church Side – Joseph Stainforth 65y, described as pauper, Labourer and Sexton of the parish, w Harriet 63y and son-in-law William Hollings 22y Butcher, w Martha 20y Dressmaker. John Farrar 46y Innkeeper and Farmer of 80 acres with three Agricultural Labourers, w Charlotte 41y. Thomas Wright 35y Tailor, w Hannah 34y.

Holmes Villa – John Holmes 37y Draper, Shoemaker & possibly Farmer of 100 acres.

Railway Bridge – George Uttley 26y Grain Dealer, his mother Mary 56y, brother William 23y Grain Dealer.

National School House – Girls – Emma Maddams(?) 25y Schoolmistress.
Boys – Joseph Wilkinson 29y Schoolmaster, w Harriet 26y.

Pinder Green – Thomas Robinson 30y Farmer of 100 acres with two men, w Ann 30y.

Popple Hole – John Marshall 36y Engine Tenter, w Mary 32y.

Pinder Green – Mary Robinson 65y Widow & Proprietor of Houses, s Thomas 35y Mineral Surveyor – Colliery Viewer.

Hazel House – Robert Smirthwaite 27y Farmer of 174 acres with 4 labourers, w Sarah 34y, d Sarah 3y, s Robert 1y, with 4 servants, John Freeman 19y, John Sykes 15y, Mary Ann Smith 21y, Annie Freeman 14y.

Watergate – Joshua Greaves 35y Organist & Shopkeeper, w Mary 34y with 2 children & his father John 82y. Henry White 60y Beer House Keeper & Gardener. John Bentley 60y Wheelwright & Robert White 27y Butcher.
Stephen Elliott 71y farmed 56 acres with 3 men. Elizabeth Pickersgill 65y Schoolmistress, also Mary Ann Tomlinson 38y Widow, with d Elizabeth 13y, s John 10y, d Maria 2y. Peter Nettleton 30y Innkeeper & Farmer of 15 acres.
Joseph Robinson 43y Gamekeeper. Nathan Wilson 46y Farmer of 111 acres with 2 labourers, w Grace 34y with 3 children & 3 servants.

West Lane – Mary Ann 65y Widow Farmer of 55 acres. Benjamin Burnley 51y Coal Proprietor employing 138 labourers, also Farmer of 200 acres with 5 labourers, w Mary 53y, s Benjamin, Agent in pit, d Margaret 29y, d Hannah 17y and Domestic Servant Sarah Hollings 29y. William Greaves 39y Shoemaker & Postmaster.

The Rectory – Philip Yorke Savile 36y Rector, w Emily Mary 32y, d Alice Mary 6y, s George 3y, s Henry William 1y, with William Goulden 23y Servant, Jane Smith 29y Lady's Maid, Elizabeth Hipwell 28y Nurse, Mary Roberts 34y Cook, Marriane Wilkinson 30y Housemaid, Mary Ann Sibley 16y Nursery Maid Alice Smith 39y Laundry Maid.

Houses 85, Males 205, Females 209, Total Persons 414.

Area covered – Church Lane, Holmes Villa, Railway bridge, Pinder Green, Popple Hole (1 house), Hazel House, Watergate, Scholey Hill, Fox Hole Colliery, Bottomboat Lane, West Hall.

PARISH OF METHLEY CENSUS 1851 Ref. HO/107/2329/Area 1B

All the township of Methley that lies to the West of the railway from Leeds to York and bounded by the Wakefield road on or towards the South-East including the West side of Scholey Hill, Hungate and Woodrow.

Woodrow – Thomas Garnett 39y Groom, Mary Haram(?) 55y widow/pauper with s George 11y Labourer at Corn Mill. Thomas Wilson 43y Grocer, w Hannah 39y. Joseph Braime 50y Master Carpenter, with 11 men. Clayton Murray 37y Manufacturer at Leeds employing 40. George Beavers 65y Dealer in Flour. Joseph Braime 26y Boat Builder. John Turpin 33y Boot & Shoe Maker. Joseph Cheeseborough 41y Tailor. Daniel Rogers 32y Innkeeper of United Kingdom, w Elizabeth 32y, with 4 children & 2 servants, also William Turpin 34y Master Butcher. William Cress 77y Farmer of 174 acres with 4 men.

Moscar House – John Pullein 54y Farmer of 122 acres with 1 man.

Lanes – Thomas George Gilderdale 24y Farmer of 90 acres with 2 men.

Hungate – Matthew Atkinson 46y Boot & Shoe Maker, also Joseph Scott 40y.

Scholey Hill – Robert Hirst 47y Great Northern Rly Station Master.

Houses 65, Males 139, Females 147, Total Persons 286.

PARISH OF METHLEY CENSUS 1851 Ref. HO/107/2329/Area 1C

All that part of Methley which lies to the South of the road leading from Allerton Bywater ferry through Mickletown to Wakefield and bounded by the railway from Leeds to York on the South including the South side of Mickletown.

Mickletown – John Charlesworth 27y Publican. Moses Tompson 37y Surgeon & Apothecary. Robert Smirthwaite 65y Farmer of 70 acres. John Wright 32y Fellmonger.

The Common – Henry Waddington 40y Farmer of 102 acres, w Hannah 38y with 7 children & 3 servants.

Green Lane – John Atack 43y Shoemaker with Martha Atack 77y widow/Housekeeper. Charles Hardcastle 40y Tailor.

Dunford House – Thomas Dean 63y Farmer of 170 acres with 4 labourers, w Jane 60y, 1 daughter and 4 servants.

The Mires – Samuel Backhouse 42y Ag. Labourer, w Sarah 42y, sons Joseph 16y, Thomas 14y, Samuel 12y Coal Miners, also 4 other children Grace 9y, another child 3y, James 2y, George 2 mths. John Shillito 55y Farmer of 104 acres with 3 labourers.

Boat Staithe – James Parker 34y Potter. Giles Denison 58y Farmer of 70 acres.

Mickletown – Samuel Charlesworth 27y Farmer of 64 acres. Abraham Cheesebrough 32y Tallow Chandler. William Gill 40y Cordwainer. John Taylor 53y Farmer of 88 acres with 12 men. Charles Howson 64y Ships Carpenter.

Houses 122, Males 291, Females 274, Total Persons 565.

PARISH OF METHLEY CENSUS 1851 Ref. HO/107/2329/Area 1D

All that part of Methley which lies to the North of the road from Allerton Bywater ferry through Mickletown to Wakefield and bounded by the rivers Aire and Calder towards the North and the railway from Leeds to York and including the North side of Mickletown.

Mickletown – John Wray 70y Chelsea Pensioner, w Hannah 70y. Nicholas Wild 65y Queen's Pensioner. Joseph Charlesworth 57y Farmer of 60 acres with 1 labourer. Joshuah Hall 70y Chelsea Pensioner, w Hannah 60y with step-d Martha Buttrick 22y. James Watkinson 63y Ship Owner, w Henrietta. Elizabeth Wrigley 19y School Mistress, d of David Wrigley Coal Miner. William Robinson 36y Farrier. Amy Pollard 49y widow Farmer of 15 acres, s Edmund(?) 20y Butcher near Silver Row. Samuel Perkins 56y widower with s David 28y Basket Makers. Thomas Wilson 50y Coll. Banksman, sons Thomas 12y & Frederick 9y Coal Miners. Joseph Braime 42y Joiner with 5 men, s George 16y Pupil Teacher. James Taylor 68y Farmer of 49 acres, w Hannah 65y. Richard Peaker(?) 39y Corn Miller. Samuel Ripley 28y Brick Maker. Benjamin Idle 51y Coal Engine Tenter. James Waide 48y Farmer of 54 acres with 2 men, w Mary 48y. John Ripley 33y Brick Maker. Richard Braime 38y Grocer. Henry Denison 34y Farmer. William Hick 55y Farmer of 110 acres with 3 men, w Sarah 45y. Christiana Pickersgill 37y widow with d Mary 17y Straw Bonnet Maker. Richard R Denison 39y Wagoner, w Ann 42y. James Fletcher 27y Butcher, brother Richard 18y School Master.

Parsonage House – Edward Russum(?) 40y Commercial Traveller.

Butcher Row – John Clarkson 39y Butcher. Mark Micklefield 52y with sons James & Joseph both 13y Coal Hurriers. George Connell 28y Corn Miller of Mill Lane. John Hollins 25y Boat Builder with b-in-law Thomas Atkinson 21y. Robert Hollings 43y Farmer of 220 acres with 4 men, w Sarah 37y. Richard Taylor 36y Booking Clerk at Station House. Francis Brook 63y Lock Keeper.

Area covered – Mostly North side of Mickletown.

Houses 148, Males 337, Females 324, Total Persons 661.

TABLE OF HOUSES, PEOPLE AND OCCUPATIONS FROM THE 1851 CENSUS

	Houses	Male	Female	Total
Area 1A	85	205	209	414
Area 1B	65	139	147	286
Area 1C	122	291	274	565
Area 1D	148	337	324	661
Total	420	972	954	1926

OCCUPATIONS

Occupation	No.	Occupation	No.
Annualant	9	Gamekeeper	4
Banksman (Colliery)	2	Gardener	22
Basketmaker	2	Glass Blower	1
Blacksmith	11	Grain Dealer	4
Builder	2	Grocer	6
Boatbuilder	4	Groom	1
Bookeeper/Clerk	1	Inkeeper	5
Bricklayer	4	Labourer-General	26
Brickmaker	4	Labourer-Mill	3
Butcher	10	Landagent	1
Canalworker	4	Laundress	4
Carpenter-General	13	Lockeeper	1
Carpenter-Master	1	Maid	2
Carpenter-Ship	9	Mason	5
Carter	1	Miller	1
Chemist	1	Nurse	1
Clergy	1	Organist	1
Cloth Manufacturer	1	Painter	3
Coal Dresser	3	Parish Relief	15
Coal Hurrier	2	Pauper	23
Coal Miner	164	Post Master	1
Cordwainer	4	Potter	4
Cornmiller	2	Railway Worker	5
Doctor/Surgeon	1	Railway Plate Layer	1
Domestic Servant	28	Railway Pointsman	1
Domestic Cook	4	Railway Stationmaster	1
Dressmaker	15	School Master	2
Draper	1	School Mistress	3
Engine Tenter	7	Shoemaker	12
Engineer-Coal	1	Surveyor	1
Farrier	1	Tailor	8
Farmer	19	Draper	1
Farm Labourer	78	Waterman	2
Fellmonger	1	Wheelwright	6
Flour Dealer	1	Yeoman	1

PARISH OF METHLEY CENSUS 1861 Ref. RG9/3431/Area 12

Part of the parish of Methley which lies South-West of the railway from Leeds to York and bounded by the Wakefield road on or towards the North-West including Watergate and the East side of Scholey Hill

Church Lane – George Lilley 29y Railway Pointsman, w Ann 27y. John Holmes 46y Linen Draper & Shoe Manufacturer, w Sarah, d Edith 8y, Ann Platt 46y Housekeeper, Jane Bell 19y Housemaid. Thomas Brunt 42y Carter & Sexton, w Sarah 46y, also John Longbottom 16y stepson & Thomas Longbottom 22y lodger. Thomas Longbottom 50y Wheelwright employing 1 boy, w Martha 39y. Sarah Rowlandson 60y widow Schoolmistress, d Sarah Jane

23y, d Mary A 20y Assistant Teachers. William Redfern 31y West Riding Police Constable. Henry Burton 28y Corn Miller, w Mary 26y Milliner. John Idle 28y Engine Tenter, W Sarah 27y their 3 day old son Samuel, m-in-law Sarah Pickersgill 57y. Charlotte Goodall 46y Shopkeeper. David Arundell 28y Colliery Carpenter, w Sarah 27y.

Church Side – Rose & Crown Inn - John Farrar 56y Innkeeper & Farmer of 58 acres with 2 men, w Charlotte 51y, s John 17y, s Richard 11y. Sarah Greaves 51y widow Postmistress, nephew William James 22y Parish Clerk. Philip Yorke Savile 47y Rector of Methley, w Emily Mary 42y, d Alice Mary 16y, s George 13y, son William H 1y, James Blackburn 16y Page, Martha Lewsey(?) 41y Lady's Maid, Mary Bunnell(?) 30y Cook, Mary Leatru(?) 32y Parlour Maid, Margaret Stephen 30y Laundry Maid, Mary Bannister 21y House Maid, Jane Metcalfe 26y Nurse, Jane Speed 29y Governess. Sarah Fox 29y Schoolmistress, sister Margaret 25y Housekeeper and Louisa Hill 18y Pupil Teacher.

Popple Hole – Thomas Craven 41y Blacksmith, w Jane 39y, also boarders Benjamin Dawson 42y Labourer, Richard Dawson & Samuel Day, Brick Makers. Richard Arundell 35y Coal Mine Underviewer, w Sarah 29y. William Holdsworth 54y Colliery Agent, w Martha 54y, s William 16y, d Ellen 14y.

Pinder Green – Edwin Chadwick 45y Farmer of 86 acres with 2 men & 1 boy, w Susannah 37y, sons Edmund 12y, Thomas W 7y, George 9y, Henry 7y, Arthur 5y & 10 month old twins Mary & Sarah, William Kay 20y Farm Servant. Joseph Wilkinson 39y Schoolmaster, w Harriet 37y, 2 daughters, 2 sons & 2 week old twins, names not shown. Mary Robinson 75y widow Proprietor of Houses. John Pullein 65y Farmer of 175 acres, with 4 men & 2 boys, w Rachael 62y.

Watergate – Mary White 71y widow Beer Shop Keeper.

Scholey Hill – Stephen Elliott 82y widower Farmer of 26 acres, with 2 men. Thomas Webster 65y Boat Carpenter, w Sophia 58y. George B Keighley 24y Plumber/Glazier, w Jane 24y. John Webster 35y Gamekeeper, w Mary 25y. Jane Buckley 62y widow Shopkeeper. Richard Matthew 40y Innkeeper & Farmer of 12 acres, with 1 man. Joseph Taylor 27y Farmer of 107 acres, with 2 men & 1 boy, w Ann 21y.

Methley Lane – John Raynor 39y Colliery Owner, with 154 men & 26 boys, w Sarah 29y, s Samuel 5y, d Dinah 3y, d Emily 1y, Alfred Bellerby 23y Groom, Grace Booth 18y Cook, Ann Longfield 18y House Maid. Thomas Colbert 40y Coal Waggoner, w Mary 42y Dressmaker. Thomas Nettleton 23y Farmer of 21 acres, his sister Mary 37y Housekeeper. James Wheatley 37y Gardener employing 1 man, w Nancy 36y.

Pot Oven House – Edward Clayburn 53y Blacksmith, w Hannah, s George 19y Blacksmith.

Cringlesworth House – Joseph Wilby 48y Coal Fitter, w Elizabeth 47y, d Hannah 23y.

Fox Hole – John Blackburn 42y widower Pit Engine Tenter, with 6 children, Elizabeth Pawson 25y Housekeeper. Benjamin Idle 61y Engine Tenter, w Sarah 59y, s Timothy 21y, grand-daughter Estha 10y.

Wilks House – Joshua Greaves, 45y Organist, w Mary 44y Shopkeeper.

Boats-			
Providence	Reg. Beverley	crew 2	45 tons coal
The Vine	Reg. Beverley	crew 2	40 tons coal
Sarah	Reg. Selby	crew 2	60 tons coal
Rhoda	Reg. Knottingley	crew 3	60 tons coal
Elizabeth	Reg. Beverley	crew 3	45 tons coal
Martha Ann	Reg. Leeds	crew 2	70 tons coal
Three Sisters	Reg. Leeds	crew 1	50 tons coal

Houses 97, Males 235, Females 218, Total Persons 453.

THE PARISH OF METHLEY CENSUS 1861 Ref. RG9/3431/Area 13

Part of the parish of Methley which lies to the West of the railway from Leeds to York and bounded by the Wakefield road and towards the South East including the West Side of Scholey Hill, Hungate and Woodrow.

Woodrow – United Kingdom, Crispin Teal 31y Innkeeper, w Elizabeth 29y, boarder at the inn David Milnes 40y Gamekeeper.

Templar Coattage – George Nelson 35y Cashier of the Leeds Trade Protection Society, w Lucy 32y.

Woodrow – Joseph Braime 35y Boat Builder, w Hannah 33y. Murray Clayton 47y Proprietor of Houses, w Mary 44y, d Eliza 19y, d Amelia 10y, s Murray 10y, Emma Clark 16y General Servant. John Hornes 34y Brick Maker, w Mary 32y. William Wood 49y Whiting Mill Labourer, w Ann 47y, with 3 children, a visitor was Thomas Ward 19y late of the Queen's Guards. Benjamin Braime 57y Waterman/Keelman, w Hannah 57y, s Joseph 19y Ships Carpenter. Joseph Braime 60y Boat Builder, with 4 men & 5 boys, also a Brick Maker with 1 man, w Elizabeth 62y. Charlotte Burton 69y pauper. Thomas Wilson 53y Shopkeepr & Farmer of 47 acres, with 2 men & 1 boy, w Hannah 48y, s Edwin 26y Woollen Draper. Joseph Braime 59y Joiner/Cabinet Maker, w Rebecca 54y Dressmaker.

Royal Oak – John Ream(?) 59y Gardener & Publican, w Mary 58y.

Woodrow/Leeds Road – Matthew Amery 40y Farmer of 145 acres, with 2 men & 2 boys, w Selina 33y.

Alms Houses – Elizabeth Smith 61y Washerwoman with Mary Wright 49y pauper. Elizabeth Etherington 59y. Sarah Longbottom 79y widow/pauper. Hannah Wright 73y widow/pauper. Mary Pickersgill 75y widow/pauper. Elizabeth Watson 77y widow/pauper.

Woodland Cottage – Edward Jowett 60y Land Agent to Earl of Mexborough.

Woodside – Hester Firth 39y Proprietor of Houses.

Leeds Road – The Lodge – Dickinson Swann 39y Head Gamekeeper, w Eliza 41y.

Methley Hall – Titus Salt 57y Alpaca Mnfr., also Deputy Lieutenant of the West Riding of

Yorkshire and a Magistrate, w Caroline 48y, s Herbert 20y, s Titus 17y Scholar, Harriett Stables(?) 51y Housekeeper, Elizabeth Rainer(?) 36y Cook, Margery McPherson 30y Laundry Maid, Mary Ward 20y Laundry Maid, Ann Darnborough 35y, Ann (?) 28y, Hannah (?) 23y & Ann Rogerson 22y House Maids, Mary Fawkes 24y & Eliza Walker 21y Kitchen Maids.

Methley Park –
The Dairy House – Hannah Atkinson 59y Housekeeper, John Hall 55y a boarder and a late nobleman's servant.
The Stables – George Kirby 49y Gentleman's Coachman, w Hannah 52y, d Mary 16y House Servant.
Clumpcliffe House – Francis Armitage 43y Farmer of 180 acres, with 2 men & 3 boys, w Jane 47y, step-son George Sykes 26y, Mary Sykes 21y & Ann Sykes 19y House Assistants, Sarah Sykes 13y, Ellen Sykes 11y & Emma Sykes 9y Scholars.

Moscarr House – Peter Curtis 64y Farmer of 122 acres, with 1 man & 2 boys, w Sarah 58y, Sarah Turner 15y General Servant, William Poole 23y Carter, William Connell 15y Ploughboy.

Methley Lanes – Solomon Idle 37y Colliery Engine Tenter, w Martha 37y. John Bennett 44y Colliery Blacksmith, s Robert 16y Groom. William Wood 39y Coal Proprietor & joint Farmer of 300 acres, with 10 men & 2 boys, w Hannah 27y.

Hungate – Richard Taylor 45y Horse Keeper in coal mine, w Margaret 54y Schoolmistress. John Roberts 56y Bookkeeper. John Hird 52y Gas Engineer. Joseph Ellis 12y Hurrier in coal mine. Christopher Holgate 33y Shepherd. Joseph Ellis 40y Under Colliery Viewer, w Nancy 40y, with 6 children. Thomas Wilde 37y Gentleman's Butler, w Agnes 38y.

Hungate/Scholey Hill – John Atkinson 53y Joiner/Builder, with 5 men. Thomas Rider 65y Gardener/Groom. Thomas Robinson 45y Mineral Surveyor & Colliery Owner, w Jane 40y Proprietress of Houses.
Sand Hill Cottage No 1 – Alice Lord 51y Proprietress of Houses.
Sand Hill Cottage No 2 – Admiral Pepper 59y Proprietor of Houses, his niece Mary Gill 20y Housekeeper.

Houses 74, Males 149, Females 154, Total Persons 303.

Area covered – Woodrow, United Kingdom Public House, Templar Cottage, Royal Oak, Woodrow/Leeds Road, Wood Side Alms Houses, Wood Side, Leeds Road – The Lodge, Methley Park – the Gardens, the Dairy House, the Stable, Clumpcliffe, Clumpcliffe House, Moscarr House, Methley Hall. Methley Lanes, Hungate, Park Lodge Wakefield Road, Mount Pleasant Leeds Road, Sand Hill Cottages.

PARISH OF METHLEY CENSUS 1861 Ref. RG9/3431/Area 14

Part of the parish of Methley which lies to the South of the road leading from Allerton Bywater ferry through Mickletown in Methley to Wakefield and bounded by the railway from Leeds to York on the South including the South side of Mickletown.

Mickletown – John Wright 42y Fellmonger, w Elizabeth 33y, s Arthur 15y Coal Miner, s George 11y Hurrier in mine. Thomas Bell 28y Boot Maker. Mark Micklefield 62y Coal

Shipper. Robert Smirthwaite 75y widower Farmer of 50 acres, with 1 man & 1 boy. Mary Ann Woodhouse 64y widow Schoolmistress, her son George 20y Coal Miner, w Matilda. George (?) 44y Farmer, employing 4 men, w Margaret 35y, d Elizabeth 9y, s John 2 mths, Jane Hanson 16y Housemaid. Joseph Lister 65y widower Farmer of 28 acres, with 1 man, d-in-law Mary Bickersdyke 37y, s-in-law John Bickersdyke 33y Butcher, Sarah Walton 14y House Maid, George Atkinson 29y Engine Driver. At Garden House lived Arthur Bartlett 48y Land Surveyor. Moses Thompson 49y Surgeon & Apothecary, w Annie 46y. John Charlesworth 39y Farmer & Beer House Keeper, w Sarah 39y. John Bland 79y Vestry Clerk, w Grace 79y. Thomas Burton 41y employed 4 men & 1 boy, w Marth 39y. Benjamin Illingworth 49y Cordwainer. Charles Howson 42y unmarried Boat Builder. Samuel Appleby 38y Brick Maker. Walter Wright 53y Builder. John Taylor 63y Farmer of 147 acres, with 2 men, w Mary 57y. Joseph Pyrah 46y Shopkeeper & Coal Miner, w Mary 44y, s John 19y Coal Miner, d Ann 14y, s James 12y Hurrier in Coal Mine, s Jason 11y, d Alice 8y, s James 6y, s Joseph 2y, s Jesse 1 mth. Low Green Farm – Joseph Lumb 48y Coal Miner, w Abigail 42y, s Thomas 19y Coal Miner, s Richard 12y Hurrier in Coal Mine. George Pollard 28y Wheelwright, w Martha 25y. John Hick 57y Joiner/Cabinet Maker, w Mary 41y. Abraham Cheeseborough 42y Tallow Chandler, w Isabella 42y. Samuel Charlesworth 40y Farmer of 100 acres, with 1 man, w Ann 40y. Austin Westerman, 54y Colliery Agent.

Boat Staithe – Thomas Denison 36y Farmer of 75 acres, w Ann 33y, Ann Rogerson 16y Dairy Maid.

Mickletown – Benjamin Norton 68y Sawyer, w Ann 65y. Peter Milner 39y Bookkeeper, w Lucy 38y. William Palmer 43y Potter. Willow Cottage – John Shillito 68y Farmer of 106 acres, with 4 men & 2 boys, w Martha 55y. Coney Moor – James (?) 41y widower Gamekeeper. Dunford House – John Hollings 26y Farmer of 172 acres, w Jane 26y. Moorhouse Farm – Henry Waddington 55y Farmer of 145 acres, w Hannah 49y.

Burnley Place – Benjamin Gunnerson(?) 33y Engine Driver, w Caroline 24y.

Lancashire &Yorkshire Railway Station – Robert Hirst 36y Stationmaster.

Mill House Cottage – Henry Denison 49y Farmer of 20 acres. Thomas Robinson 42y Veterinary Surgeon, w Ann 39y.

Carr Houses – John Carr, 77y Retired Publican, w Mary 66y.

Houses 185, Males 481, Females 430, Total Persons 911.

Area covered – Mickletown, Primitive Methodist Church area (2houses(?)), Garden House, Farm House, Low Green Farm, Boat Staithe, Willow Cottage, Coney Moor, Dunford House, Green Lane (20 houses), Moor House, Burnley Place (26 houses shown in the census – was this the first part of Methley Junction to be built?), Lancashire & Yorkshire Railway Station, Common Side, Mill House Cottage, Carr Houses.

PARISH OF METHLEY CENSUS 1861 Ref. RG9/3431/Area 15

All the remaining part of the parish of Methley which lies to the North of the road from Allerton Bywater ferry through Mickletown to Wakefield and bounded by the rivers Aire and

Calder towards the North and the Leeds-York railway on the West including the North side of Mickletown and Carr Hall.

Midland Railway Station – George Maudsley 44y, w Jane 44y, d Hannah 17y, d Alice 15y, d Margaret 2y.

Farm House – Robert Hollings 54y Farmer of 150 acres, with 3 men & 1 boy, w Sarah 48y, grand-d Sarah 1y, Sarah Ward 18y General Servant, Frank Spence 19y Carter, Rhoda White 13y Nurse Maid.

Mill Lane, Mickletown – Henry Atkinson 36y Corn Miller. John Ripley 52y widower Corn Miller. Abraham Lister 35y Drapers Shopkeeper, w Elizabeth 31y.

The Bay Horse Inn – Samuel Popplewell 36y Innkeeper, w Sarah 31y.

The Lord Nelson – Phil Connell 47y Innkeeper, w Henrietta 43y.

Stocks Hill – George Charlesworth 29y Grocer/Tea Dealer, w Caroline 30y. William Hick 67y Fellmonger. Benjamin Burnley 34y Fundholder. Mary North 43y widow Grocer, s Edwin Bellwood 17y Telegraph Clerk. Moses Popplewell 54y Drapers Shop Owner, w Jane 47y. Richard Braime 48y Grocer/Tea Dealer & Wesleyan Local Preacher. John Atack 57y Mason & Builder, w Ann 57y. James Waide 58y Farmer of 50 acres & Mnfr of Sulphuric Acid, employing 7 men. Richard Bayldon 58y Road Surveyor.

Wesleyan Reformed Church – Mary Ann Merton 45y widow Schoolmistress, s William 19y Pot Maker. Edwin Pickersley(?) 43y Attorney, w Hannah 44y.

Parsonage House – Mary Cheap 61y widow Fundholder.

Mickletown (cont'd) – Thomas Bell 48y Tailor. Richard Tate 23y son of Henry Tate, Watchman at Railway Station. Amy Pollard 59y widow Land Proprietress. Elizabeth Briggs 34y widow Land Proprietress & Fundholder.

The Queen Inn – James Wilkinson 73y Innkeeper, w Henrietta 66y.

Houses – 171, Males 380, Females 406, Total Persons 786.

Area covered – Lemon Royd Lock, Brickyard House, Midland Railway Station, Farm House, Carr Hall, Mill Lane, Butcher Row(?), Bay Horse Inn, Lord Nelson Inn, Lord Nelson Yard, Stocks Hill, Chapel Square, Wesleyan Methodist Chapel & School House, Wesleyan Reformed Chapel, Red House, Parsonage House, New Row(?), The Queen Inn, Ratten Row, Engine House, Farm House.

The rest of this part of the census could not be microfilmed because the pages were too tightly bound. Because of this I have been unable to complete a list of people in employment together with occupations.

All that part of Methley commencing at the United Kingdom Inn including Woodrow, Woodrow Hill, Woodside (Oulton Lane) and the Park district, Clumpcliffe, Moscarr, West Hall, West Hall Colliery, part of Methley Lanes, Hungate and part of Scholey Hill, bounded on the North by Oulton Beck, on the West by the township of Oulton and Royds Green, on the South by the township of Bottomboat and the Methley/Wakefield road and on the East by the Midland Railway.

Woodrow – Crispin Teal 41y United Kingdom Innkeeper, w Elizabeth 39y. James Nicholson 31y Surgeon (not practising), w Jane 26y, s James 2y, s Arthur 1y, Ethel Prest 12y General Servant. Robert Hollings 64y retired Farmer, w Sarah 58y. Joseph Braime 45y Boat Builder and Grocer, w Hannah 43y. Murray Clayton 58y retired Manufacturer, w Mary 55y, d Amelia, s Murray, Machine & Tool Maker. William Cundall 23y Rly Telegrapher/Signalman. Sarah Newell 46y widow Charwoman, d Emma 20y Seamstress, s George 15y Ag. Labourer, s Stephen 13y Hurrier in coal mine. George Conyer 46y Sawyer, bachelor, boarding with him George Ward 33y Whitening Maker, w Fanny 29y Dressmaker, d Mary 8y, s William 4y, s Ephraime 2y, d Alice 4 mths. William Spencer 29y Blacksmith's Striker, w Maria 22y. Charles Kidd 56y Rly Platelayer, w Jane 58y, s William 15y Painter & Plumber.

Royal Oak Inn – Thomas Burton 51y Innkeeper & Master Builder employing 7 men & 4 boys, w Martha 44y, sons John 15y, Walter 12y, d Maria 9y.

Woodrow – Joseph Whittaker 41y Road Contractor, w Harriett 40y. Joseph Braime 69y Master Joiner with 1 man, w Rebecca 66y, d Emma 26y. Jessie Sutcliffe 52y Commercial Traveller in Rope & Hemp, w Sarah 42y, s Walter 12y.

Woodrow Farm – Matthew Amery 52y Farmer of 145 acres with 4 men, d Elizabeth 19y, d Sarah 17y, s Thomas 11y.

Alms Houses – Elizabeth Swales 80y, Elizabeth Hetherington 70y, Ann Illingworth 70y, Ann Raby 76y, Martha Arran(?) 76y, Hannah Wright 75y, Mary Firth 61y.

Wood Lane Cottage – John Richardson 39y Civil Engineer & Land Agent, w Sarah 31y, Sarah Wales 20y General Servant.

The Lodge, Oulton Road – Simon Prest 36y Head Gamekeeper, w Mary 34y.

Methley Hall – John Savile Earl of Mexborough 60y Land Owner & JP, w Agnes 33y, d Mary 8y, d Ann 6y, s John 2y, Henry Irish 36y Butler, Dominich Pagliarine(?) 53y Footman, Sarah Bowlam 16y Nurse, Harriett Fletcher 36y Housemaid, Jane Stainthorpe 29y Housemaid, Sophia Sady(?) 32y Maid, Caroline King 32y Maid, Annie Illingworth 61y Cook, Anne Howaye(?) 19y Cook.

Clumpcliffe Farm – Jane Armitage 58y widow Farmer of 177 acres with 4 men & 1 boy, living as a boarder Patrick Slattery 40y Gas House Labourer.

Moscarr Farm – Peter Curtis 70y Farmer of 124 acres with 3 men & 2 boys, w Sarah 55y, d

Alice 25y, d Emma 22y, grand-s Edwin 15y, William Bateman 13y Servant, James Burnett 50y Ag. Labourer.

West Hall Gate – James Wheatley 47y Market Gardener of 21 acres with 4 men & 2 boys, w Nancy 46y, s John 20y, s Joseph 18y, d Jane 16y.

The Lanes – Joseph Cass(?) 32y Coll. Agent, w Christiana 31y, s William 5y, d Fanny 3y, s Charles 2y, s Joseph 2 days.

Hungate – Matthew Atkinson 65y Farmer of 10 acres, w Elizabeth 60y, m-in-law Sarah Smith 86y. John Atkinson 30y and Jesse Ryder 32y Joiners/Journeymen.

Park Farm – Robert Smirthwaite 22y Farmer of 210 acres with 3 men & 2 boys, w Lydia 22y, s Robert 2y, d Florence 1 mth. Park Farm Stable Yard – William Ince 49y Coachman.

Scholey Hill – John Atkinson 63y Master Joiner with 3 men & 2 boys, w Margaret 59y, d Rosetta 19y, s William 17y

Woodrow Hill – Admiral Pepper 67y Annuitant, w Mary 30y, d Sarah 6y, d Ann 2y. Thomas Brunt 56y Sexton & Market Gardener with 2 men, w Sarah 56y.

Houses 95, Males 216, Females 211, Total Persons 427.

PARISH OF METHLEY CENSUS 1871 Ref. RG10/4640/Area 11.

The boundaries of this area were not shown in this census.

Church Lane – George Sharpe 25y Rly Porter, w Kate, John Case 27y boarder & Rly Pointsman, w Elizabeth 23y. George Thompson 51y Police Officer born Mildenhall. Suffolk, w Sarah 34y. Thomas Longbottom 60y Wheelwright with 2 boys, w Martha, d Jane 21y, s Arthur 19y, s Edwin 11y, d Ann 8y, s Walter 5y, Sarah Ann Hirst 8y lodger.

Grove Villa – Thomas Taylor 32y Surgeon, w Annie 23y, s Thomas 2y, Mary Ann Webster 17y Servant.

Holme Villa – John Holmes 56y Master Draper with 4 men & 2 boys, w Sarah Ann 52y, d Edith Ann 17y, Ann Platt 56y widow Cook/Nurse, Emma Scott 18y Kitchenmaid.

Church Lane – David Farrar 56y Retired Bank Messenger, w Ann 55y. Matthew England 26y Coal Miner, w Esther 27y, d Georgiana 8y, d Ada 4y, s Walter 3 mths. Alfred Atkins 26y Rly Signalman, w Fanny, John Atkins 29y Platelayer & lodger, John Walls 26y Porter & lodger. John Cheeseborough 32y Ships Carpenter, w Martha 34y, d Prudence 3y, s Samuel 2y. George Lilly 39y Postman, w Ann 37y, d Emma 11y, s George 5y, s Frederick 1y.

Church Side – The Rose & Crown – John Farrar 66y Farmer of 40 acres with 2 men & 1 boy, w Charlotte 61y, s Richard 20y, Elizabeth Tremellin 17y Servant.

Church Side – Richard Goodall 49y Coll. Banksman, w Charlotte 50y, s Paul 24y, s Richard 16y. Sarah Greaves 61y widow Sub-Postmistress.

The Cedars – Thomas William Embleton 61y Viewer of Collieries, born Newcastle-on-Tyne, w Caroline Ann 59y, d Caroline Ann 34y, d Isobel Adelaide 32y, d Emma 31y, d Louisa 29y, s Thomas William 28y Viewer of Collieries, s Denis Maud 25y Engineer, d Emily Maud 20y, s Henry Cawood 16y, (there was another son, James, who died 2/8/68), Elizabeth Rockfort(?) 23y Cook, Mary Ration(?) 23y Housemaid, John Hollins 19y Groom.

Church Side – Church Side School – Alice Jane Bryning 24y National Schoolmistress born Lancaster, Emma Dean 18y Pupil Teacher & boarder.

Church Side – The Rectory – Philip Yorke Savile 56y Rector of Methley, Elizabeth Williams 39y Cook, Martha Barret 23y Housemaid.

Pinder Green – Joseph Williamson 49y Schoolmaster, w Harriet 47y, s George 15y, s Alfred 11y, s Arthur 10y, s Walter 5y, d Ann 13y, d Ellen 10y. Edward Chadwick 53y Farmer of 100 acres with 1 man, w Susannah 46y, s Edward 22, s Arthur 13y, d Mary Ann 10y, d Sarah Elizabeth 10y, d Alice Jane 8y, s John Edwin 5y. Peter Roe 60y Retired Farmer, his sister Mary Ann 54y Housekeeper. William Hall 28y Tailor/Draper, his mother Mary 62y widow/Housekeeper. William Kershaw 37y Gardener, w Mary 37y, s Chrispin 15y, s Leonard 13y Coachhorse driver. Arthur Bartlett 58y Asst. Overseer of the Poor, w Frances 57y, d Sarah 24y.

Watergate –Hazel House – James Bailey 29y Coll. Manager, w Elizabeth 27y, s Ernest 7y, s James Thomas Herbert 5y, d Mary Elizabeth 4y, s Arnold Neal 2y, d Julia Margaret 10 mths., Ann ? 25y Servant, Edith Ripley 12y Nurse.

The Junction Inn – Thomas Ward 44y Innkeeper/Grocer, w Emma 48y, d Sarah 18y, s Stephen 16y, d Alice 14y, d Mary 11y, s Amos 9y.

Watergate – Joshua Greaves 55y Retired Organist, w Mary 54y, s John 27y, s Thomas 26y. John Barker 58y Gamekeeper, w Mary 55y, s Joseph 37y, d-in-law Ann 31y, grand-d Elizabeth 14y.

The Rising Sun Inn – Joseph Smith 48y Publican/Gardener, w Mary 46y, d Hannah 16y, s Henry 12y, d Sarah 9y, d Fanny 7y.

Scholey Hill – Robert Kendall 26y Coachman, w Sarah 35y, s Ruben 11 mths.

The Mexborough Arms Inn – Richard Matthews 53y Farmer of 15 acres, w Martha 45y.

Scholey Hill – John Parkin 54y Farmer of 110 acres with 2 men, w Mary 49y, Thomas Stanley 16y and Sarah Hewett 14y Servants. John Idle 38y Engine Driver, w Sarah, s Samuel 9y, d Emily 5y, s Arthur 5 mths.

Fox Holes – Solomon Idle 47y Engineer, w Martha 47y, s John 20y Engine Driver, d Elizabeth 19y, s Walter 6y, grand-d Clara 1y. William Walker 65y Weighman, w Bertha 48y. George Waring 56y Coll. Underviewer, w Elizabeth 54y, s Alexander 15y.

West Lane – Sarah Waring 54y widow/Gardener of 5 acres.

Fox Holes – Joseph Wilby 59y Pit Weighman, w Elizabeth 58y, d Hannah 33y.

Fox Holes Staithe – vessel "Jane", Master James Foster 31y born Hull.

Houses 116, Males 237, Females 235, Total Persons 472.

Area covered – Church Lane, Grove Villa, Holme Villa, Church Side, Pinder Green, Watergate, Scholey Hill, Fox Holes, West Lane.

PARISH OF METHLEY CENSUS 1871 Ref. RG10/4640/Area 12

All that part of the parish of Methley commencing at Methley Junction including Mr Waddington's farmhouse and cottage, Dunford House, and the whole of Methley Common bounded on the West by the Midland Railway, on the South by the river Calder, on the East by the river Aire, on the North by the Leeds/Barnsdale turnpike.

Moor House – Henry Waddington 62y Farmer of 160 acres with 3 men & 2 boys, w Hannah 59y, s Henry 25y, s William 21y, s George 18y, s John 16y, d Emily 19y, William Jessop 17y and Christina Tricket 16y Servants.

Dunford House – John Hollings 36y Farmer of 198 acres with 3 men & 3 boys, w Jane 36y, d Sarah 11y, s Robert 10y, d Jane 8y, s John W 6y, s Roger 4y, s Edwin 2y, and Elizabeth Fletcher 20y, Sarah Birkinshaw 15y, George Bland 20y, George Shillito 15y Servants.

Low Common – Henry Dennison 39y Publican & Farmer of 140 acres, w Mary 48y, d Elizabeth 22y, d Ann 14y.

Windmill House – Thomas Robinson 51y Cattle Doctor, w Ann 50y, d Sarah 15y.

Low Common – Samuel Bastow 34y Deputy Coll. Steward, w Elizabeth 22y Dressmaker, d Lilian 1y.

Methley Junction – Richard Robinson 38y Deputy Coll. Steward, w Hannah 34y. Matthew Bastow 60y Coll. Viewer, w Sarah 56y. Robert Hirst 46y Station Master Lancashire &Yorkshire Railway Station, w Mary 41y. John Gill 49y Coll. Manager, w Elizabeth 27y. Matthew Smith 30y Grocer, w Jane 30y. Joseph Mosby 42y Grocer, w Elizabeth 55y. Jacob Fore(?) 13y Pit Pony Driver. Joseph Hanley 41y Miner & Grocer, w Ann 49y. Thomas Hanley(?) 27y Boot/Shoe Maker, w Sarah 25y Dressmaker. William Webster 12y (son of Robert Webster 36y) is described as a coal miner. Joseph Bentley 31y Coll. Foreman Blacksmith, w Mary 28y, d Emma 7y, s Jesse 2y. John Inman 45y Coll. Horsekeeper, w Nancy 48y, s William 27y.

There were now 104 houses at Methley Junction with 290 males of all ages, 151 worked in the mines, 3 on the railways and the remainder of working age worked in agriculture and sundry other occupations.

Methley Junction Staithe – No boats named but John Oldfield 23y and Marshall Barker 20y were boat men.

Houses 133, Males 372, Females 306, Total Persons 678.

Area covered – Moor House, Dunford House, Common Side, Windmill House, Methley Junction.

PARISH OF METHLEY CENSUS 1871 Ref. RG10/4640/Area 13

All that part of the parish of Methley commencing East of the Midland Railway bridge, Church Lane, and taking the whole of the South side of Mickletown, also the Boat Stake, Coney Moor and Green Lane, bounded on the west by the Midland Railway, on the North by the North side of Mickletown and Boat Lane, on the East by the river Aire, on the South by the Leeds/Barnsdale turnpike road, and Green Lane including any boats etc. which may be on the West side of the river Aire.

Boat Stake – John Smith 37y Basket Maker, w Mary Ann 45y. Thomas Dennison 45y Maltster & Farmer of 80 acres.

Willow Grove – John Farrar 28y Farmer of 110 acres with 1 man & 2 boys.

Mickletown – William Wilson 41y Cordwainer, w Harriet 38y. William Stevenson 61y Farmer of 12 acres, w Sarah 58y. Joseph Charlesworth 43y Farmer of 65 acres with 2 men & 2 boys, w Mary 41y. James Sheil 36y Master Grocer, w Ann 36y. William Hollings 77y, w Mary 76y on Parish Relief. Ann Atkinson 63y, d Emma 28y Dressmakers. Joseph Taylor 37y Farmer of 110 acres, w Ann 31y, d Alice 10y, d Amelia 7y, s Henry 5y, d Mary 3y, d Frances 2y, also Ann Dolphin 17y Domestic Servant, William Parsons 16y Farm Servant.

Poor Houses – Martha Morris 46y widow/pauper, d Leah 14y, s Joseph 12y, s John 9y, d Mary 1y. Ann Bilton 64y widow/Washerwoman.

Dennison Houses – William Dickinson 27y Ship Builder, w Elizabeth 20y. William Greenwood 30y Boat Carpenter, w Margaret 33y. John Charlesworth 48y Publican & Farmer of 70 acres, w Sarah 48y. Dinsley Pickles 39y Fruiterer, w Margaret 40y. John Bickersdyke 43y Butcher, w Sarah 37y.

Smithson House – Robert Heath 37y Butcher, w Emma 34y. Robert Collins 24y Policeman, w Margaret 25y.

Houses 152, Males 383, Females 351, Total Persons 734.

Area covered – Boat Stake, Willow Grove, Coney Moor, Green Lane, Mickletown, Low Green Terrace, Field Top, Poor Houses (12), Dennison Houses, Butte Cottage, Summer House, Smithson House.

PARISH OF METHLEY CENSUS 1871 Ref. RG10/4640/Area 14

All that part of Methley commencing at Woodrow Railway Station taking in Lemon Royd brickyard and lock, also the dry dock house, Bowers Coal Staithe, Kippax Lock, and the whole of the North side of Mickletown bounded on the North by the river Aire, on the West by the Midland Railway and on the South by the North side of Mickletown and Boat Lane.

Ferry Road – William Palmer 57y Potter, w Emma 50y. William Arundel 32y Miner, w Hannah 31y. Joseph Robinson 27y Moulder at Iron Foundry. Samuel Charlesworth 50y Farmer of 86 acres, no servants, w Annie 50y, also her father Joseph 81y Retired Farmer.

Queen Inn – Samuel Foster 36y Coal Miner, w Eliza 28y.

Ferry Road – George Stephenson 29y Butcher, w Elizabeth 23y. Amos Wright 37y Bricklayer, w Drucilla 35y. William Micklefield 63y widower Pit Engine Tenter.

Mickletown – Thomas Ward 28y Joiner & Builder, w Mary 22y. Isabella Cheeseborough 50y widow, s Benjamin 23y Carrier, John Ward 44y Ship's Carpenter, w Sarah 43y. George Atack 42y Coal Miner, w Emma 43y, s Joseph 18y Greengrocer. Riley Cheeseboro 81y, s Thomas Cheeseborough 30y Ship Builder, Julia Wood 49y Grocer. George Schofield 49y Pit Deputy, w Ann 46y, d Elizabeth 16y, s William 20y, s Benjamin 13y, d Sarah 11y, d Emma 6y, also father-in-law William Green 78y widower. Christina Webster 52y, s Albert 12y Hurrier in coal mine. Elizabeth Aylward(?) 63y Schoolmistress. William Inman 34y Carrier, w Mary 32y. George Bowman 56y Boot & Shoe Maker, w Mary 47y. Joseph Braime 62y widower Farmer. Henry Atkinson 50y Butcher, w Fanny 44y. William Taylor 23y Farmer of 36 acres, with 1 man. Joseph Armitage 42y Rector of Whitwood, aunt Hannah 81y widow, cousin Sarah Ackroyd 51y. Thomas Wilson 63y Farmer of 56 acres, with 2 men, w Hannah 58y.

Red House – John Much(?) 34y Ship's Carpenter, w Mary 28y, s Job 7y, s James 6y, s John 2y, d Eliza 6 mths.

Mickletown – Thomas Braime 33y Butcher, w Eliza 34y, d Rosetta 6y, d Clara 4y, s Hamilton 2y and niece Hannah Slack 3y.

Commercial Hotel – Joseph Waring 36y Innkeeper, w Sarah.

Chapel Square – Jonathon Pickersgill age(?) Ship's Carpenter, w Mary 60y, s Alfred 31y Weighman.

Mickletown – Arthur Waide 32y Farmer of 50 acres, with 1 man & 1 boy, Maria Goodwin 45y widow Housekeeper, Emma Fremming 22y Domestic Servant. James Dickinson 61y Shoemaker, w Elizabeth 57y, d Martha 18y, s George 16y Shoemaker, s Thomas 11y, s-in-law John Ward 26y Carpenter, w Hannah 20y, s Benjamin 2 mths. Moses Popplewell 66y Draper, w Jane 57y, d Mary 21y Milliner, s Arthur 19y Ship's Carpenter, d Ester 17y, s Walter 12y, also his mother Sarah Wilson 86y. William Ibbotson 31y Miner, w Sarah 33y, s Albert 12y Pit Pony Driver, s Joseph 8y, s John 6y, s David 4y, s Samuel 2y, d Ellen 1 mth. Thomas Bell 58y Tailor/Draper, w Mary 52y, s William 19y Boat Builder, s Walter 15y Bricklayer. Robert Sawyer 61y widower Wheelwright, d Love 20y was the Housekeeper, s Alfred 18y Bricklayer, s William 15y Wheelwright. James Chantry 67y Colliery Bookkeeper, w Caroline 60y.

Skinner Lane – Harriet Baildon 70y widow, d Elizabeth 35y & d Henrietta 26y Teachers, grand-d Elizabeth 7y was a pupil as were Emily Lister 11y, Mary Kitchen 10y, Sarah Dennison 9y, Sarah Woolscroft 9y, Jane Denison 9y, Annie Parks 7y.

West (?) Cottage – John Hicks 76y widower Retired Farmer, Jane Crawford 44y widow Housekeeper.

Mickletown – Henry Sharp 33y Coal Miner, w Ann 39y, s George 6y, d Hannah 4y, s Alfred 3y, s Robert 1y, step-children Joseph Aldridge 19y Coal Miner, William 17y, Betsy 11y. Francis Bartfell 33y Shopkeeper, sister Jane 18y Schoolmistress.

Lord Nelson Inn – Philip Connell 37y Innkeeper, w Elizabeth 53y.

Mickletown – William Parrott 27y Coal Miner and a local preacher from Somerset, w Eliza 23y, d Sarah 2y, d Annie 3 mths. Richard Hopton 30y Clock/Watch Repairer, w Annie 30y. Thomas Winterburn 47y Grocer, w Eliza 48y, s Levi 20y Coal Miner, s Joseph 12y Pit Pony Driver, Sarah Inman 15y Domestic Servant. John Dixon 42y Secretary of the Miners' Union, w Mary 40y.

Mill Lane – John Hollings 45y Boat Builder, w Hannah 44y. Sarah Atkinson 42y Corn Miller. Amos Ward 35y Boat Builder, w Elizabeth 35y. Moses Thompson 60y Surgeon/G.P., w Ann 56y, Ann Parrott 20y Domestic Servant.

Caroline Inn – George White 57y Landlord, w Elizabeth 57y, s Robert 20y Farm Labourer, s Watson 18y, d Emily 15y.

Carr Hall Houses – There were 12 houses occupied by miners.

Carr Hall – George Richardson 50y widower Night Colliery Deputy Steward, d Mary 17y, Housekeeper, s Timothy 13y Pit Horse Driver, d Ruth 16y scholar.

Shann House – John Clarkson 59y Farmer of 110 acres, with 2 men.

Shann Cottage – William Beecroft 31y Farm Labourer, w Ruth 28y Dressmaker.

Midland Railway Station House – John Hayward 25y Stationmaster.

Lemon Royd Lock – Thomas Parkin 50y Lockkeeper, w Jane 50y.

Dry Dock House – William Barker 51y Pit Labourer, w Ann 39y, d Mary 16y, s George 19y Miner/Local Preacher, d Frances 5y, d Elizabeth 2y, sister-in-law Frances Hague 23y Machine Hand, nephew Tom Robertshaw 5y.

Kippax Lock – John Abson 44y Lockkeeper, w Elizabeth 46y, d Emily 13y, s John 11y, s Tom 8y, s Harry 5y, d Rhoda 3y.

Astley Staith – Three boats, no details given.

Area covered – Ferry Road, Queen Inn, Mickletown, Red House, Commercial Inn, Skinner Lane, West (?) Cottage, Lord Nelson Inn, Mill Lane, Caroline Bridge & Inn, Astley Staith, Carr Hall Houses, Shann House, Shann Cottage, Midland Railway Station, Lemon Royd Lock and Dry Dock, Kippax Lock.

Houses 197, Males 488, Females 478, Total Persons 966.

TABLE OF HOUSES, PEOPLE AND OCCUPATIONS FROM THE 1871 CENSUS

	Houses	Male	Female	Total
Area 10	95	216	211	427
Area 11	116	237	235	472
Area 12	133	372	706	678
Area 13	152	383	351	734
Area 14	197	488	478	966
Total	693	1696	1581	3277

OCCUPATIONS

Occupation	Number
Basketmaker	1
Blacksmith	18
Boatbuilder	8
Bookmaker/Clerk	3
Boot/Shoemaker/Repairer	5
Bricklayer	1
Butcher	10
Canal Lock Keeper	2
Carpenter/Cabinet Maker	1
Carpenter General	20
Carpenter Master	2
Carpenter Ships	9
Cattle Doctor	1
Clergy	1
Clockmaker/Repairer	1
Coachdriver	2
Coachman	2
Colliery Agent	1
Colliery Banksman	5
Colliery Blacksmith/Foreman	1
Colliery Coal Dresser	1
Colliery Deputy	1
Colliery Engineer	1
Colliery Engine Tenter	10
Colliery Hurrier	8
Colliery Horse Keeper	1
Colliery Manager	2
Colliery Miner	556
Colliery Pony Driver	8
Colliery Steward (Deputy)	2
Colliery Steward (Night Deputy)	1
Colliery Steward (Under)	1
Colliery Viewer	3
Colliery Under Viewer	1
Colliery Union Secretary	1
Colliery Weighman	1
Commercial Traveller	1
Cordwainer	3
Cornmiller	1
Engineer Mechanical	2
Factory Hand	1
Farmer	26
Farm Labourer	92
Farm Manager	1
Fruiterer	1
Gamekeeper	1
Gas House Labourer	1
Grocer	16
Groom	2
Housebuilder/Mason	10
Innkeeper	7
Land Agent	1
Machine Hand	1
Market Gardener	3
Mechanic	1
Moulder (Iron Foundry)	1
Overseer of the Poor	1
Painter	1
Parish Relief	3
Plumber	2
Police Officer	2
Postman	1
Postmaster Assistant	1
Potter	3
Railway General Worker	3
Railway Plate Layer	6
Railway Pointsman	5
Railway Porter	2
Railway Signalman	1
Railway Stationmaster	2
Road Contractor	1
Roadworker	1
School Master	1
School Mistress	6
School Pupil Teacher	1
Sexton	1
Solicitors Clerk	1
Solicitors Articled Clerk	1

Doctor/Surgeon	3	Tailor	5
Draper	6	Telegraphist	2
Dressmaker	27	Tool Maker	1
Engine Driver	2	Wheelwright	9
Engineer Civil	1	Whitening Maker	1

PARISH OF METHLEY CENSUS 1881 Ref. RG11/4592/Area 7

All of that part of Methley commencing at the United Kingdom Hotel including Woodrow, Woodrow Hill, the Park district, Clumpcliffe, Moscar, West Hall, West Hall Colliery, part of Methley Lanes, Hungate bounded on the North by Oulton Beck, on the West by the township of Oulton and Royd Green, on the East by the Midland Railway and on the South by the Methley-Wakefield road.

United Kingdom Hotel – Joseph Prime(?) 48y Innkeeper, w Louisa 50y, d Louisa 21y, s Joseph 19y Wine/Spirit Merchant/Commercial Clerk, s Francis 17y Publican's Assistant, d Helena 14y.

Woodrow – Robert Hollings 74y Yeoman & widower, lived at the Bond House. Murray Clayton 68y Retired Machine Maker, lived at Clayton Villa, w Mary 65y, s Murray 24y Machine Tool Maker. Thomas Cheeseboro 40y Boat Builder with 2 men & 3 boys, w Helena 42y, d Sarah 7y. Thomas Fitton 33y Coal Mine Deputy, w Henrietta 33y. George Keighley 45y Plumber/Painter, w Jane 43y, d Sarah 18y Pupil Teacher, d Catherine 16y Pupil Teacher, d Emily 14y, d Edith 12y, s James 10y, d Ellen 1y.

Royal Oak Inn – George Marshall 29y Innkeeper, w Eunice 27y, d Eleanor 6y, s George 3y, Mary Wilson 16y General Servant.

Woodrow – Daniel Jennings 41y Colliery Engine Driver, w Sarah 41y, s Arthur 18y Colliery Engine Driver, s William 16y Engine Stoker, s Enoch 15y Pupil Teacher, s John 10y, d Mary 8y, d Ester 5y, d Eva 3y, d Georgiana 1y. Samuel Fellingham 64y Welted Cloth Mnfr, born Mirfield, w Mary Ann 65y, d Mary 23y, Sarah Braime 19y General Servant. Jessie Sutcliffe 62y Commercial Traveller in Flax Trade, w Sarah 52y, s Walter J. 22y Clerk/Sub Manager for Cloth Mnfr. Thomas Brunt 62y Market Gardener, w Ann 66y, step-d Ellen Brooke. John Hollings 72y Retired Farmer, w Elizabeth 66y. Thomas Burton 61y Builder, w Martha 59y, s John 25y Stonemason, d Maria 19y Milliner, d Clara 11y. John Jackson 51y Cornmiller & Farmer with 12 men & 1 boy, lived at Bellwood House, s Thomas 19y Student.

Alms Houses – Ann Wright 63y widow. Ann Illingworth 77y widow. Sarah Carr 84y widow. Mary Backhouse 66y widow. Elizabeth Chadwick 72y widow. Ann Spurr 78y widow. Ann Bilton 75y widow. Ann Hirst 46y widow.

Woodland Villa – John Richardson 49y widower Land Agent/Surveyor, Sarah Richardson 69y m-in-law, Catherine Holder 19y Housemaid, Mary A Slater 19y Cook.

The Lodge, Oulton Road – Simon Prest(?) 44y widower Gamekeeper, d Esther 22y Dressmaker, d Clara 12y, d Tryphena(?) 8y, s Alexander 6y, d Ethel 2y, God-s Clarence 2y.

Clumpcliffe – Jane Armitage 67y widow Farmer of 201 acres with 2 men & 2 boys, s George

Sykes 43y Farmer, d Ann 39y, d Jane 35y, d Harriett 33y, Harriett Byram 18y Domestic, Henry Stones 18y Farm Servant, William Harrison 16y Farm Servant.

Mosscar – George Hanley 44y Farmer of 122 acres, father John 63y, mother Ann 65y, brother John 28y, brother Richard 24y, nephew William W Hanley 17y. Nancy Wheatley 56y widow Market Gardener, s John 30y Manager for mother, d Hannah 22y, God-d Margaret 3y.

The Lanes – James Turner 64y Colliery Head Blacksmith, w Elizabeth 58y, s James 23y Blacksmith, s Frederick 20y Coal Miner, s John 16y Coal Miner.

Park Farm – Robert Smirthwaite 31y Farmer of 150 acres with 2 men & 1 boy, w Lydia 29y, s Robert 11y, d Florence E 10y, d Elizabeth 7y, d Mary 4y, Annie Gillet 23y Governess.

Houses 102, Males 226, Females 225, Total Persons 451.

Area covered – Woodrow, Bond House, Templar Cottage, Clayton Villa, Royal Oak Inn, Alms Houses, Wood Side, Woodland Villa, The Lodge Oulton Road, The Park, Clumpcliffe, Mosscar, West Hall, The Lanes, Hungate, Park Farm, Scholey Hill.

PARISH OF METHLEY CENSUS 1881 Ref. RG11/4592/Area 8

All that part of the township of Methley which lies to the West side of the railway bridge Church Lane, bounded on the North by Park Lane and the Methley-Wakefield road, on the West by Bottomboat Beck, on the East by the Midland Railway, on the South by the River Calder.

Church Side – Richard Farrar 31y Farmer of 60 acres, also Maltster, w Emma 29y, s John Richard, 3y, s Percy Robinson 1y, John Farrar 76y Retired Farmer & Innkeeper, w Charlotte 71y. Crispin Teal 76y Innkeeper at the Rose & Crown Inn, w Elizabeth 49y, s Fred 20y Clerk, d Clara 30y ex Pupil Teacher, d Florence Mary 9y. Richard Goodall 59y Sexton, w Charlotte 60y. William Goulden 52y Incapacitated Butler (born Alverthorpe) was a lodger with Sarah Baldry 73y widow and her sister Martha Woodcock 84y. Sarah Greaves 77y widow Sub-Postmistress.

The Cedars – Thomas W Embleton 71y widower Mining Engineer, d Caroline Ann 44y, d Isobel Adelaide 42y, d Emma 41y, d Louisa 39y, s Thomas William 37y Mining Engineer, d Emily Maud 30y, s Henry Cawood 26y Mining Engineer, Jane Hollings 21y Cook, Thomas Haw 49y (born Escrick, York) Groom. All the children of Thomas W Embleton were born at Middleton, Leeds.

The Rectory – Charles Abrams 28y Coal Miner, w Alice 24y, d Emma 3y, d Annie 8 mths, (?) Newell 18y Gardener, Emma Wood 13y Domestic.

National School House – Elizabeth Clough 22y Schoolmistress.

Pinder Green – Edwin Chadwick 65y Farmer of 96 acres, w Susannah 56y, s Edmund 32y, s Henry 25y, s Arthur 23y Chemist, d Mary Ann 20y, d Sarah E 20y. Harriet Wilkinson 57y widow, s George 25y Limestone Keeper, d Annie 23y, s Alfred 22y Bank Clerk, d Ellen 20y, s Walter 15y Bank Clerk.

Hazel House – Walter G Jackson 34y Mining Engineer, w Marion 23y, d Edith 8 mths, Clara Wall 35y Cook, Sarah Owen 25y Nurse, Sarah Burton 19y Housemaid.

Hazel Farm – John Cockcroft 50y.

Junction Inn – Thomas Weston 34y Miner (born Worcestershire), w Elizabeth 32y, s Eli 11y, Scot Bullock 43y (from S Milford) Groom & Coachman. Joshua Greaves 65y Organist, w Mary 64y, s Thomas 36y Bricklayer.

Scholey Hill – Richard Illingworth 41y Miner, w Ann 38y, s Harrison 15y Miner, s William 14y Miner, d Mary 14y, s John 11y, d Eliza 9y, s Joseph 7y, s Kitson(?) 5y, d Emma 3y, s Richard 2y. Benjamin Stephenson 58y Farmer of 30 acres, w Susannah 54y, s James 21y Farm Worker, s Amos 19y Saddler. Arthur Atkinson 38y Builder & Joiner employing 3 men & 2 boys, w Elizabeth 39y, d Rossetta 16y, d Elizabeth 14y, s Christopher 13y, d Alice 9y, s John 5y, s Frederick 3y, d Mabel 1y. Richard Matthews 64y Farmer of 16 acres & Innkeeper, w Martha 56y. Margaret Ashworth 36y widow Schoolmistress, d Charlotte 11y.

Fox Holes – George Waring 66y Deputy at Coal Mine, w Eliza 64y. Peter Taylor 50y Pit Deputy, w Eliza 46y, s John 19y Pony Driver, d Ellen 12y, d Alice 5y. Robert Hayson 54y Shepherd, w Rebecca 51y.

Houses 136, Males 350, Females 326, Total Persons 676.

There were also 13 vessels at Fox Holes Staithe with 26 men and 9 women, no more details.

Area covered – Church Lane, Church Side, Rose & Crown Hotel, The Cedars, The Rectory, Pinder Green, Hazel House and Farm, Junction Inn, Watergate, Scholey Hill.

PARISH OF METHLEY CENSUS 1881 Ref. RG11/4592/Area 9

All that part of the parish of Methley commencing at Methley Junction including Mr Waddington's Moorhouse Farm and cottages, Dunford House, the whole of Methley Common bounded on the West by the Midland Railway, on the South by the River Calder, on the East by the River Aire, on the North by the Leeds-Barnsdale road.

Moorhouse Farm – William Hardcastle 32y Mine Inspector, w Rebecca 31y, d Eleanor 10y.

Dunford House – John Hollings 46y Farmer of 190 acres with 5 men, w Jane 46y, s Robert 20y Student, d Jane 18y, s John 16y Farm Bailiff, s Roger 14y, s Edwin 12y, s George 9y, d Phebe 7y, d Gertrude 5y, Eliza Fletcher 18y & Jane Hodgson 14y Domestic Servants, Thomas Thackray 21y & John Whitehead 14y Farm Workers.

Low Common – Annie Street 28y (husband in USA), s James 2y, d Ann 7 mths, living as boarder Hannah Jackson 32y (husband in USA), s John 8y, s Frank 3y s Edward 8 mths. Samuel Taylor 27y Huntsman/Horse Clipper, w Mary, d Mary, s William, d Eliza.

Mill Moor Tavern – Henry Dennison 69y, w Mary 58y.

Windmill House – Thomas Robinson 66y Cattle Doctor, w Ann 61y, Elizabeth Baldwin 17y Domestic Servant.

The Old Hospital – Thomas Rees 36y Mechanical Engineer, w Catherine 33y, d Lily 9y, s Edwin 7y, s Alfred 5y, s Herbert 2y.

Methley Junction – William Totty 40y Blacksmith, w Patience 35y, s Joe 15y, d Polly 13y, s Charles 10y, s Benjamin 8y, s Willie 6y, s Thomas 1y, d Annie 9 mths. Joseph Hough 49y Methley Junction Colliery Steward, w Ellen 39y, d Mary 4y, s Joseph 2y. Charles Beech 34y Police Constable, w Eliza 31y, s William 3y.

Great Northern Railway Station – Robert Miller 39y Stationmaster, w Mary 38y, d May 7y.

Front Row

No 1 – William Singer 37y Colliery Clerk, w Ann 33y, s George 12y, d Mary 9y, d Christina 7y, s Thomas 4y, d Margaret 2y, Hanna Swan 60y widow Monthly Nurse.

No 2 – Charles Naylor 43y Colliery Blacksmith, w Sarah 35y, d Harriet 12y, s George 10y, d Sarah 6y.

No 3 – Smith Wilson 41y Miner, w Elizabeth 35y.

No 4 – Daniel Barnes 38y Miner, w Mary 39y, s Thomas 16y Coal Hurrier, s Samuel 14y, d Elizabeth 12y, s John 8y.

No 5 – John Deville 33y Miner, w Ellen 28y, d Alice 6y, & boarders William Barker 21y Miner, William Jackson 28y Bricklayer.

No 6 – Joseph Wilson 32y Miner, w Betty 25y, d Sarah 6y, s Arthur 4y, & boarders John Collinson 36y Miner, John Ellis 23y Miner.

No 7 – John Grice 33y Miner, w Hannah 38y, d Jemima 13y, d Emma 11y, s George 8y, s Robert 6y, s John 8 mths.

No 8 – William Crossley 29y Colliery Blacksmith, w Ann 23y, d Sarah 9 mths.

No 9 – Charles Murgatroyd 39y Colliery Carpenter, w Ruth 36y, s Thomas 4y, d Emma 2y, & boarder Richard Toft 42y Miner.

No 10 – Ellis Broadhead 61y, & boarder Jeremiah Beech 60y Miner.

No 11 – Joseph Wood 33y Colliery Carpenter, w Elizabeth 29y, s George 9y, d Amelia 6y, d Annie 4y.

No 12 – David Gray 31y Railway Shunter, w Isabella 38y, d Mary 2y.

No 13 – Charles Dickinson 63y Carting Agent, w Mary 62y, s Andrew 18y Engine Cleaner, grand-s Andrew Ripley 7y, & boarder Tom Idle 37y Miner.

Middle Row

No 1 – Jim Tremelling 29y Miner, w Ann 24y, d Mary 8y, d Florence 4y.

No 2 – Edwin Rickers 30y Miner, w Mary 30y, s George 2y, s Ben 5 mths, d Harriet 4y, Ben Rickers (Father) 50y Miner, John Kirkham (Brother) 23y Miner.

No 3 – John Meek 31y Miner, w Maria 29y, d Eve 12y, d Sarah 10y, d Susane 8y, d Gwen 6y, s Isiah 5y, s William 3y, s Ernest 9 mths.

No 4 – William Roberts 33y Miner, w Sarah 34y, s Thomas 14y Miner, d Maria 10y, d Matilda 8y, s Emanuel 3y, d Selena 3 mths.

No 5 – Thomas Reed 43y widower Miner, s William 20y Miner.

No 6 – George Houghton 37y Miner, w Ann 35y, s George 10y, d Sarah 8y, d Martha 5y, d Alice 2y, d Mary 4 mths.

No 7 – Edwin Boycott 30y, Miner, w Sarah 27y, d Zilpah(?) 9y, s Landale 2y, d Eliza 6 mths.

No 8 – James Webster 40y Miner, w Mary 36y, d Polly 14y, s James 5y, d Annie 3y, d Susannah 2y, & boarder George Greenwood 33y Miner.

No 9 – John Herrington 23y Miner, w Annie 17y, d Ida 2 mths.

No 10 – Edwin J Powell 40y Miner, w Rose 29y, s Edward 17y Miner, d Elizabeth 15y, d Ester, d Mary, d Lucy, s Thomas, d Alice, d Ada (no ages shown).

No 11 – Uninhabited.

No 12 – John Hawes 51y Miner, w Eliza 51y, s William 23y, d Rhoda 14y, s George 12y, d Emily 9y.

No 13 – Uninhabited.

No 14 – George Lumb 45y Miner, w Drusilla 49y, s Samuel Dyson 20y Miner.

No 15 – Thomas Hodget 33y Miner, w Sarah 38y.

No 16 – Henry Horton 29y Miner, w Mary 28y, d Silvia 4y, d Pheobe 4 mths, brother Frederick F Horton 17y Miner, sister Elizabeth Horton 14y.

Burnley Row

No 1 – Samuel Williamson 35y Miner, w Sarah 33y, s Samuel 9y, d Mary Jane 5y, s William 3y.

No 2 – Eli Weston 30y Miner, w Jane 28y, d Alice 7y, d Clara 5y, d Gertrude 4y.

No 3 – Christopher Robinson 42y Miner, w Emma 38y, s Richard 18y Miner, d Mary 10y, d Emily 2y, d Rosetta 3 mths.

No 4 – Francis Dunnill 37y Colliery Carpenter, w Mary 37y, d Amy 14y, s Joseph 11y, d Florence 9y, d Ellen 7y.

No 5 – William Ellwood 29y Colliery Horsekeeper, w Alice 30y, s Walter 3y.

No 6 – John Dunnill 38y Colliery Engineman, w Mercy 40y, s William 14y, s Fred 12y, s Frank 2y, s Holland 1mth.

No 7 – William Bennett 24y Colliery Engineman, w Ester 23y, d Eva 3y, s James 1y, s George 2 mths.

No 8 – William Innman 37y Miner, w Rhoda 30y, d Mary 10y, s Joseph 8y, d Linda 3y, s William 10 mths, John Innman (father) 55y widower Miner.

No 9 – John Evans 27y Miner, w Margaret 30y, d Alice 5y, s Enoch 2y, s George 2 mths, & boarders William H Vickers 20y Miner and Levie(?) Bowen 18y Miner.

No 10 – James Dickinson 31y Miner, w Emma 32y.

No 11 – Jonah Parker 39y Miner, w Betsy 40y, d Mary 19y, s Daniel 17y Miner, s Jonah 16y Miner, d Sarah 12y, d Susannah 10y, s Job 9y, d Clara 6y, s Joseph 4y, s James 1y.

No 12 – George Connell 28y Miner, w Emma 27y, s Walter 7y.

No 13 – George Slater 38y Miner, w Hannah 37y, d Levina 15y, d Henrietta 12y, s Samuel 11y, s John 5y, s Albert 4y, niece Georgina 10y, and boarder Samuel Tomlinson 31y Miner.

No 14 – Henry Mosby 28y Miner, James Mosby 22y Miner, Jane Mosby 19y.

No 15 – William Pugh 24y Miner, w Catherine 27y, s William 5y, s John 13y, s Elija(?) 11 mths, and boarder Joseph Haywood 18y Miner.

No 16 – Henry Tremelling 49y Miner, w Alethea 53y, grand-d Charlotte Roper 5y, & boarders Charles Hoyland 40y, Charles Hill 35y, Tom Pickering 22y Miners.

No 17 – Joseph Mosby 54y Butcher/Grocer, w Elizabeth 64y, sister Ruth 28y.

The following 3 families are shown in the Burnley Row returns but have no house numbers, could they be the back-to-back houses in Burnley Row?

House – Timothy Roper 33y Miner, w Hannah 31y, s Timothy 10y, d Mary 12y, d Alethea 7y, d Rose 2y, & boarders James Cooper 28y & Enoch Lane 30y Miners.

House – John Tranter 39y Miner, w Elizabeth 38y, s William 18y Miner, s Samuel 17y Miner, d Elizabeth 13y.

House – Henry Addinell 21y Miner, w May 20y.

Green Row

No 1 – Uninhabited.

No 2 – William Herrington 59y Miner, w Mary 56y, s Samuel 17y Pit Pony Driver, and boarders John Bastow 20y, James Smith 25y Miners.

No 3 – John Pots 59y widower Miner, d Annie 25y, d Mary 17y, s Albert 19y Agricultural Labourer, d Jane 14y, d Maggie 30y married with s John 9 mths.

No 4 & 5 Uninhabited.

No 6 – George King 46y Miner, w Elizabeth 43y, d Sarah 17y, s George 12y.

No 7 – Mary Clarkson 57y widow, s Benjamin 25y Miner, s Ralph 21y Miner, s John 14y, with boarder Joseph Fell 24y Miner.

No 8 – John Ellis 32y Miner, w Mary 30y, d Hannah 11y, s Arthur 5y, d Eva 2y, s David 1y.

No 9 – Edwin Mincher 43y Miner, w Rachael 39y, s Thomas 14y Miner, d Sarah 11y, s Albert 7y, s Edwin 6y, s Herbert 1y.

No 10 – George Websdale 60y Miner, w Mary 54y, s Walter 22y Miner, s Jonathon 15y Miner.

No 11 – Walter Hawkes 40y Miner, w Mary 36y, s Walter 16y Miner, d Elizabeth 12y, s George 9y, d Rhoda 7y, d Harriet 4y, d Sarah 1 mth.

No 12 – George Mosby 38y Miner, w Elizabeth 35y, d Annie 15y, d Elizabeth 12y, d Margaret 9y, d Louisa 1y, Jane Mosby 73y widow & mother of George.

No 13 – Thomas Turner 40y Miner, w Margaret 41y, s Joseph 16y Miner, d Eliza 15y, s Thomas 12y, d Pheby 11y, d Elizabeth 9y, d Sarah 5y, s John 2y, d Margaret 4 mths.

No 14 – Uninhabited.

No 15 – Henry Johnson 37y Colliery Engineman, w Sarah 32y, d Ada 3y, d Frances 1y.

No 16 – Samuel Jackson 46y Miner, w Margaret 44y, s James 19y Miner, d Ann 16y, s Charley 14y, s Christopher 12y.

No 17 & 18 – Uninhabited.

No 19 – Samuel Farrar 60y Miner, w Martha 60y, s John 22y Miner, s Charles 18y Miner, d Jane 11y.

No 20 – Joseph Hebberley 41y Miner, w Hannah 38y, s with initials A.E. 14y, daughters with initials C.J. 8y, E.M.4y.

No 21 – Emma Laycock 51y widow Shopkeeper, s Solomon 24y Colliery Engineman, d Ester 26y, d Elizabeth 15y.

No 22 – George Garforth 52y Colliery Deputy, w Jane 49y, s George 21y Railway Number Taker, s Thomas 14y, s James 12y, s Alfred 3y.

Low Row – consisted of ten back to back houses, housing twenty families.
No 1 – Elizabeth Bennet 46y widow Farm Labourer, d Sarah 12y, s Thomas 9y, s Albert 2y.

No 2 – Uninhabited.

No 3 – Thomas Cox 27y Miner, w Mary 20y, d Mercy 1y.

No 4 & 5 Uninhabited.

No 6 – Samuel Bold 32y Miner, w Emma 30y, s William 12y, d Annie 10y, d Emily 3y.

No 7 – Charles Dennett 33y Miner, d Eliza 5y, d Anna 3y, s George 1y.

No 8 – William Jarrard 34y Miner, w Elizabeth 30y, s George 9y, d Mary 5y, d Sarah 4y, s James 2y, s Walter 5 mths.

No 9 – John Drury 61y Miner, w Ann 63y.

No 10 – Uninhabited.

No 11 – James Lee 45y Miner, w Ellen, s William 23y Miner, s Joseph 21y Miner, d Mary 12y.

No 12 – William Wood 74y, w Jane 65y.

No 13 – James Websdale 23y Miner, w Annie 20y.

No 14 – Richard Broadbent 20y Miner, w Eliza 26y, s John 3y, s Joseph 6 mths.

No 15 – John Clay 32y Miner, w Eliza 28y, d Mary 4y, s John 1y.

No 16 – Mathew Smith 40y Grocer, w Jane 40y, d Mary 16y.

No 17 – William Herrington 25y Miner, w Emma 23y, s Joseph 2y.

No 18 – Joseph Herrington 21y Miner, w Martha 19y.

No 19 – Whitley Hastley 29y Miner, w Clara 26y, d Martha 5y, s Henry 2y.

No 20 – Samuel Birch 40y Miner, w Emma 46y.

The following details follow the Low Road returns, could they have been the railway cottages near the bridge crossing the Barnsdale road and shown on the map of Methley Junction?

House – Samuel Thurlkettle 32y Rly. Platelayer, w Sarah 31y, d Alice 4y, s Herbert 2y, s Fred 1y.

House – George Gibson 27y Labourer, w Sarah 26y, s Frederick 4y, s Nevile 2y.

House – Joseph Scarr 41y Labourer, w Elizabeth 38y, d Mary 11y, d Sarah 9y, s Frederick 7y, s Walter 3y, s Edward 10 mths.

Lancashire & Yorkshire Railway Station – James Graham 27y Station Master, w Ann 23y.

Also shown on the Methley Junction returns are the following 2 families no addresses shown:

House – Elisha Harrison 29y Coll. Lamp Cleaner, w Charlotte 22y, d Maria 2y, s Benjamin 6 mths, Ann Ward 60y (mother).

House – Robert Powell 32y Miner, w Ann 42y, s Robert 8y, d Hannah 3y.

Houses 153, Males 415, Females 358, Total Persons 773

Area covered – Moor House, Dunford House, Low Common, Mill Moor Tavern, Windmill House, Carr House, Old Hospital, Methley Junction.

PARISH OF METHLEY CENSUS 1881 Ref. RG11/4592/Area 10

All that part of the parish of Methley East of the Midland Railway bridge at Church Lane, taking the whole of the South side of Mickletown, also the Boat Stake, Coney Moor, Green Lane, bounded on the West by the Midland Railway, on the North by the North side of Mickletown and Boat Lane, on the East by the river Aire, on the South by the Leeds/Barnsdale turnpike road and Green Lane.

Top Fold – William Collinson 46y Letter Carrier. William Evans 32y Police Constable, w Caroline 32y, d Annie 2y, s George.

Smirthwaite House – George William Higgin 35y Surgeon, brother Robert Smirthwaite Higgin 29y Solicitor, John Higgin 20y Solicitor, Mary Stead 41y Housekeeper, Arthur Walker 20y Coachman.

Denison Square – Henry Parker 51y Grocer, w Abigail 51y, s Henry 18y Miner, s Tom 16y Miner, d Annie 14y, s Alfred 12y, d Sarah 10y, s Walter 7y, s William 5y, Frances Grayson 20y Domestic. Martha Hill 38y widow/Grocer, d Caroline 10y, s Edward 9y, d Lily Maude 7y, d Gertrude 3y, s Fred 1y. Sarah Waite 18y Dressmaker. John Grayson 14y Shopboy. Thomas Bell 48y Shoemaker, w Sarah 39y, s Henry 19y Miner, s William 14y Miner, d Emma 12y, d Elizabeth 11y, d Mary 9y, s John 6y, s Tom 5y, s Benjamin 11 mths. Thomas Chadwick 27y Grocer, w Betsy 25y, d Ellen 4y, s Edward 3y, s Arthur 7 mths. There were 40 houses in Denison Square.

Smithson House – Robert Heath 47y Butcher, w Elizabeth 44y, d Elizabeth 19y, d Emma 10y, d Violet 7y, s Greenwood 2y.

Mickletown – John Bickerdyke 51y Farmer of 22 acres, w Sarah 47y, s James 19y, d Sarah 14y, d Margaret 9y. Jane Pickles 51y widow/Grocer. James Stead 58y Blacksmith & Farmer of 11 acres, w Annie 43y, s John 32y Blacksmith, d Eliza 29y, d Maude 10y, s James Oswald 7y, s Fred 3y.

Malt Shovel Inn – John Charlesworth 57y Publican & Farmer of 60 acres with 1 man & 1 boy, w Sarah 57y.

Pinfold Lane – Board School – Robert Goodacre 36y School Master, w Elizabeth 34y School Mistress, niece Florence 16y, Charlotte Dixon 13y Domestic.

Butts House – Samuel Denison 55y Retired Farmer, w Elizabeth 45y, s Sydney 4y.

Pinfold Lane Police Station (was at North end of Pinfold Lane) – George Askew 32y Police Sergeant (born Croft, Lincs.), w Jane 35y, s William 10y, d Mary 8y, s John 6y, d Annie 2y, s George 6 weeks, boarder Bartholomew Walker 71y Travelling Showman & Conjuror (from Edinburgh).

Lumbs Cottage – Harriet Asquith 64y widow/Board School Cleaner.

White House Farm – Thomas Charlesworth 28y Farmer of 100 acres with 1 man and 1 boy, w Ruth 27y, s Samuel 11 mths, m-in-law Margaret Naylor 68y widow, b-in-law George Naylor 40y widower.

Mickletown – Samuel Hague 49y, w Catherine 40y Dressmaker. James Pyrah 26y Butcher, his father Joseph 66y Grocer. William Dickinson 68y Rly. Gatekeeper, w Elizabeth 69y, s John 30y Miner. John Hick 71y Joiner/Cabinet Maker, s William Miner, s Samuel 28y, d-in-law Mary Alice 21y Milliner. John Firth 50y widower/House Painter. George Atack 51y Greengrocer, w Louisa 50y, s George 22y Miner, s Arthur 21y Miner, s Sam 18y Miner, d Ada 17y, s Albert 15y, d Annie 12y, d Florence 9y, d Sarah 8y. James Sheil 45y Grocer, w Ann 45y, d Catherine Dressmaker.

Coney Moor Farm – Joseph Charlesworth 53y Farmer of 80 acres with 2 men & 1 boy, w Mary 51y, d Sarah 24y Infant School Mistress, d Ellen 22y, d Frances 21y, s George 15y, d Annie 13y.

Mickletown – William Wilson 41y Grocer/Draper/Shoemaker, w Harriet 48y, s George 23y Miner, s Herbert 14y. George Minett 29y Traction Engine Driver, w Sarah 27y, s George 2y, s James 9 mths.

Methley Grange – Thomas Denison 55y Farmer of 90 acres with 2 men, w Ann 50y, d Sarah 20y, d Jane 19y, d Frances 18y.

Willow Grove – John Farrar 36y Farmer of 100 acres with 1 man & 1 boy, Ann Askwith 27y Housekeeper.

Green Lane – John Robinson 32y Blacksmith, w Lily 27y, d Mary 4y, s George 2y, d Annie 1y, his mother Ann Robinson 71y widow. Squire Westmoreland 33y Miner, w Margaret 33y, d Emma 13y, d Alice 11y, s William 8y, s Harry 5y, s Tom 3y, s Donald 2y.

Pinfold Lane – Thomas Taylor 40y Surgeon, w Annie 34y, s Benjamin 2y, Emily Robinson 17y & Clara Robinson 14y Domestics, Ezra Thompson 18y Coachman/Domestic.

Houses 185, Males 510, Females 440, Total Persons 950.

Area covered – Mickletown, Top Fold, Smirthwaite House, Dennison Square, Garden Cottage, Malt Shovel Inn, North end of Pinfold Lane, Board School House, Butts House, Lumbs Cottages, Police Station, White House Farm, Coney Moor Farm, Methley Grange, Boat Stake, Willow Grove, The Mires, Green Lane.

PARISH OF METHLEY CENSUS 1881 Ref. RG/11/4592/Area 11.

All that part of Methley commencing at Woodrow Station taking in Lemon Royd, Brick Lane, Lock House, also the Dry Dock House, Bowers Coal Staithe, Kippax Lock and the whole of the North side of Mickletown bounded on the North by the river Aire, on the West by the Midland Railway, on the South by the South side of Mickletown and Boat Lane.

Woodrow Station – James Fearns 39y Station Master, w Dora 36y, s James 8y, s Willie 2y.

Shan House – John Clarkson 69y Farmer of 109 acres with 2 men & 1 boy, w Ann 65y.

Caroline Inn – George White 63y Licensee, s Robert 26y Miner, s Watson 26y Miner, d Emily 24y Housekeeper, d Ellen 13y.

Kippax Lock – James Brandford 55y Lockkeeper, w Annie 46y, s Robert 23y, Fireman on canal staithe, s Benjamin 21y Bricklayer, s Richard Coal Screener, s Joseph 6y, mother Elizabeth Matthews 71y widow.

Mickletown –Samuel Charlesworth 60y Farmer of 86 acres with 1 man & 1 boy, w Annie 60y, d Sarah 30y, s Joseph 19y. William Atack 58y Insurance Agent, w Mary 57y, d Emily 14y. John Edwin Brook 31y Glass Blower, w Henrietta 26y, d Laura 4y, s William 6 mths.

Queen Inn – James Green 63y Innkeeper, w Martha 61y, s Arthur 31y Miner.

Mickletown – Joseph Pickersgill 39y Miner, w Mary 37y, d Alice 18y Milkmaid, s William 16y Miner, s James 10y, s Samuel 6y. William Talbot 57y Rly. Platelayer, w Ann 62y, d Sarah Waring 39y widow, d Kate 27y, s Bertram 7y, grand-s William Waring 11y, father Denis Talbot 82y widower. William Henry Taylor 33y Farmer of 30 acres with 1 man. Thomas Braime 43y Butcher, w Eliza 43y, d Rosetta 16y Pupil Teacher. Thomas Wilson 73y Farmer of 50 acres with 1 man & 1 boy, w Hannah 68y.

Commercial Inn – George Pollard 48y Publican/Blacksmith, w Martha 48y, s Alfred 14y, d Martha 12y, d Mary 10y. Louisa S Goodwin 36y School Teacher, niece of Maria L Goodwin 56y Housekeeper. William Dickinson 39y Ships Carpenter/Grocer, w Elizabeth 30y. John Elstop 50y Accountant, w Elizabeth 50y, d Jane 20y, s Thomas(?) 18y Coll. Weighman, d Mary 16y, d Paulina.

The Lord Nelson Inn – Phillip Connell 49y widower Licensed Victualler, s-in-law Henry Shillito 21y, d-in-law Mary Shillito 18y, grand-s Phillip Shillito 10 mths, Mary Bowman 57y widow/Housekeeper.

Bay Horse Inn – Sarah Wright 58y Licensed Victualler.

Mickletown – Eli Atack 29y Newsagent, w Hannah 25y. John Henry Phillips 40y Accountant, w Jessie 39y, d Dorothy 5y.

Houses 242, Males 636, Females 587, Total Persons 1223.

Area covered – Woodrow Station, Shan House, Carr Hall, Lemon Royd, Dry Dock, Caroline Bridge, Bowers Row Staithe, Kippax Lock, and parts of Mickletown.

TABLE OF HOUSES, PEOPLE AND OCCUPATIONS FROM THE 1881 CENSUS

	Houses	Males	Females	Total
Area 7	102	226	225	451
Area 8	136	350	326	676
Area 9	153	415	358	773
Area 10	185	510	440	950
Area 11	242	636	587	1223
Totals	818	2137	1936	4073

OCCUPATIONS

Accountant	2	Farm Bailiff	1
Baker	1	Farmer	25
Blacksmith	27	Farm Labourer	60
Boatbuilder	2	Flour Dealer	1
Bookkeeper/Clerk	20	Gamekeeper	1
Bricklayer	12	Glassblower	1
Brickmaker	1	Grocer	21
Builder/Mason	8	Groom	3
Butcher	10	Huntsman	1
Canal Lockkeeper	3	Inkeeper	11
Canal Others	3	Insurance Agent	1
Carpenter/Cabinetmaker	2	Landagent/Surveyor	1
Carpenter/General	4	Limestone Keeper	1
Carpenter/Ships	10	Milkmaid	1
Carter/Carrier	3	Newsagent	1
Cattle Doctor	1	Nurse	2
Chemist	1	Market Gardener	4
Clergyman	1	Painter	2
Cloth Manufacturer	1	Plumber	1
Coach Driver/Man	4	Police Constable	2
Coal Steward	1	Police Sergeant	1
Colliery Banksman	4	Postman/Woman	4
Colliery Deputy	6	Potter	1
Colliery Engineer	3	Railway Gatekeeper	1
Colliery Engine Driver	3	Railway General	1
Colliery Engine Man/Tenter	4	Railway Platelayer	18
Colliery Fireman	2	Railway Porter	5
Colliery Hurrier	3	Railway Signalman	9
Colliery Mine Inspector	1	Railway Stationmaster	3
Colliery Miner	782	Roadworker	2
Colliery Ponydriver	22	Saddler	1

Colliery Weighman	5	School Master	1
Commercial Traveller	1	School Mistress	5
Cordwainer	2	School Pupil Teacher	5
Cornmiller	1	Sexton	1
Doctor/Surgeon	2	Shepherd	1
Draper/Tailor	14	Shoemaker	5
Dressmaker	11	Solicitor	2
Engine Driver	2	Toolmaker	1
Engine Tenter	15	Yeoman	1
Engineer Mechanical	8	Wheelwright	4

PARISH OF METHLEY CENSUS 1891 Ref. RG12/3762/8/Area 8

All that part of the parish of Methley commencing at the United Kingdom public house, including Woodrow, Woodrow Hill, Clumpcliffe, Moscar and all the Park district, West Hall, West Hall Colliery and part of Methley Lane and Hungate, bounded on the North by Oulton Beck, on the West by the township of Oulton and Royds Green, on the East by the Midland Railway, on the South by the Methley-Wakefield road.

Woodrow Hill – Thomas Brunt 71y Market Gardener, w Ann 73y. Thomas Burton 71y Builder, w Martha 69y Railway Parcel Clerk, d Clara 21, Fred B Frickley 29y widower lodger Railway Parcel Clerk.

Bond House – Robert Hollings 84y widower, s Edwin 22y Medical Student, grand-d Sarah Heptinstall 30y Housekeeper.

Woodrow – United Kingdom Hotel – Joseph Prime 55y, w Louisa 67y, d Louisa 30y, s Francis 27y, d Helena 24y, all Assistant Innkeepers

Templar House – Thomas Wilson Heptinstall 69y of independent means, w Sarah 54y, s Thomas Hollings Heptinstall 32y Brewer's Agent.

Woodrow – Thomas Cheeseborough 50y Ship Builder, w Helen 52y, d Sarah Louise 17y.

Royal Oak Inn – George Marshall 39y Innkeeper, w Eunice 38y, d Helenor 16y, s George 13y.

Woodrow – Alfred Braime 48y Pattern Maker, w Maria 45y, s Alfred 14y. George Bywater Keighley 53y Plumber/Painter, w Jane 53y, d Sarah 28y Assistant Schoolmistress, d Emily 22y, s James Plumber, d Ellen 16y.

Woodrow House – Walter Kaye 52y Dry Salter, w Rhoda 33y, s George 23y Brewer's Traveller, s George Downing 21y Architect's assistant.

Woodrow – Samuel Fellingham 74y widower Felt Cloth Manufacturer, d Mary Alice 33y.

Albert Place – William Robinson 57y Platelayer, w Jane 60y, d Mary 17y Schoolteacher, d Minnie 15y Schoolteacher. Henry Swift 59y Mine Railway Engineer, w Sarah 56y, s George Railway Stoker.

Methley Park – John Richardson 59y, Civil & Mining Engineer/Land & Mineral Agent/Surveyor/Valuer, w Mary 37y, s Joe 8y, s John 6y, s Thomas 4y, s Charles 1y, mother Sarah 79y widow, Laura Slathers 20y Domestic, Edith Acron 21y Governess, Matilda Smith 22y Cook, Lily Prellensworth(?) 19y Nurse.

Ellwood House – John Jackson 60y widower Farmer, Ann Finnian(?) 48y Housekeeper, Margaret Langley 16y Domestic, John Giblin 23y Domestic

Woodrow – Herbert Prime 33y Grocer, w Harriet 36y, s Frank 9y, d Minnie 8y, Harry Hale 12y Domestic.

Albert Place – John Cass 46y Shoemaker, w Pricilla 50y, s Joseph 26y Shoemaker.

The Lanes – Edward Nixon 53y Certificated Colliery Manager, w Sarah 42y, d Bertha 24y, Alice Stephenson 24y Servant.

West Hall – John Wheatley 40y Market Gardener, w Hannah 39y, d Mary 13y, d Nancy 9y, s Joseph 7y, d Bertha 5y, s Horace 3y, d Evelyn 2y, mother Nancy 66y widow.

The Lanes – William Field 41y Colliery Deputy, w Esther 40y, s John 18y Colliery Driver, d Harriet 17y, s Harry 16y Colliery Driver, s Tom 14y Colliery Trammer, s Joseph 11y, s Albert 9y.

Clumpcliffe – Paul Sherrand, 47y Farmer, w Rebecca 37y, d Margaret 19y, s Joseph 18y, d Jane 15y, d Catherine 13y, d Maria 11y, s Thomas 8y, d Julia 5y, d Sarah 1 mth, Maria McFaddon 22y Domestic, John Cowan 29y Farm Servant.

Methley Hall – John Savile Earl of Mexborough 80y JP, d Annie 23y, s John H 21y Officer of Militia, s George 18y, Francis Eves 33y Butler, Elise Lee 39y Lady's Maid, Hermann Furrer(?) 24y Cook, Thomas Hayton 43y Footman, w Harriet 56y Housemaid, Frances Drake 43y Housemaid, Ada Egg 23y & Alice Taylor 15y Domestics, Jules Tahler(?) Assistant Cook.

Wood Side – The Lodge – Thomas Crowther 36y Gamekeeper, w Sarah 35y, d Lucy 11y, d Florence 9y, s Charles 7y.

Houses 104 (of which 67 had less than 5 rooms), Males 253, Females 238, Total Persons 491.

PARISH OF METHLEY CENSUS 1891 Ref. RG12/3762/9/Area 9

All that part of the parish of Methley commencing at the West side of the railway bridge, Church Lane, bounded on the North by Park Lane and the Methley-Wakefield road, on the West by Bottomboat Beck, on the East by the Midland Railway, on the South by the River Calder including all boats on the North side of the River Calder and Cringlesford and Foxholes Staithes.

Church Lane – Alfred Langham 49y Rly Porter, w Clara 43y, d Ellen 14y. William Getliffe 44y Rly Signalman, w Emma 42y, s Thomas 19y Blacksmith, s Joseph 16y Rly Porter. Edwin Longbottom 31y widower Wheelwright/Blacksmith. William Atkinson 38y widower Colliery Cashier, sister Eliza 34y Housekeeper, d Sarah 11y, d Annie 5y. Edward Henshall 33y Civil

Engineer (Assoc.M.I.C.E.), w Jane 32y, d Dorothy 1y, s Edward 1 mth, father Samuel 74y Ret. Draper, mother Julie 63y, Annie Bowen 17y Domestic.

Church Side – Rose & Crown Inn - Crispin Teal 61y Licensed Victualler, w Elizabeth 59y, d Clara 30y Schoolmistress, s John 28y Grocer, d Florence 19y, Martha Anderson 25y Domestic, John Renard 20y boarder/Ag. Lab. Jane Bowman 54y unmarried Sub-postmistress. William Goulding 62y bachelor of independent means. Thomas Embleton 81y widower Mining Engineer, d Emma 52y, d Louisa 50y, s Thomas 48y Mining Engineer, s Dennis 46y Tool Maker, d Emily 41y, s Henry 37y Mining Engineer, Lucy Massey 24y Domestic, Sarah Burnett 26y Domestic, Mary Jane Jones 16y Domestic, William Skenitt(?).

Hazel Farm – John Cockroft 60y Farm Bailiff, w Sarah 49y, d Alice 21y Schoolteacher, s John 15y Office Boy, s Herbert 13y, sister Elizabeth Shaw 52y, Mary Home 19y boarder/Schoolteacher, Fred Walker 20y, Joseph Ansell 21y, John Brazier 15y, George Baxter 15y, Patrick Thornton 53y, John Thornton 41y all Ag Labs.

Hazel House – John Phillips 50y Company Secy., w Jessie 48y, d Dorothy 15y, s James 13y, Emma Walsh 19y and Elizabeth Walker 18y Domestics.

Watergate – William Westerman 39y Licensed Victualler, w Ann 36y, Lilly Armitage 17y Domestic, niece Amy Nettleton 4y. Thomas Illingworth 51y Mine Deputy, w Martha 55y, s William 25y Mechanic, d Emma 23y, s Henry 21y Clerk, s John 18y, and s Thomas 15y both Apprentice Carpenters. Sarah Idle 57y widow Laundress, s Samuel 30y Engine Driver. Sarah Greaves 74y married of independent means. Joseph Smith 67y Licensed Victualler, s John 19y Miner, s-in-law Charles Travis 35y Coll. Banksman, w Elizabeth 34y, grand-d Annie Elizabeth Travis 12y, grand-s George H Travis 10y.

Scholey Hill – Jessie Rider 52y Joiner, w Margaret 34y, s Thomas 29y Painter, d Elizabeth 17y Milliners Apprentice, s Charles 13y, d Annie 11 mths, grand-s Jessie 3y. Thomas Green 47y Licensed Victualler, w Emily 48y, s Albert 22y Ag.Lab., d Marjery(?) 15y, s John 10y, d Emily 7y. Margaret Ashworth 47y widow Schoolmistress, d Charlotte 21y Schoolmistress, s Sidney 20y Clerk, s Norman 15y, Rosetta Speight 14y Domestic.

Fox Holes – Joseph Edmondson 50y Farm Bailiff. Ephraim Jackson 41y Engineer,w Fanny 44y, s Arthur 21y Engineer, d Louisa 19y Dressmaker, s Joseph 17y Engineman, s Willie 8y, d Lucy 6y, s George 4y. Christopher Shillito 61y Coll. Horsekeeper, w Mary 62y, d Ester 28y Domestic, s Charles 24y Boat Carpenter, s John 21y Blacksmith. John Idle 40y Winding Engineman, w Annie 35y, s Percy 10y. James Hartley 52y Coll. Deputy, w Martha 51y, s Edwin 23y, s Harry 21y both Checkweighmen, d Charlotte 18y Dressmaker, d Dora 16y, d Ethel 10y. Richard Arundel 65y Coll. Manager, w Sarah 55y.

There were 4 boats at Fox Holes Staithe.

Houses 140 (of which 95 had less than 5 rooms), Males 332, Females 328, Total Persons 660.

PARISH OF METHLEY CENSUS 1891 Ref. RG12/3762/Area 10

All that part of the parish of Methley commencing Methley Junction including Moor House

Farm and cottages, Dunford House and the whole of Methley Common bounded on the West by the Midland Railway, on the South by the river Calder, on the East by the river Aire, on the North by the Leeds/Barnsdale turnpike road.

Methley Junction:
Low Row
No 1 – Thomas Walshaw 55y Miner, w Martha 48y, lodger John Bennett 36y Miner.

No 2 – John Mullard 28y Miner (b Staffordshire), w Mary A 25y, s John 7y, d Elizabeth 2y, d Florrie l mth.

No 3 – John W Hudson 33y Miner, w Sarah A 31y, d Ann 5y, d Mabel 4y, d Charlotte 2y, s James 1y.

No 4 – William Taylor 23y Miner (b Cambridgeshire), w Phoebe 21y, s James 3 mths.

No 5 – Charles Henry 23y Miner, w Florence 19y.

No 6 – Thomas Beards 38y Miner (b Great Bridge, Staffs.), w Susannah 37y, s William 18y Pit Bottom Worker, s Enoch 14y Pit Pony Driver, s Joseph 9y, s Thomas 7y, d Susannah 5y, d Sarah 1y.

No 7 – James Websdale 33y Miner (b Tibenham, Norfolk), w Annie E 30y, s Jathan 8y, d Ellen 6y, s George 4y.

No 8 – Alfred Smart 41y Miner, w Mary A 39y, d Sarah 7y, d Lily 6y, s William 3y, s Ethelbert 11y, s Henry Firth 13y Pit Pony Driver, s Thomas Firth 12y, s Arthur Firth 8y.

No 9 – James R Booth 20y Coll. Labourer (b Walsall, Staffs.), w Elizabeth 23y, s Leonard 5 mths.

No 10 – John Bailey 37y Miner (b Darlaston, Staffs.), w Mary 38y, s John 10y, d Priscilla 2y.

No 11 – Joseph Pickersgill 50y Miner, w Mary 47y, s James 20y Miner, s Sam 16y Miner, s Alfred 5y.

No 12 – Thomas Spencer 39y Miner (b West Bromwich), w Rebecca 36y (born Tipton, Staffs.), d Elizabeth 13y, d Louisa 12y, s Alfred 11y, d Annie 2y.

No 13 – Joseph Turner 26y Miner (b Darlaston, Staffs.), w Elizabeth 22y (born London), d Florence 2y, s George William 9 mths.

No 14 – Thomas Goodall 28y Miner, w Sarah 28y, d Ethel 2y.

No 15 – Robert D Horsfield 27y Coll. Fireman, w Mary 29y, s George W 2y, d Emma 6 mths.

No 16 – Thomas Moore 25y Miner, w Jane 25y, s Harry 4y.

No 17 – Isaac Crew 25y Miner (b Kidsgrove, Staffs.), w Eliza 25y, s Isaac 4y.

No 18 – Charles Morris 29y Miner, w Louisa 30y, s Sydney 6y, d Bertha 4y, d Maude A 1y.

No 19 – George Haigh 29y Miner, w Louisa 28y, s William 7y, d Edith 2y, s Herbert 9 mths.

No 20 – William Carr 26y Miner, w Emily 24y, d Gertrude 2 mths.

Green Row
No 1 – William Smith 57y Miner, w Connie 57y, s Henry 31y Miner, s Richard 16y Miner, grand-d Ellinor 5y, boarder Solomon Laycock 35y Miner.

No 2 – Amos Dooley 53y Greengrocer (b Lane End, Staffs.), w Mary A 51y, s Thomas 24y Miner, s William 17y Miner, d Eliza 13y, boarders Thomas Williams 27y Miner (b Derbyshire), Joseph Bennett 36y Miner (b Nottinghamshire), Samuel Harris 50y Miner (b Gloucester), William Wright 21y Miner (born Bristol).

No 3 – John Wright 49y Miner, w Annie 44y, s George William 17y Miner, s Thomas 16y Pit Pony Driver, s Richard 14y Coll. Deputy Boy, s Fred 12y, d Mary Ann Green 22y, s-in-law Joseph Green 24y Miner.

No 4 – Mary Limbert 48y widow, s Edwin 19y Coal Hurrier, d Edith M 17y Tailoress, d Kate 15y Tailoress, d Florence 13y Domestic, s Robert 9y, boarders Joseph Towers 27y Miner, Arthur Waring 33y Miner.

No 5 – Samuel Crew 60y Miner (b Framlington, Gloucester), w Mary A 66y (born Gloucester).

No 6 – Thomas Turner 55y Miner (b Darlaston, Staffs.), w Margaret 53y, s Thomas 23y Miner, d Sarah A 15y Domestic, s John William 12y, d Margaret 10y, d Mary A 7y.

No 7 – Thomas Goodall 50y Miner, w Ann E 46y, s John 17y Miner, d Jane 10y, d Almeda 8y, d Lilly 5y, grand-d Eleanor 3y.

No 8 – Henry C Wright 38y widower Miner (b Donisthorpe, Leics.), s William 15y Pit Pony Driver, d Mary M 15y Domestic at home, s Joseph 11y, d Ada 9y, s George 7y, niece Sarah A Whittaker 27y widow/Housekeeper & her d Mary E 8y.

No 9 – Thomas Crew 49y Miner, w Mary E 48y, s John 28y Miner, s Harry 21y Miner, s Admiral 17y Miner, d Mary 15y, d Louisa 13y Domestics at home, d Rhoda 9y, d Edith 9y.

No 10 – Charles Stather 68y Blacksmith, w Esther 60y, s Willim 21y Miner, s Charles 17y Miner.

No 11 no details

No 12 no details

No 13 – George Walsh 50y Blacksmith, w Maria 50y, s Isaac 21y Miner, d Annie 17y Domestic, s Arthur 15y Coal Screener, d Sarah 12y, s Alfred 10y, s Tom 8y, grand-s George E 2y.

No 14 – John Wooton 51y Miner (b Staffs.), w Eliza 52y, s Walter 18y Miner.

No 15 – Henry Johnson 48y Engine Driver, w Sarah 40y, d Ada 13y, d Frances 11y, s Arthur 6y.

No 16 – William Hartshorne 48y Miner (b Bilston, Staffs.), w Martha 44y (b Bilston), s Isaiah 18y Miner (b Bilston), s William 16y Miner (b Bilston), d Maria 13y (b Featherstone), s John Henry 6y (b Staffs.), s Alfred 2y (b Clay Cross, Derbyshire).

No 17 – Christopher Robinson 53y Miner, w Emma 49y, d Emily 12y, d Eetta(?) 10y, s Alfred 8y, d Bertha 5y, boarder Forest C Robinson 27y Miner (b Warwickshire).

No 18 – Joseph Farrar 48y Miner, w Sarah 44y, d Sarah E B Smith 16y Domestic, d Annie B Smith 14y Domestic at home, s Samuel Farrar 13y Coll. Labourer, boarder Robert Bleasby 55y Labourer.

No 19 – Martha Farrar 74y widow, boarders William Bernard 40y Labourer & Anna Bernard 31y.

No 20 – Samuel Crew 31y Miner (b Bristol), w Hannah 30y (b Shropshire), & daughters Beatrice 10y, Ethel H 9y, Ella 5y, & s Samuel 8y (all b Normanton), d Laura 4y (b Methley).

No 21 – James Smith 42y Grocer, w Susan 41y, m-in-law Christiana Elliott 73y widow, nieces Mary E Elliott 5y & Susannah A Elliott 14y Domestic.

No 22 – Thomas Jubb 66y widower, s William 33y Miner, Mary A Byford 47y Housekeeper.

Burnley Row:

No 1 – Samuel Williamson 45y Miner (b Nuneaton, Warwickshire), w Sarah 42y (b Bilston, Staffs.), s Samuel 19y Miner, s William Henry 13y, d Julia H 9y.

No 2 – Charles Bellwood 40y Mine Lamp Keeper (b Staffs.), w Isabella 34y (b Glasgow), s Herbert 14y.

No 3 – William Jackson 39y Miner (b Foles Hill, Warwickshire), w Hannah 35y (b Burntwood, Staffs.), d Emma 11y, s William 10y, d Eliza 6y, s John 4, s George 1y, boarder William Blake.

No 4 – Francis Dunnill 44y Mine Carpenter, w Mary A 46y, s Joseph H 21y Miner, d Ellen 18y Domestic at home, grand-s Herbert 6y.

No 5 – Andrew Thornton 30y Miner, w Maria 27y (b Radford, Notts.), s Major A 8y, s George H 6y, d Fanny M 4y, d Mahala 2y, s Eli 1 mth.

No 6 – John Dunnill 49y Engine Tenter, w Mercy 50y (b Leamington Spa), s Frank 12y, s Holland 10y.

No 7 – Atkinson Sawyer 41y Miner (b Oldham, Lancs.). w Mary 43y, d Minnie 11y, s Jabez 10y, d Edith 8y.

No 8 – William Inman 44y Mine Deputy, w Rhoda 40y, s Joseph 18y Mine Brakesman, s William J 10y, d Charlotte 7y, d Rhoda 4y, s John 2y, d Ruth 1 mth.

No 9 – John Evans 40y Mine Deputy (b Dudley, Staffs.), w Emma 41y (b Madeley, Staffs.), s Enoch 12y (b Burntwood, Staffs.), s George William 10y, d Miriam 8y, s John J 3y, s Arthur 1y.

No 10 – James Dickinson 41y Miner, w Emma 41y, d Mary E 9y.

No 11 – William Smith 24y Miner, w Annie 25y, d Annie E 3y, d Elizabeth 1y.

No 12 – William Whitaker 40y Miner (b West Bromwich, Staffs.), w Elizabeth 34y (b Walsall), s William 14y Miner, d Emily 15y Domestic, d Ann 12y, d Mary 10y, s Albert 8y (all b Chase Terrace, Staffs.), d Elizabeth 3y, d Louisa 1y (b Methley), boarder Thomas Winter 24y Miner (b Nailsey. Somerset).

No 13 – Robert Milner 40y Miner, w Sarah A 42y, s Robert 17y Coll. Labourer, s Tom 16y Coll. Labourer, d Maria 13y, s James 10y, s William 7y, d Edith 4y, s Charles 2y.

No 14 – Mary Mosby 65y widow, s Henry 38y Miner.

No 15 – William Wright 27y Miner, w Harriet 22y, d Martha 3y.

No 16 – Alethea Tremelling 65y widow (born Bilton, Staffs.), boarders Richard Roden 60y widower, William Roden 52y, George Mercer 28y Labourers & Fred Spilman 21y Farm Labourer.

No 18 – Herbert Wilson 25y Grocer, w Henrietta 30y, boarder David Ainley 14y Grocer's Apprentice.

No 19 – No information

No 20 – James Newbrook 39y Miner (b Worcs.), w Elizabeth 46y, s Edwin 13y Miner, d Caroline 11y, d Emma 9y.

No 21 – Joseph Fellows 46y Miner (b Pellsall, Staffs.), w Mary A 38y (b Walsall), d Elizabeth 18y, d Lily 13y, s John 9y (b Clay Cross, Derbyshire), s Eli 6y, d May 3y (b Methley), married d Fanny Sunderland 19y, boarder Harry Drinkwater 24y Miner (b Worcs.).

No 22 – Joseph Herrington 32y Miner (b Staffs.), w Martha 29y, d Elizabeth 9y, d Eleanor 7y, d Eva 5y, s James 3y.

No 23 – William Perry 56y Miner (b Wolverhampton), w Sarah 50y, boarder Samuel Rhodes 53y Miner.

No 24 – William Pickersgill 26y Miner, w Emily 29y, s Joseph 2y, d Mary E 3 mths.

No 25 – John Kirkham 30y Miner (b Ironbridge, Salop), w Alice 28y, s John 2y, boarder Alan Parker 26y Miner.

Middle Row

No 1 – George Grice 41y Miner (b Bilston, Staffs.), w Hannah 44y (b Halbrook, Staffs.), s George 20y Miner & Robert 18y Miner (b Cannock, Staffs.), s John J 11y.

No 2 – Edwin Rickers 41y Miner (b Salop), w Mary J 41y (b Salop), d Harriet 15y Home Domestic, s George 14y Miner, s Ben 11y, d Emma 4y, s Edwin 1y.

No 3 – Joseph Smith 52y Miner (b Tipton, Staffs.), w Mary A 54y (b Tipton), s Job S 21y Miner (b West Bromwich).

No 4 – John Kirkham 25y Miner (b Madeley, Staffs.), w Sarah J 27y (b Staffs.), d Sarah E 1y, boarder George Warrander 40y (b Shropshire).

No 5 – James Durwall or Dunnall(?) 26y Miner (b Madeley, Shropshire), w Emma 21y (b Sedgley, Staffs.), d Agnes 2y.

No 6 – John Whittaker 38y Miner (b West Bromwich), w Agnes 34y (b St George's, Shropshire), s William 16y Pit Pony Driver (b Donnington), d Martha 14y (b Chase Terrace, Staffs,).

No 7 – Robert Adams 45y Miner, w Mary A 38y.

No 8 – Enoch Gill, 34y Miner (b Penistone), w Catherine 24y (b West Bromwich), d Mary A 5y, s George 1y.

No 9 – Arthur Pickersgill 35y Miner, w Mary A 39y, s Walter K Yates 16y, d Harriet 15y.

No 10 – John Jones 45y Miner (b Hall Green, Staffs.), w Elizabeth 44y, d Elizabeth 15y Domestic at home, s John H 9y, s Isiah 6y, d Mary 4y.

No 11 – Robert Powell 50y Miner (b N. Wales), w Ann 52y (b Mould, Wales), s Robert 17y Miner, d Hannah 13y.

No 12 – Esther Spencer 37y widow (b Bilston, Staffs.), s Henry 12y (b Dudley Port, Staffs.), d Esther 10y, d Mary 7y, d Emily 5y, d Elizabeth 1y, boarders Richard Led(?), 49y Miner (b Molesworth, Staffs.), William H Tunningley 22y Engine Fireman.

No 13 – James Webster 56y Miner (b Edwinstowe, Notts.), w Mercy 48y (b Heckington, Derbyshire), s Jim 16y Pit Pony Driver, d Susannah 11y, s Riley 8y, grand-d Mary A 1y.

No 14 – James Cooper 38y Miner, w Mary A 41y, s Alfred Leek 21y Miner, s George 17y Pit Pony Driver, s John 16y Bricklayer, s Foster 13y.

No 15 – Joseph Millard 36y Miner (b Great Bridge, Staffs.), w Mary A 34y (b West Bromwich), d Elizabeth 14y, s John 12y Hanger-on in pit, s William 10y, s Samuel 7y, s Stephen 2y, d Bertha 9 mths.

No 16 – Luke Kirkham 27y Miner , w Jemima 23y (both b Rates Hill, Staffs.), d Emma 4y, d Elizabeth 2y, s James 6 mths, boarder Jack Kirkham, 20y Miner (b Rates Hill).

Front Row (Back to back houses)

No 1 – John Ellis 43y Miner, w Mary 38y, s Arthur 14y, d Eva 12y, s David 11y, d Sarah 9y, s Fred 4y, s John R 3y, d Mary E 11 mths, mother Elizabeth Milner 63y widow.

No 2 – Charles Naylor 53y Blacksmith (b High Byland), w Sarah 45y, s Charles 3y,

The compiler of this census return then showed No 2 Front Row again as follows:

No 2 – Samuel Sykes 21y Miner, w Harriet 22y, s George H 6 mths.

No 3 – Smith Wilson 51y Miner (b Methley), w Elizabeth 45y (b Tryddyn(?) Flintshire).

No 4 – William Sunderland 46y Miner, w Ellen 44y, s Friend 12y, s Percy 9y, d Honor 6y, s Jewell 1y.

No 5 – John Jackson, 27y Miner (b Foleshill, Warwickshire), w Amy 24y, s Albert 6 mths.

No 6 – George Gledhill 25y Miner, w Annie 35y, s Spawforth 3y, s Arthur Wilson 14y Coal Hurrier.

No 7 – William Simpson 36y Miner, w Jane 36y, s Harry 5y, d Emma 2y.

No. 8 – John Curry 56y Miner, w Elizabeth 52y.

No 9 – Joseph Wood 43y Carpenter, w Elizabeth 40y, s George William 19y Railway Porter, d Amelia 16y Apprentice Dressmaker, d Annie E 14y Domestic at home.

No 10 – Ellis Broadhead 70y widower, nephew George H Simpson 19y Box Maker, boarder William Carter 29y Miner (b Portobella, Staffs.).

No 11 – Aaron Church 37y Miner (b London), w Sarah H 37y, s Alfred B 11y, s Samuel 9y, d Sarah E 8y, d Louisa R 6y, s John E 4y, d Alice 2y.

No 12 – Samuel Laycock 39y Miner, w Ruth 39y, s John Henry 8y, s William Henry 5y, mother Mary Booth 75y.

No 13 – William Ellwood 39y, w Alice 40y, s Walter 13y, s Robert 9y, s George 8y, d Annie 3y, s Albert 2y.

Station House – Charles Haigh 44y Rly Station Agent, w Frances D 40y, d Florence B 13y, s Thomas P R 7y.

Station House – John Gosling 33y Rly Stationmaster, w Sarah J 33y, d Eleanor 7y, d Evelyn 4y, d Constance 8 mths, Elizabeth Wright 17y Domestic.

Common Side – John Scott 34y Police Constable, w Ellen 35y, d Ellen M 14y.

Moorhouse Farm – William Hardcastle 43y Coal Inspector, w Rebecca 41y, d Eleanor 20y Domestic at home, s William H 2y.

Methley Junction Pit Yard – George Morrison 59y Colliery Steward (from Sherburn Grange), w Emma 61y.

Fever Cottage – Richard Evans 53y Miner (b Donnington, Salop), w Selina 48y, s John 5y.

Carr Houses – William Scott 44y widower Engine Tenter (from Horncastle, Lincs.), s Frederick William 21y Boat Builder, d Sarah A 18y Housekeeper.

Mill Moor Tavern – Charles Beech 44y Publican (from Dorset), w Eliza 41y, s William 15y, Annie Etherington 17y Domestic.

Dunford House – Henry Pycock 41y Farm Manager, w Maria 43y. Albert Guise 46y (from Droitwich, Worcestershire) Clerk to Chemical Mnfr., w Sarah 43y (from Worcester) with their 8 children and m-in-law Elizabeth Whittington 75y widow.

Water Side – John Totty 57y widower Blacksmith (from Royston), children Polly 24y married, Fred 24y married, Job 25y Blacksmith, Benjamin 18y Blacksmith, Charles 20y Blacksmith, William 16y Engine Fireman, Thomas 12y, Harry 8y, Annie 10y, Jane 9y, grand-s Albert 2y.

Houses 169 (of which 156 had less than 5 rooms), Males 487, Females 407, Total Persons 894.

PARISH OF METHLEY CENSUS 1891 Ref.RG12/3763/Area 11

All that part of Methley East of the Midland Railway bridge, the Boat Stake, Coney Moor and Green Lane, bounded on the West by the Midland Railway, on the North by the North side of Mickletown and Boat Lane, on the East by the river Aire, on the South by the Leeds/Barnsdale turnpike road and Green Lane.

Smithson Building – William Jarvis 27y Police Constable.

Smirthwaite House – George William Wigan 45y Doctor, Maria Tate 55y widow Housekeeper, Jesse Platt 19y Coachman.

Dennison Square – Henry Parker 62y Grocer, w Grace 42y. George Waterburn 42y Grocer, w Sarah Ann 40y. William Gamble 57y Grocer, w Isabella 38y. John Braime 21y Butcher. Herbert Cox 29y Greengrocer, w Elizabeth 27y.

Dennison Yard – Mary Ann Stainthorpe 61y widow/Caretaker of Board School.

Police Station – George Carter 42y, w Jane 45y.

Malt Shovel Inn – Charles Haywood 49y, w Sarah Ann 47y.

Mickletown – Francis Wilkinson 50y Hairdresser, w Elizabeth 41y. Sarah Charlesworth 69y widow/Farmer.

Lumb's Cottage – William Jennings 31y Coll. Engineman, w Emma 28y, d Anna 6y, s Albert 2y.

Workhouse Yard – Thomas Houson 63y Coal Dealer, w Ellen 58y.

Greenfield Terrace – Jason Pyrah 41y Coll. Deputy, w Emily with 7 children. Joseph Hetherington 27y Life Assurance Asst. Superintendent, w Mary Ann 25y, s Bertie 2 mths.

Low Green Terrace – Martha Pollard 55y widow/Laundress, s Alfred 24y Coll. Labourer. James Langley 35y Deputy, w Mary 36y with 7 children.

Shiels Yard – James Shiel 54y Grocer, w Ann 55y, d Agnes 20y Dressmaker.

Rose Villa – Thomas Waide 36y Printer/Stationer, w Sarah 31y and 5 daughters.

Clara Villa – Ann Robinson 71y widow, d Elizabeth 35y.

Butts House – Elizabeth Dennison 54y widow.

Victoria Cottage – Maria Waide 69y widow, d Maria 32y.

White House Farm – Thomas Charlesworth 38y, w Ruth 37y, with 4 sons & 1 daughter.

Oaklands – Thomas Taylor 50y Medical Practitioner, w Annie Dobson.

Coney Moor Farm – Joseph Charlesworth 63y, w Mary 61y.

Coney Moor – William Stevenson 81y, s Benjamin 41y Farmers. John Thomas Wood 47y Miner, s Jackson 17y Teacher.

Boat Stake – William Addy 30y Insurance Agent (b Hemsworth), w Lavinia 30y (b Hunslet), d Alice 6y (b Illinois USA), s George 3y (b Pontefract), s Frank 1y, mother Elizabeth 69y widow (b Whitby).

Methley Grange – Thomas Dennison 60y Farmer, w Ann, d Jane 29y, d Frances 28y.

Area covered – Top Fold, Dennison Yard, Smithson Fold and Building, Wigans Building, Smirthwaite House, Dennison Square, Smithson Row, Mickletown, Stocks Hill, Lumbs Cottage, Workhouse Yard, Field Top, Field Head, Greenfield Terrace, Low Green Terrace, Shiels Yard, White House Farm, Clara Villa, Butts House, Victoria Cottage, Oaklands, Coney Moor, Green Lane, Willow Grove Cottage, Boat Stake, Methley Grange.

Houses 197 (of which 167 were houses with less than 5 rooms) Males 517, Females 435, Total Persons 952.

PARISH OF METHLEY CENSUS 1891 Ref. RG12/3763/Area 12

All that part of Methley commencing at Woodrow Station taking in Lemon Royd Brickyard and Lock House, Dry Dock House, Bowers Coal Staithe, Kippax Lock and the whole of the North side of Mickletown, bounded on the North by the river Aire, on the West by the Midland Railway and on the South by the South side of Mickletown and Boat Lane..

Woodrow Railway Station – James Fearns 47y Stationmaster.

Shann House – John Clarkson 79y Farmer.

Lemon Royd Lock – Joshua Goodyear 55y Lockkeeper.

Mill Lane – John Arundel 35y Carpenter, w Ada 33y, s Herbert 9y, s William 3y, d Kate. John Hollins 65y Ships Carpenter, w Hannah 63y. Richard Shillito 52y Miner, w Annie 49y, s Henry 29y, s Asker 20y. s Ezra 18y, s Elija 15y, d Millah(?) 27y, d Annie 11y, d Eva 9y. Frederick Bilton 47y Miner, w Elizabeth 47y, with 5 sons & 3 daughters. Joseph Hough 59y Coll. Manager. John Elstop 61y Asst. Coll. Manager, w Elizabeth 61y, s Thomas 28y, d Mary, d Pauline(?) 20y. Eli Atack 39y Newsagent, w Hannah 35y. Thomas Asquith 44y Grocer/Draper, w Ann 38y.

Bay Horse Inn – Gerry Risker(?) 36y Publican.

Lord Nelson Inn – Phillip Connell 57y widower/Landlord.

Mickletown – William Dickinson 47y Ship Builder, w Elizabeth 40y, with 3 sons & 1 daughter. Walter Wright 34y, w Ellen 33y, step-d Gertrude Stoker 14y described as a teacher. Thomas Bedford 46y, w Mary Ann 45y, with 5 sons & 5 daughters. Thomas Braime 53y Butcher, w Elizabeth 52y, d Annie 15y described as a schoolteacher, lodging with them was the Church of England curate James C B Hall, 32y bachelor. Elizabeth Dickinson 71y widow/Shoe Dealer, s Thomas 31y Shoemaker. John Howes 31y Draper, w Mary 31y Dressmaker. Charles Worth 26y Miner, w Sarah 23y Dressmaker. Rockley(?) Brooke 54y Miner, s James 27y Asst. Schoolmaster. Braushy(?) Fisher 50y Miner, d Mary 23y Schoolteacher. William Laycock 49y Wagon Builder. John Ripley 46y Grocer, w Ann 47y. Thomas Ward 48y Wheelwright, w Mary 42y, d Bertha 20y Dressmaker, d Minnie 16y Board School teacher & 2 sons. William Wright 41y Miner, w Mary 42y Dressmaker. Ann Rhodes 51y widow, s Walter 20y Insurance Agent. Samuel Charlesworth 70y Farmer/Maltster, w Ann 70y, d Sarah 39y, s Joseph 28y, grand-d Gertrude 14y, and Annie Threadgold 18y, Joseph Threadgold 15y, Joseph Kitchen 21y Servants. George Hepworth 58y Pit Deputy, w Ann 57y, s Alan 22y. William Freeman Collinson 56y Letter Carrier/Postman.

The Old Rectory – Clifford Dunn 45y Solicitor, w Marrion Jane 25y.

Commercial Hotel – William Wilson 33y Landlord, w Emma 36y

Queen's Hotel – Arthur Green 41y Landlord, w Hannah 49y, father James 74y Retired Innkeeper.

Caroline Inn – George White 77y widower/Publican, s-in-law John Asquith 32y Engine Driver, w Emily 33y.

Kippax Lock – James Balmforth 65y Lockkeeper, w Annie 56y, s Joseph 16y, s Benjamin 20y, d Hannah 23y, d Sarah 21y, d Letitia(?) 19y, d-in-law Kate 25y, grand-sons James 5y, Frederick 2y.

There were 4 barges at the Savile Coal Staithe and 7 at Bowers Coal Staith manned by 22 men and 7 women.

Houses 260 (of which 42 had less than 5 rooms), Males 694, Females 638, Total Persons 1332.

Area covered – Station House, Shann House, Woodrow, Boatyard House, Lemon Royd Lock, Carr Hall, Mill Lane, the Old Rectory, Kippax Lock, and Mickletown.

TABLE OF HOUSES, PEOPLE AND OCCUPATIONS FROM THE 1891 CENSUS

	Houses	Males	Females	Total
Area 8	104	253	238	491
Area 9	140	332	328	660
Area 10	169	487	407	894
Area 11	197	517	435	952
Area 12	260	694	638	1332
Totals	870	2283	2046	4329

OCCUPATIONS

Blacksmith	20	Gamekeeper	1
Boatbuilder	2	Gashouse Labourer	2
Bookeeper/Clerk	14	Grocer	27
Bricklayer	19	Groom	1
Butcher	11	Hairdresser	2
Canal Lockkeeper	4	Inkeeper	10
Canal Boatman	4	Insurance Agent	1
Carpenter/General	13	Landagent/Surveyor	1
Carpenter/Ships	6	Market Gardener	2
Carter/Carrier	10	Lodging House Keeper	2
Clergy/Rector	1	Newsagent	2
Clergy/Curate	1	Pattern Maker	1
Coachman	3	Plumber	2
Coal Shipper/Dealer	3	Police Constable	2
Coal Steward	2	Police Sergeant	1
Colliery Banksman	11	Postman	2
Colliery Deputy	12	Printer	2
Colliery Engineer	3	Railway Booking Clerk	1
Colliery Engine Driver	2	Railway General Worker	6
Colliery Engineman/Tenter	27	Railway Plate Layer	16
Colliery Firemen	1	Railway Pointsman	1
Colliery Hurrier	3	Railway Porter	8
Colliery Mine Inspector	1	Railway Signalman	7
Colliery Miner	851	Railway Station Agent	1
Colliery Pony Driver	56	Railway Station Master	3
Colliery Union Secretary	1	Roadworker	2
Colliery Weighman	6	Saddler	2
Confectioner	5	Schoolmaster	4
Doctor/Surgeon	2	Schoolmistress	3
Draper	1	School Pupil Teacher	5
Dressmaker	3	Shoemaker/Repairer	2
Engine Driver	1	Solicitor	2
Engineer Civil	1	Surveyor	2
Farmer	18	Toolmaker	1
Farm Labourer	40	Waggonbuilder	4
Farm Manager	1	Wheelwright	10

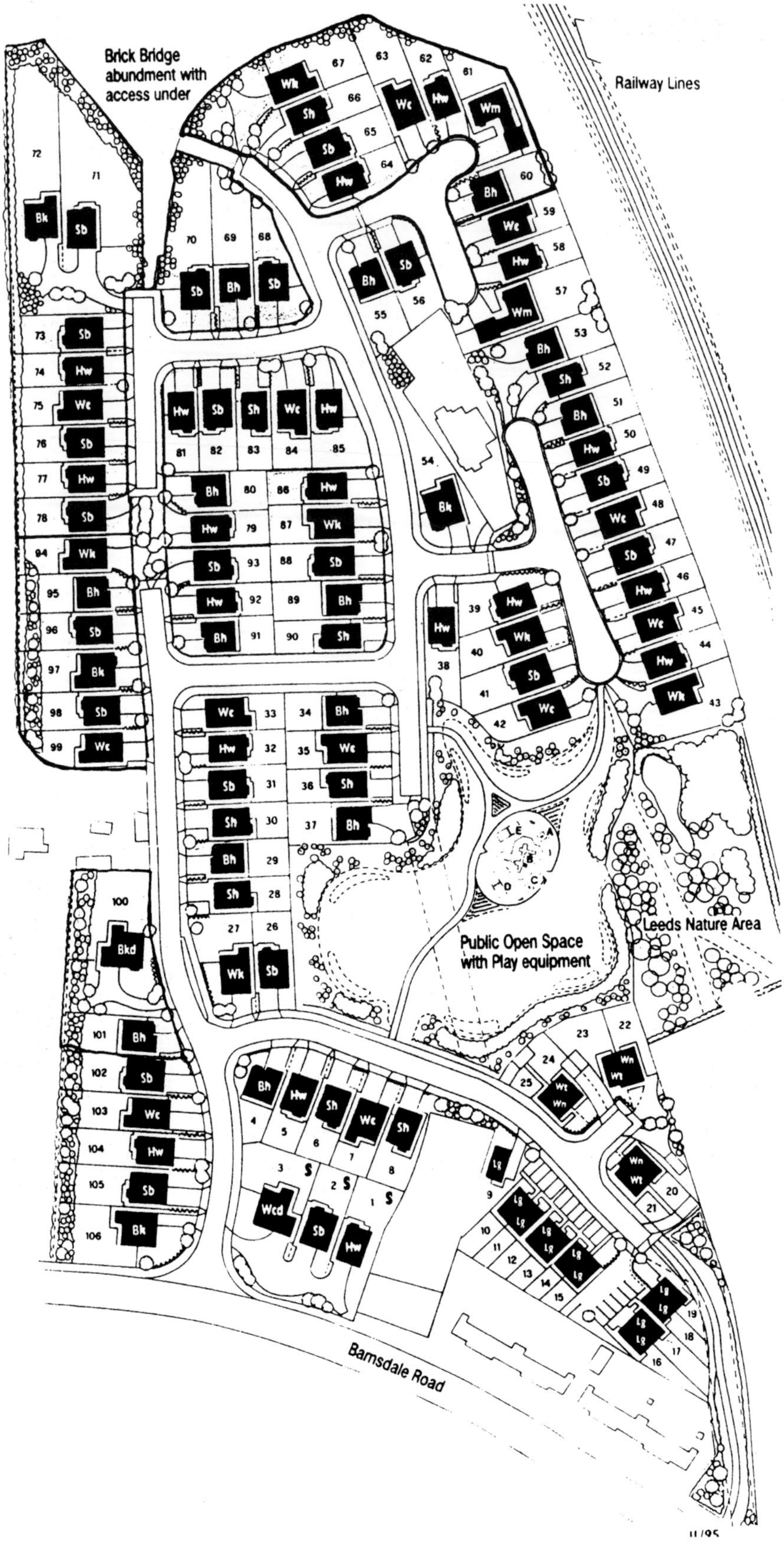

Barnsdale Meadows (not to scale)

By kind permission of McLean Homes Northern Ltd.

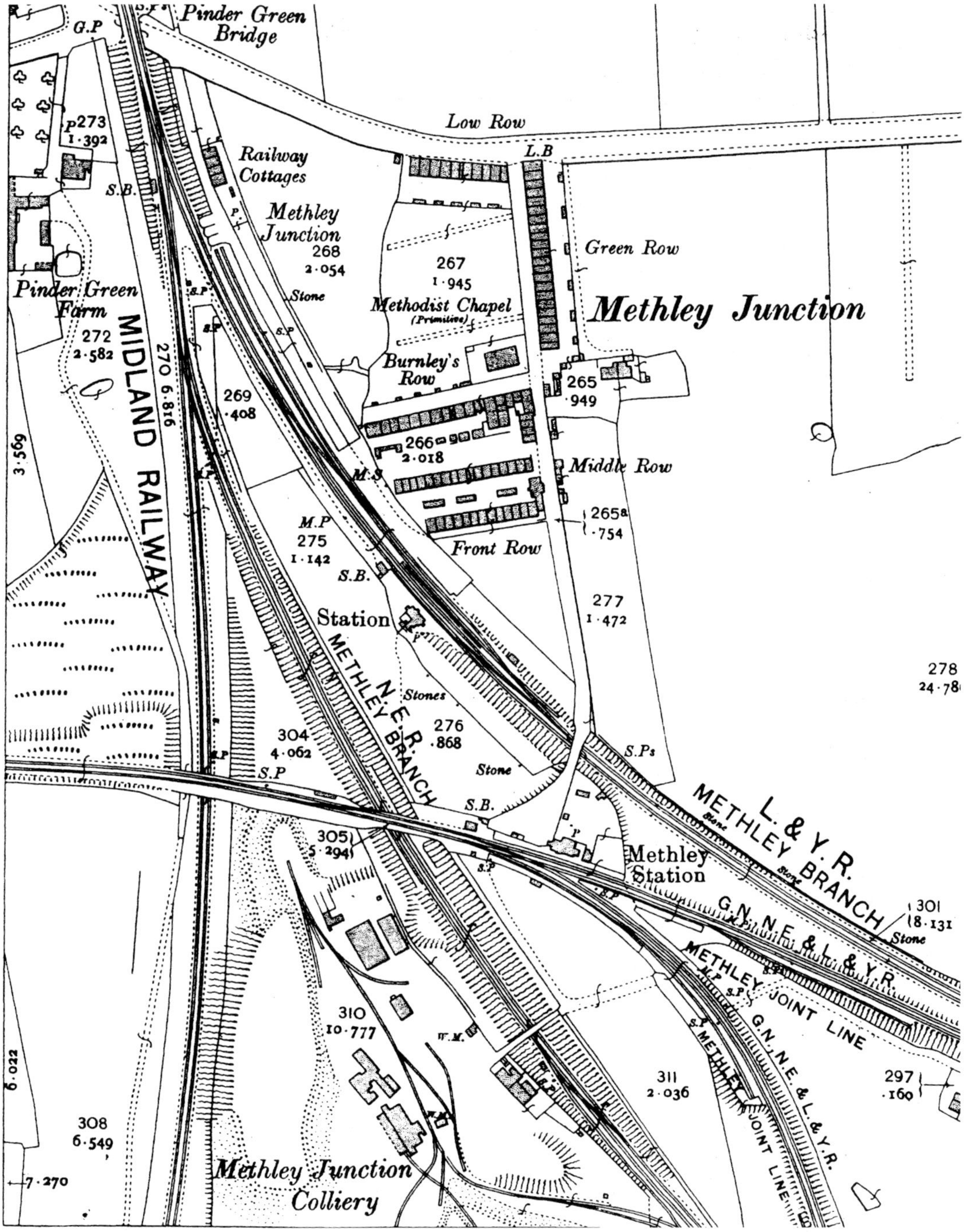
Pinder Green Bridge
Low Row
Railway Cottages
Methley Junction
Green Row
Methley Junction
Methodist Chapel (Primitive)
Burnley's Row
Middle Row
Front Row
Pinder Green Farm
MIDLAND RAILWAY
Station
N.E.R. METHLEY BRANCH
L. & Y. R. METHLEY BRANCH
Methley Station
G.N. N.E. & L. & Y.R. METHLEY JOINT LINE
Methley Junction Colliery

Methley Junction 1985.

Barnsdale Meadows 2000.

View of Methley Junction showing L & Y Railway Station

COLLIERY HOUSES (H. BRIGGS & CO.) METHLEY
TENANTS & RENTS 1874 - 1919

METHLEY JUNCTION

Front Row

1874 – Rent 3s.0d. a week

No. 1	William Singer	No. 2	Joseph Sykes
No. 3	S Wilson	No. 4	William Sunderland
No. 5	Jas. Wigley	No. 6	M Coleman
No. 7	William Walker	No. 8	Thomas Dixon
No. 9	Charles Murgatroyd	No. 10	Jos. Green
No. 11	George Cookson	No. 12	Job Farrer
No. 13	George Garforth		

1880 – Rent 3s.0d.a week

No. 1	William Singer	No. 2	C Naylor
No. 3	S Wilson	No. 4	Jas. Barker
No. 5	Jona. De-ville	No. 6	I Ellis
No. 7	J Grise	No. 8	Jonathon Inman
No. 9	Charles Murgatroyd	No.10	J Broadhead
No.11	Jas. Wood	No.12	D Grey
No.13	C Dickinson		

1910 – Rent 4s.0d. a week

No. 1	Henry Totty	No. 2	Alfred Walsh
No. 3	Wilson Smith	No. 4	Ellen Sunderland
No. 5	Thomas Firth	No. 6	Mofforth Gledhill
No. 7	John Heaps	No. 8	Henry Livesy
No. 9	Joseph Wood	No.10	George Simpson
No.11	Herbert Dunnill	No.12	Samuel Laycock
No.13	Thomas Crewe		

1915 – Rent 4s.0d. a week

No. 1	Henry Totty	No. 2	Alfred Walsh
No. 3	Wilson Smith	No. 4	Ellen Sunderland
No. 5	Thomas Firth	No. 6	Mofforth Gledhill
No. 7	John Heaps	No. 8	Ed. Livesy
No. 9	Joseph Wood	No.10	George Simpson
No.11	M. Thornton	No.12	Samuel Laycock
No.13	J. Harrison		

In the rent book for 1919 the Clerk entered the initials of what seems to be the place of work.

MS = Methley Savile
WH = Water Haigh
S = Savile
MJ = Methley Junction
SS = ?

1919 – Rent 4s.0d. a week

No. 1	Emma Lightowler	No. 2	Alfred Walsh - MS
No. 3	Alfred Jackson – Sav	No. 4	Jewel Sunderland – Savile
No. 5	Henry Livesey - MS	No. 6	Mofforth Gledhill – WH
No. 7	Geo. Bilsborough MJ	No. 8	Alfred Poulter – S
No. 9	Joseph Ward – MJ	No.10	George W Simpson – MJ
No.11	Thomas Hanson – SS	No. 12	Samuel Laycock – S
No.13	John Harrison – SS		

Middle Row

1874 – Rent 3s.0d.

No. 1	J Morris	No. 2	S Houghton
No. 3	James Mills	No. 4	Francis Burgoyne
No. 5	Charles Varley	No. 6	James Bennett
No. 7	Joseph Walker	No. 8	James Hardy
No. 9	William Fremelling	No.10	Robert Powell
No.11	James Farrer	No.12	J Hughes
No.13	A Thomas	No.14	James Webster
No.15	Joseph Simpson	No.16	Samuel Walker

1880 – Rent 3s.0d.

No. 1	P Williamson	No. 2	E Kirkham
No. 3	E Banks	No. 4	C Cooper
No. 5	J Bulmer	No. 6	G Houghton
No. 7	T Hardman	No. 8	Jas. Webster
No. 9	?	No.10	J Mason
No.11	A Hamilton	No. 12	Jonathon Hughes
No.13	Jas. Hale	No.14	P Lockett
No.15	?	No.16	H Horton

1910 – Rent 4s.0d.

No. 1	Alfred Leake	No. 2	Edward Rickers
No. 3	Benjamin Day	No. 4	William Wright
No. 5	William Taylor	No. 6	Daniel Haries
No. 7	William Taylor	No. 8	Peter Gallagher
No. 9	Charles Morris	No.10	William Williamson
No.11	Joseph Turner	No.12	Jacob Cox
No.13	Riley Webster	No.14	Thomas Anderson
No.15	Job Smith	No.16	William Whittaker

1915 – Rent 4s.0d.

No. 1	Alfred Leake	No. 2	Edward Rickers
No. 3	Benjamin Day	No. 4	C Robinson
No. 5	William Taylor	No. 6	Daniel Haries
No. 7	William Taylor	No. 8	Peter Gallagher
No. 9	Charles Morris	No.10	William Williamson
No.11	Joseph Turner	No.12	D Holland
No.13	Benjamin Addy	No.14	Thomas Anderson
No.15	Job Smith	No.16	Edgar Wright

1919 – Rent 4s.0d.

No. 1 Alfred Leake S	No. 2 E Rickers S
No. 3 Benjamin Day S	No. 4 John Inman S
No. 5 Harry Wright S	No. 6 Daniel Harries WH
No. 7 Wm. Green Taylor S	No. 8 Peter Gallagher R
No. 9 Charles Norris S	No.10 Wm. Williamson S
No.11 Joseph Turner S	No.12 Holland Dunnill MS
No.13 Benjamin Addy WH	No.14 Arthur Hains MS
No. 15 John Smith MS	No.16 Edward Rickers WH

Burnley Row

1874 – Rent 3s.2d.

No. 1 Sam Ripley	No. 2 Jonathon Wroe
No. 3 Ed Flockton	No. 4 F Dunnill
No. 5 M Handley	No. 6 J Dunnill
No. 7 Jonathon Inman	No. 8 William Inman
No. 9 Alf Anson	No.10 Robert Webster
No.11 William Smith	No.12 Charles Hewitt
No.13 Francis Walker	No.14 Ben Mosby
No.15 George Morrison	No.16 Matthew Smith
No.17 Joseph Mosby	No.18 Joseph Mosby
No.19 George Crooks	No.20 Thomas Sunderland
No.21 William Farrer	No.22 Thomas Taylor
No.23 George Houghton	No.24 Joseph Taylor
No.25 T King	

1880 – Rent 3s.2d.

No. 1 S Taylor	No. 2 E Weston
No. 3 L Jackson	No. 4 F Dunnill
No. 5 W Ellwood	No. 6 Jonathon Dunnill
No. 7 W Bennett	No. 8 William Inman
No. 9 I Evans	No.10 H Dickinson
No.11 James Parks	No.12 J Connell
No.13 E Tennants	No.14 Ben Mosby
No.15 T Dickens	No.16 H Fremelling
No.17 Joseph Mosby	No.18 Joseph Mosby
No.19 Joseph Mosby	No.20 Thomas Sunderland
No.21 J Hardman	No.22 Tim Roper
No.23 J Newbrook	No.24 ?
No.25 T King	

1910 – Rent 4s.2d.

No. 1 Samuel Williamson	No. 2 John Kirkham
No. 3 Thomas Moore	No. 4 Francis Dunnill
No. 5 Joseph Inman	No. 6 John Dunnill
No. 7 Charles Leake	No. 8 William Inman
No. 9 John Jackson	No.10 Benjamin Wright
No.11 William Beard	No.12 Redfern Ashton
No.13 Robert Milner	No.14 Henry Mosby
No.15 Daniel Hopwood	No.16 John Bell

No.17 Joseph Harrison
No.18 Joseph Harrison
No.19 Joseph Harrison
No.20 House demolished
No.21 House demolished
No.22 House demolished
No.23 House demolished
No.24 Thomas Turner
No.25 William ?

Nos. 17, 18 & 19 now a shop, house and warehouse at a rent of £28 p.a.

1915 – Rent 4s.2d.

No. 1	Samuel Williamson	No. 2	John Kirkham
No. 3	J Kirkham	No. 4	Francis Dunnill
No. 5	James Inman	No. 6	John Dunnill
No. 7	Charles Leake	No. 8	William Inman
No. 9	H Wilson	No.10	Benjamin Wright
No.11	M Bucknall	No.12	W Inman
No.13	C Goodall	No.14	Henry Mosby
No.15	W Jackson	No.16	John Bell
No.17	John Harrison	No.18	John Harrison
No.19	John Harrison	No.24	J Ashmore
No.25	R Taylor		

1919 – Rent 4s.2d.

No. 1	Samuel Williamson S	No. 2	Jonathon Lindley
No. 3	George Turner S	No. 4	Francis Dunnill
No. 5	Joseph Inman MS	No. 6	John Dunnill SS
No. 7	Thomas Rickers WH	No. 8	William Inman S
No. 9	Herbert Wilson S	No.10	Benjamin Wright S
No.11	Harry Bucknell S	No.12	Wm Jason Inman MS
No.13	Charles Goodall Speedwell	No.14	Henry Mosby S
No.15	Wm Jackson (Junior)	No.16	George Wright
No.17	Joseph Harrison	No.18	Joseph Harrison
No.19	Joseph Harrison	No.24	John Ashmore
No.25	Wm Richard Taylor S		

Green Row

1874 – Rent 4s.0d.

No. 1	J Totty	No. 2	Thomas Jones
No. 3	J Steel	No. 4	J Hunt
No. 5	George Morley	No. 6	George Mosby
No. 7	Mrs C Dickenson	No. 8	Jas. Cawthorne
No. 9	George Morritt	No.10	George Websdale
No.11	Walter Hawes	No.12	Jno. Goodhall
No.13	R Clayton	No.14	Jos. Lumb
No.15	Jna. Gill	No.16	Mrs Ann Barker
No.17	Jos. Thomas	No.18	George Wilson
No.19	Sam Farrer	No.20	J A Murgatroyd
No.21	Aaron Laycock	No.22	Jos. Wilkinson

1880 – Rent 4s.0d.

No. 1	T Warwick	No. 2	W Herrington

No. 3 J Potts
No. 4 H Pugh
No. 5 J Fremelling
No. 6 G King
No. 7 E Evans
No. 8 H Ellis
No. 9 W Smith
No.10 George Websdale
No.11 W Hawes
No.12 G Mosby
No.13 T Turner
No.14 J Rodgers
No.15 H Johnson
No.16 M Cox
No.17 G Chiltern
No.18 T Hughes
No.19 S Farrer
No.20 T Abberly
No.21 A Laycock
No.22 G Garforth

1910 – Rent 4s.9d.

No. 1 William Smith
No. 2 William Jackson
No. 3 John Wright
No. 4 Edward Limbert
No. 5 John Livesy
No. 6 Thomas Turner
No. 7 George Wright
No. 8 Robert Bellwood
No. 9 Jna. Wm. Robinson
No.10 Jesse Lumb
No.11 Walter Hawes
No.12 John Whittaker
No.13 Henry Crewe
No.14 Elizabeth Wooton
No.15 Charles Frobisher
No.16 Andrew Thornton
No.17 Christopher Robinson
No.18 Joseph Horsfield
No.19 James Newbrooke
No.20 George Stainthorpe
No.21 James Smith
No.22 Fenwick Moore

1915 – Rent 5s.4d.

No. 1 E Beards
No. 2 William Jackson
No. 3 John Wright
No. 4 Edward Limbert
No. 5 John Livesy
No. 6 T Turner
No. 7 George Wright
No. 8 M Hancock
No. 9 C Taylor
No.10 Jesse Lumb
No.11 H Wright
No.12 T Turner
No.13 Jacob Cox
No.14 Elizabeth Wooton
No.15 W Holt
No.16 Andrew Thornton
No.17 Thomas ?
No.18 A Milner
No.19 James Newbrooke
No.20 J Booth
No.21 G Thornton
No.22 W Wright

1919 – Rent 4s.9d.

No. 1 Emily Beards
No. 2 William Jackson S
No. 3 John Wright MS
No. 4 Edward Limbert MS
No. 5 Charles Leake MS
No. 6 Mary Turner
No. 7 George Wright MS
No. 8 Charles Frobisher
No. 9 Sam Taylor S
No.10 Jesse Lumb
No.11 Edward Banham MJ
No.12 Thomas Turner WH
No.13 Jacob Cox MS
No.14 Eliza. Wooton
No.14 William Holt MS
No.16 Andrew Thornton S
No.17 Thomas Moore MS
No.18 John Bailey (Jnr)
No.19 James Newbrooke MS
No.20 John Booth
No.21 Walter Poulter MS
No.22 William Wright S

Low Row (These were back-to-back houses)

1874 – Rent 2s.8d.

No. 1	Isaac Bond	No. 2	Jesse Phillips
No. 3	Harry Meadowcrofts	No. 4	William Goodwin
No. 5	Paul Cresswell	No. 6	Robert Bleasby
No. 7	Charles Naylor	No. 8	Joseph King
No. 9	George Ward	No.10	Ed. Dickman
No.11	? Cummings	No.12	George Websdale
No.13	R Neal(?)	No.14	R Cresswell
No.15	Thomas Walker	No.16	Paul Cresswell
No.17	I Wood	No.18	Thomas Dean
No.19	Jonathon Drury(?)	No.20	Jonathon Lewis

1880 – Rent 2s.8d.

No. 1	Mrs Bennett	No. 2	Jesse Phillips
No. 3	T Cox	No. 4	W Crossley
No. 5	N Smith	No. 6	?
No. 7	?	No. 8	W Gerald
No. 9	H Horton	No.10	H Walton
No.11	James Lee	No.12	B Ward
No.13	Ed. Thomas	No.14	T Dougan
No.15	J Wolstencroft	No.16	M Smith
No.17	W Harrington	No.18	J Ward
No.19	E Beech	No.20	J Clark

1910 – Rent 3s.5d.

No. 1	Thomas Walshaw	No. 2	Richard Jordan
No. 3	George Wm. Wright	No. 4	James Hodgkinson
No. 5	John Ashmore	No. 6	George Thornton
No. 7	George Websdale	No. 8	Henry Naylor
No. 9	Chris. Robinson	No.10	John Bailey
No.11	John Robinson	No.12	John Woodall
No.13	Alfred Byron	No.14	Benjamin Addy
No.15	William Jason Inman	No.16	John Bailey
No.17	James Webster	No.18	Edward Livesy
No.19	William Jackson	No.20	Holland Dunnill

In October 1914 work began to convert these 20 back-to-back houses to 10 single houses.

No.1 & No.20 George Stainthorpe
No.2 & No.19 Fenwick Moore
January 1915
No.3 & No.18 Robert Bellwood
No.4 & No.17 Riley Webster
No.5 & No.16 James Beech
No.6 & No.15 Harry Crewe
No.7 & No.14 Edgar Wright
No.8 & No.13 Edward Livesy
No.9 & No.12 John Evans
No.10 & No.11 John Jackson

1919 – Rent 5s.9d.

No. 1	George Stainthorpe	No. 2	Fenwick Moore MJ
No. 3	Robert Bellwood MS	No. 4	Riley Webster MS
No. 5	John Mell(?) S	No. 6	Harriet Crewe
No. 7	Edgar Wright	No. 8	William Livesy MS
No. 9	John Evans	No.10	John Jackson S

Methley Junction Pit Yard

1910 – Rent free		1915 –	Rent free
No. 1	Frederick Armitage	No. 1	Frederick Armitage
No. 2	George Haslop	No. 2	George Haslop

1919 – Rent free
No. 1 Frederick Armitage
No. 2 George Haslop

Both these men were overmen at Methley Junction colliery

Waterside

1874 – Rent 3s.2d.

No. 1	William Sander	No. 2	William Stephenson
No. 3	Hospital	No. 4	Hospital
No. 5	James Tupman (rent 3d.)	No. 6	Jno. Holdsworth (rent free)

1880 – Rent 3s.2d.

No. 1 J Totty — No. 2 J Leatham

No. 3 & 4 no longer hospital but is known as Laburnam Cottage & occupied by Thomas Rees rent free.

No. 5 J Herrington – (rent 3d.) — No. 6 Jno. Holdsworth – (rent free)

1910 – Rent 3s.9d.

No. 1 William Totty — No. 2 Frederick Haigh

1915 – Rent 3s.9d.

No. 1 William Totty — No. 2 Frederick Haigh

1919 – Rent 3s.9d.

No. 1 William Totty — No. 2 Frederick Haigh

Pinder Green

1910 – Rent 3s.9d.
No. 1 William Forbes Singer
1915 – Rent 3s.9d.
No. 1 William Forbes Singer
1919 – Rent 3s.9d.
Pinder House Wm Forbes Singer

Mill Lane

1910
John David Burlington – Rent free — Antony Barran Rent 6s.0d.
1915 – Rent free
John David Burlington — J Marker
1919- Rent free
John David Burlington — James Harrison
Victoria House

Church Lane (now Little Church Lane)
1910 – Rent free
Holme Villa Joseph Wilson
1915 – Rent free
Holme Villa Joseph Wilson
1919 – Rent free
Holme Villa Fred Adams
This is the end of the 1919 rent book. Not known if later rent books available.

List of cottages with occupants under Mr Whiteley's charge for rate purposes & shown in Briggs Colliery rent book for 1919

Foxholes Farm	William Cushings	Hazel House	?
	William Gibson		Christopher Bielby
	M Naylor		Edward Banham
Farm House	George H Travis		Charles Goodall
Savile Farm	M Warrington	Moorhouse Farm	James Blackburn
	W Hallowfield		John Fletcher
Old Pit Yard	Robert Chapman		Charles Flanaghan
	Walter Dunnington	Churchill Farm	Septimus Sawyer
	George Hallowfield		James Webster
	Fred Higgins		William Spink
Parkin Farm	W Gustave Passurant(?)	Millwood Farm	Mark Green
	Thomas Walker		Edwin Duckels(?)
			Jonathon Hanley
		Shann House Farm	Robert Farrer
			Edwin Beilby

THE METHLEY JUNCTION I REMEMBER

The Lankie Line

It was a warm day in summer early in the war and a long train of carriages stopped on the railway line which ran past and very near to one end of Front Row, Middle Row and Burnley Row at Methley Junction. Trains were common on that line but they either went straight through the station or stopped for just a few minutes. This train, however, stood there for a very long time.

The train stood for so long on the line that the local women became curious and went to investigate. The train turned out to be crammed full of very dirty and unshaven khaki-clad soldiers. The men asked the women if they could bring them a drink and perhaps some food as they had had nothing for a long time.

The news flashed around the houses and in no time at all the women were loading baskets with sandwiches, cake, cigarettes, tea, lemonade, etc. and even fresh strawberries, and taking them to the train, which involved a climb up a fairly steep embankment.

The year was 1940, the month was June, and the soldiers were part of the British Expeditionary Force who, only hours before, had been landed at an English port after being rescued from Dunkirk.

NOTE: Burnley Court is situated where the Lankie Line used to run.

JTM

The 'Police News'

When I was 6 or 7 years old I sometimes visited an aged relation who lived at Methley Junction. I was an avid reader, I would read anything, even, or particularly the 'Police News'. This was a tabloid size newspaper, but there were no words (or hardly any), only very dramatic pictures. One picture took up the whole of the front cover and it was usually of an attractive young woman with long flowing hair and dressed in a lovely long, filmy dress or nightgown, and she was running in obvious terror through a wood. There were similar pictures inside the paper, all connected with criminal acts.

It was a long time before I realised that my relation could not read or write. The 'Police News' was produced for people who were illiterate and with no radio at that time (70 years ago) it was the only way they could get any kind of interesting or exciting news. The pictures told a story.

JTM

James Butcher

He came to the Junction most Friday afternoons and parked right outside my parents' house at the back of Green Row. He came in a vehicle with short sides and back that had a tarpaulin draped over hoops to keep out the rain. I learnt that his name was James Butcher, that he was Jewish, and that he lived at Leeds where there was a considerable Jewish community. But I only ever remember him being called either Jimmy or 'Jimmitherjew'.

Jimmy was a short, stocky man. He always wore the same 3-piece navy blue suit that had acquired a shine over the years. After ringing a hand bell he would lower the tail gate and stand in the back of the vehicle. By this time all the women who were interested would be standing behind the vehicle.

Jimmy sold just about everything – second-hand, of course. There was clothing, shoes, clocks, mirrors, oil paintings, beds, bedding, chairs, I even remember a suite of furniture with a sort of day bed and about six matching chairs all upholstered in green velvet, the sort of thing that collectors are interested in these days. My mother and my aunt were into lace. At the merest suggestion of lace they put up their hands to show that they were interested and wanted a closer look and Jimmy would hand these things down to them. I'm fairly sure that I have in my house now some lacy cover bought from Jimmy and left by my mother when she died. Many items cost only a few pence.

Jimmy stopped coming at the outbreak of war, I think. He was greatly missed.

JTM

The Reading Room

I lived at Methley Junction as a child, in fact I lived in the first house down the steps in Front Row and the reading room actually adjoined my parents' house. The reading room was popular with the miners. It was like a club and the men could get out of the house and talk away from the pit.

There were certain rules to be obeyed, like no drinking, no bad language and no gambling. Card games were played for matches (and no doubt sometimes for ha'pennies and pennies).

Women did not go into the reading room, but being a small girl I didn't count. Sometimes my mother would send me on an errand there. I was afraid of all these men and I poked just my head round the door and to the first man to notice me I said "Will yer tell mi dad 'is dinner's ready". He always seemed to know who 'mi dad' was and he would call out "Sam, tha's to go 'ome, thi dinner's ready".

Inside the room I could glimpse men sitting at small tables playing cards or reading a newspaper and if I pushed the door open further I could see men playing billiards.

Just inside the entrance was a door behind which was a very small room with a bath in it for the use of the miners.

JTM

The Primitive Methodist Chapel

The chapel was situated opposite the end of Green Row. My mother worked hard for the chapel – cleaning and baking – and we all went to service on a Sunday, and took part in the social life of the chapel. When I was still a little girl the chapel closed and the Salvation Army took it over. We supported them but they didn't seem to last long and the building was then left empty and stayed empty. Finally it was knocked down.

JTM

DESCRIPTION OF THE CHURCH OF ST OSWALD

There has been a place of worship on this site since Saxon times. In a response of love and thanksgiving to God people have built, extended and improved the present church and cared for it over the centuries. It has become part of our treasured Christian heritage.

By the time of the Domesday Survey (1086) Methley had become part of the Domain of Ilbert de Lacy, Lord of the Honour of Pontefract, but late in the 13th century the Manor of Methley had come into the tenure of the de Methley family, probably as tenants of the de Lacys.

The church of Methley is named for St Oswald, King of Northumbria, who was killed in the fight against Penda, King of Mercia A.D.642.

No early original masonry survives above the ground, and successive rebuildings and enlargements have left us an edifice consisting of chancel with south chapel and north vestry and organ chamber, nave, with north porch, and a south aisle of three bays with south porch and a western tower.

Probably the church standing at the time of the Domesday Survey was rebuilt in the 12th century and then consisted of the chancel and an unaisled nave.

In the course of renovation work undertaken in 1900-01 remains of ancient foundations 5 ft wide were discovered beneath the pavement towards the west end of the nave near the north door.

In the 14th century the chancel may have been re-modelled but retaining the old dimensions and part of the masonry. Curious carvings are sculptured on the stone corbels that support the roof timbers of the chancel. The corbels supporting the nave roof have shields with the symbols of the Passion: in the north-west corner is one showing the left ear of Malchus cut off (not the right ear – see St John's Gospel, Cap. XVIII, v 10, 11). An aisle of three bays with well pointed arches supported on low octagonal piers with well moulded capitals was thrown out on the south side of the nave and the nave extended westward to its present length (1300-1350).

About 1357-1400, or later, came the south porch and western tower. The porch has a

Photograph of St Oswald's Church taken between 1844-1901

Plan of church in 1844 shows a different vestry, it is known that the vestry shown in the above photograph was pulled down in 1901

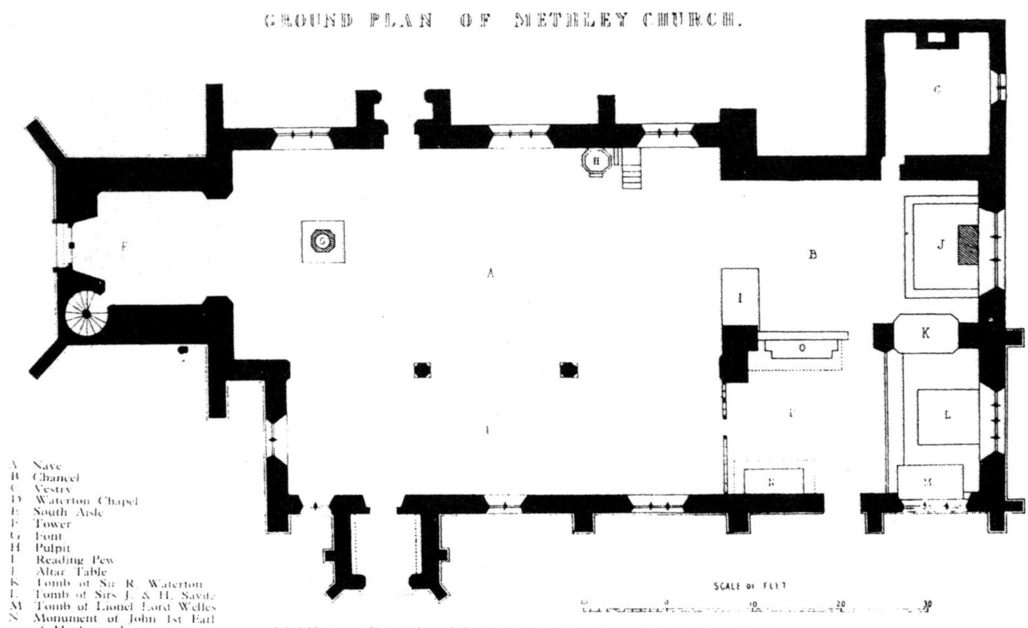

PLAN A. (Reproduced from Green's Churches of Yorkshire, 1844).

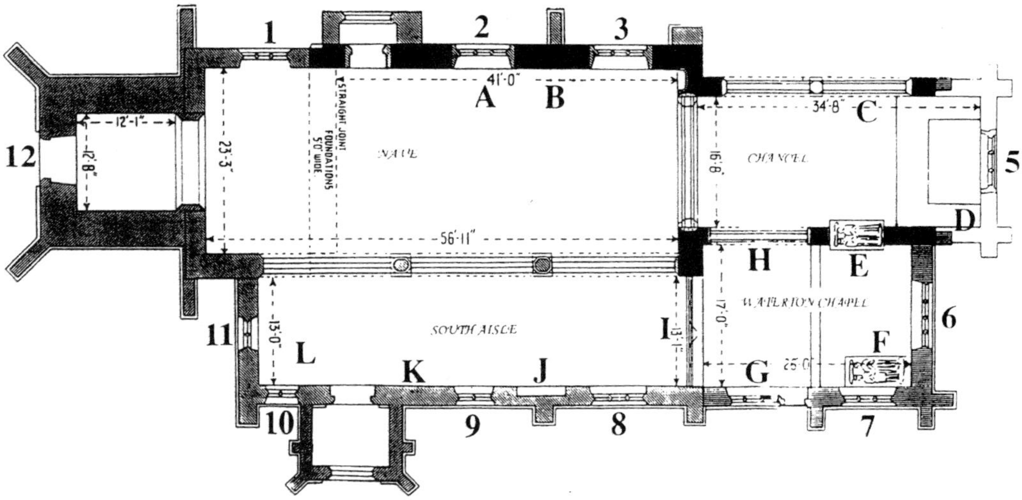

Plan of church post-1901

There was a temporary vestry of wood covered with corrugated iron sheet, which also served as an organ chamber.

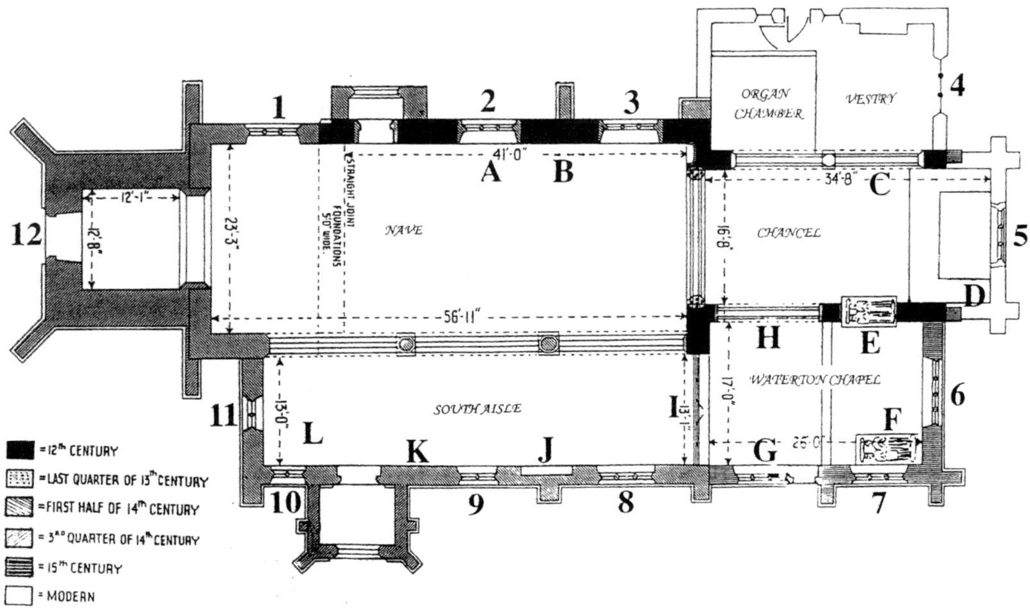

Plan of church post-1926

slabbed roof supported by stone ribs and has stone benches inside. Old doors remain at the north, south and west entrances.

Probably the latest additions to the ancient work of the church were the Waterton Chapel (about 1484) on the south side of the chancel, the clerestory, the nave roof and perhaps certain windows. The spire (re-built c.1901 and removed in 1937) is said to have been added towards the end of the 18th century. The weather cock of copper is preserved in the vestry.

There was in 1844 a gallery appropriated to the owners of Methley Park, having an external private entrance near the north porch, but by 1869 the gallery had been removed.

In 1874 work began to repair and lengthen the chancel, the east wall being entirely rebuilt with Oulton stone, and a three light window replacing the existing one, and in 1899 the weather-worn statue of St Oswald, hitherto above the south porch entrance, was placed south of the chancel arch.

During the 19th century there was much alteration to the north-east part of the church to accommodate a vestry and organ chamber. The last alteration, in 1899, meant that the vestry against the north wall of the chancel was removed and the present pointed arcade built, but it only opened to a temporary vestry of wood covered with corrugated iron sheets which served also for an organ chamber.

Under authority of a Faculty dated 1924 the east, north and south walls of the sanctuary, formed in 1874, were taken down and a new sanctuary, built of Guiseley stone, was erected in its place, and a new roof, of English oak, made over the whole chancel. A new organ chamber and vestry, faced outside with Guiseley stone, was also built. Embattled parapets were given to both chancel and vestry. The reredos, set up beneath the new east window, has a perforated canopy and in the centre are sculptured figures of Our Lord and St Mary Magdalene. The reredos is 'In Loving Memory of Charlotte Maria the Beloved Wife of George Savile. Erected to the Glory of God by her husband, brothers and sisters. A.D.1879'. This new work was mainly made possible through the generosity of Mr H C Embleton of the Cedars, Methley who died 7 February 1930. The obtuse pointed arch between the chancel and the chapel is now occupied by a light stone open screen of three cusped arches. This stone screen was dedicated in 1938 as a memorial to Mr H C Embleton.

The south, or Waterton Chapel, is a late 15th century addition to the church. Its stonework, like that of the rest of the church, has been refaced and its details renewed. A 15th century pointed arch opens from the chancel to the chapel; another of ornate character is over the Waterton tomb. There is no arch between the chapel and the south aisle, but an old traceried wooden screen with door, of 15th century character, bearing on the east side of the frieze the shields and names of Thomas Wombwell, William Skargill and John Waterton. The flat panelled roof of the chapel is conspicuously decorated on its timber framework with armorials and winged seraphim, which can be compared with those on the glass of the east window of this chapel.

Perhaps here it should be mentioned that the late Henry Moore OM, the internationally known sculptor, has recorded that at about the age of nine he became aware of sculpture for the first time whilst sketching in the chapel at Methley Church, so much so that he gave a very generous donation towards the restoration of the two alabaster tombs in the chapel in 1987-88.

The Waterton Chapel

Much is written elsewhere in this book about the Waterton Chapel and its building in the Middle Ages – see St. Oswald's Church Processional Chant, but the story of the chapel needs to be brought up to date.

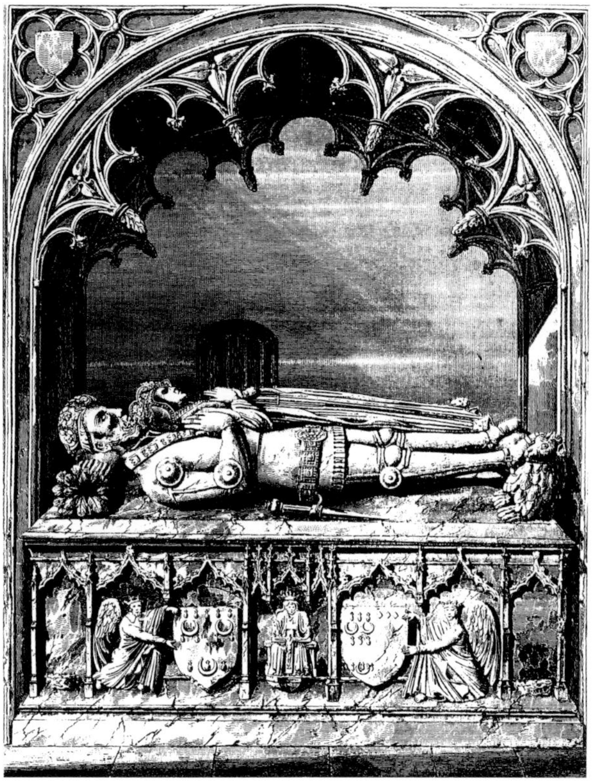

Tomb of Sir Robert Waterton and his wife.

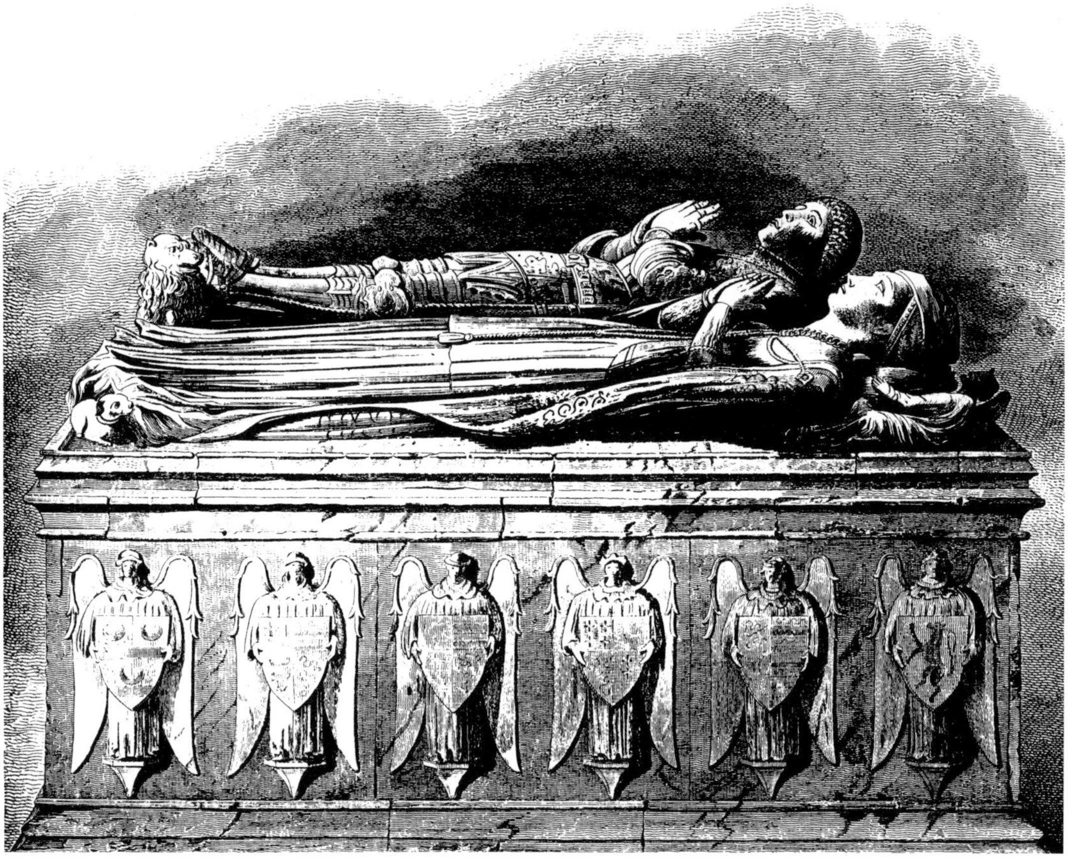

Tomb of Lionel, Lord Welles and his wife.

In 1947 the then rector suggested that the chapel be also turned into a memorial for those who died in the 2nd World War but it would be necessary to remove the huge Savile tomb from the chapel to another place so that an altar could be put in its place under the east window of the chapel. This was done at a cost of £225 and the Savile tomb was moved to its present position east of the south door. A memorial to the dead of the 1st World War was already in place at the Cenotaph in the churchyard. A memorial to the dead of the 2nd World War was affixed to the wall outside the west entrance to the chapel.

By 1976 the condition of the alabaster tombs of Waterton and Welles was giving concern; dampness was penetrating the alabaster and repairs were needed. A quote of £4,075 for repairs was submitted but no restoration work was done because of lack of funds. An appeal was launched and by 1985 the estimate for the work was £15,000. A quote was submitted and Henry Moore OM became a patron of the appeal and gave £15,000. Other donations included £1,000 from the Earl of Mexborough. The tombs were removed in January 1988 to be dried out by Harrison Hill Ltd., conservators and restorers of sculpture in Northamptonshire.

In July 1989 the tombs were returned to the Waterton Chapel and the altar floor was replaced with tiles of white Sicilian marble and Derbyshire fossil marble (commonly known as crinoid limestone) by Brian W Musson of Methley. The restoration of the tombs cost approximately £17,000 and the floor £3,500.

The Sculpture and Furniture in St Oswald's Church, Methley

'The **eight corbels** supporting the roof timbers in the chancel are thought to date from the mid-fourteenth century. They are crudely but powerfully carved, the heads and shoulders formed into grotesque human beings and animals, which grin and leer at the onlooker. The sculptor Henry Moore remembered seeing and drawing them as a boy when he went to visit his aunt in Methley and there is no wonder that he found them inspiring. They are strikingly large and have the rugged massiveness which characterised some of Moore's own work. The **two corbels** of the chancel arch, though apparently close to the others in date, are quite different in character: they are human heads, precisely carved and serene in mood. The faces are executed in the simplified, schematic manner, which Moore adopted, particularly in some of the early work of his adult life and it is difficult to believe that they did not exert some influence upon him.

The **figure of St Oswald**, King of Northumbria, the patron saint of the church, was formerly over the south door. It became badly weathered and was brought inside and cemented into the wall on the right hand (south) side of the chancel arch. The carving is a panel, executed in low relief, showing the saint crowned and holding a sceptre, seated under a Gothic canopy. A date in the late fourteenth century is suggested by the canopy architecture.

The **chantry chapel** on the south side of the chancel is regarded as the finest medieval chantry in any church in West Yorkshire. It is probably to be identified with 'Our Lady's Choir' which is known to have been added to the church in 1483-4. Sir Robert Waterton, Lord of the Manor of Methley in the early fifteenth century, had provided for the building of a chantry in this position in his will of 1425 so that masses could be said for the repose of his soul, and the building work was a tardy act of compliance with his wishes. It has a very fine **timber roof** adorned by **figures of angels**, very slim and attenuated, with spread wings. They are similar in style to those on the tomb of Lord Welles (see below), not surprising, since the two works are probably quite close in date.

The handsome wooden **lectern** bears a metal plaque on it, which states that a Mr David Leake gave it to the church in 1869. It is thought to be North European work, German or

Flemish, of the fifteenth century. This fits the appearance of the stem and the base, though the eagle book-rest may be later in date. In the base there are three statuettes of standing bearded figures. One is St John the Baptist, carrying a lamb. Another, with a book and a staff, may be St James the Less, and the third, with a book only, may be St John the Evangelist.

The octagonal oak **pulpit** of the Queen Anne period was the gift in 1708 of Gilbert Atkinson, rector. It is of plain character with panelled and moulded sides.

The **font** is of stone and lined with lead. The font cover was provided by the will dated 23 January 1584-5 of Richard Webster of Methley, painter, buried at Methley 1 March 1584. Later, the font was discarded, and when the Rev. H Armstrong Hall became rector in 1898 the bowl was found in a poultry yard and the stem was used by a mason at the other end of the village.

The **tombs** are an outstanding group, particularly that of **Sir Robert Waterton and his wife** in the arch between the chancel and the chantry chapel. The arch is splendidly embellished with vaulting in the middle and with cusps and hood moulds on both sides, the four vertical sections of the hood moulds terminating in lion masks. It forms a canopy for the tomb, a so-called 'founder's arch' for the chapel. The name is probably misleading in this case since the tomb seems to be earlier than the chapel, dating from around the time of Waterton's death; if this is so, there must have been an earlier structure where the chapel now stands.

The **effigies** and the **tomb chest** are made of alabaster. Sir Robert has an armoured body which is identical to those of the effigies of Sir Richard Redman and Sir William Ryther in the church at Harewood; it is clear that all three monuments were made in the same workshop which may have been located in York where alabaster workers are known to have been active at the time. This leaves open the question of who made the canopy arch which is of freestone and could have been carved by a different sculptor, or team of sculptors. The Redman and Ryther monuments at Harewood are also surmounted by arches and exhibit the same combination of materials.

The head of Sir Robert Waterton's effigy is very striking and unusual with deep-set eyes, a large nose and a beard and moustache composed in tight curls. His headdress is unique and takes the form of an extraordinarily large orle, a wreath of padded cloth, which was normally worn around a basinet or light helm; here it is decorated with flowers and leaves. A lion, symbolising the valour of the deceased, lies at his feet. The effigy of his wife, Cecily, who lies by his side, is a splendid fashion piece, dressed in a mantle fastened with cords attached to brooches, pointed slippers and a square headdress elaborately decorated with flowers and jewels. At her feet are two small dogs, symbols of her fidelity to her lord and master. The tomb chest has a figure of St Paul on the north side and on the south side a representation of the Holy Trinity with Christ on the cross held by a much larger, seated figure of God the Father. There would also have been a dove for the Holy Spirit but this has disappeared, so has the figure group on the north side of the chest and three of the four individual figures at the ends of the side panels, St Paul being the sole survivor.

The monument to **Lionel, Lord Welles and his wife**, which stands in the chantry chapel, is believed to have been made in the Midlands. Most alabaster work was done there in the Middle Ages and subsequently, because of the abundant local supply of the material. Welles' face, with its flat nose and prominent chin, appears to be quite individual but is, in fact, a stereotype of the workshop in which it was made, witness the very similar faces on other monuments widely scattered around the country, including those of Sir John Chideock at Christchurch, Hampshire, Lord Hungerford in Salisbury Cathedral and Richard Neville, Earl of Salisbury at Burghfield, Berkshire. The tomb chest is adorned by standing figures of angels carved in low relief, set close together and carrying heraldic shields. There is a heavy cornice moulding above their heads. The monument would probably have stood originally in the centre of the chapel, and is likely to have been displaced by the Savile tomb (see below). Its removal to the south-east corner of the chapel has resulted in the destruction of more than half the side panels and the cornice moulding which were cut away to make it fit the new space. The monument was restored with the aid of a grant from the Henry Moore Foundation in 1987-8.

In the south wall of the aisle and the north wall of the nave are **effigies of an unidentified priest and layman**, which were placed in their present positions in 1901, as stated on the inscriptions. They are carved in high relief which is integral with a supporting slab and it is clear that the slabs originally fitted together, witness the (indecipherable) inscriptions which run round the edges of the slabs and are carved in identical characters. So we have two displaced parts of a single tomb. According to an old manuscript source, the effigies represent two brothers, a lawyer and a secular priest (i.e. a priest who was not a monk or a friar) who were buried together. The record states that they 'fit damus' (built (this) house) which seems to mean that they were responsible for the building or rebuilding of all or a substantial part of the church, probably the south aisle. They could not have built the original nave and chancel as their effigies are not old enough, dating probably from the fourteenth century. Whether the priest was a rector of the church, as stated on the 1901 inscription, is not clear, but the circumstances make it probable. The effigies are in poor condition, chipped, dirty and broken across the necks.

All the other major monuments in the church commemorate members of the Savile family. **Sir John Savile** was a lawyer who became a Baron of the Exchequer (i.e. a judge in the Court of the Exchequer). He purchased the manor of Methley in 1590 and lived at Methley Park, a house of great historic interest, which had formerly been the Waterton's and was probably first built by them. It was situated some way to the west of the church and was demolished in 1963, having previously been affected by mining subsidence.

Sir John died in 1607 (1606 Old Style). His body was buried in London but his heart was removed for burial at Methley, an interesting instance of the survival of a medieval practice

Tomb of Sir John Savile.

into the early seventeenth century. His memorial is now by the west door of the church and used to be in the chantry chapel, under the window. It was erected as an act of piety by his grandson John Savile. The principal persons commemorated are Sir John himself, his son **Sir Henry Savile, Bt.** who died in 1632 and **Elizabeth Wentworth**, Sir Henry's second wife. These three are shown recumbent on a tomb chest. Sir John's effigy is placed in the middle and is raised slightly above the others, being supported on an extra slab. At Lady Savile's feet there is a kneeling effigy of a boy holding a skull, indicating that he had died, while at the bottom of the north side of the chest there is a figure of a baby, also with a skull, very charmingly carved with an air of sweet repose. The two children are identified on one of the inscriptions as Elizabeth's elder son, who is not named, and her daughter Heilena (Helen or Helena).

The portrayal of two generations on the same monument was quite common at the time in families who wished to consolidate their social position by associating themselves with the founder of their dynasty. It was also common for such families to emphasise their lineage by choosing this very traditional, medieval form of memorial. The Savile monument has been attributed to Maximilian Colt, Master Sculptor to King James 1st, who is known to have made monuments to other members of the family at Horbury and Thornhill, not far away. In the present author's opinion it is more likely to be the work of William Wright, another leading London sculptor of the period.

Next in sequence comes **Charles Savile** (d. 1741) and his wife **Aletheia** in the south-west corner of the chantry chapel. It is very much in the classical manner of its time, with effigies of white statuary marble, his being dressed as a Roman soldier. She is shown seated facing her husband in an attitude of mourning which strongly suggests that she erected the monument (it is worth noting that the date of her death, 1759, has been added to the inscription after the main text was carved). His effigy is foreshortened, and appears absurdly compressed when seen directly from the front of the memorial, which is now the natural viewpoint. If it were placed in a corner and looked at from an angle the whole composition would make perfect sense, yet there seems to be no evidence that it has ever been moved. Perhaps the sculptor, receiving his instructions in London, misunderstood where it was to stand. It must once have had a reredos or back-plate and is shown framed by a pedimented structure in a photograph taken c. 1900. The sculptor is believed, on good evidence, to have been Peter Scheemakers, a Flemish immigrant who became one of the leading lights in London.

With the next generation this branch of the Savile family acquired a series of peerage titles, the highest of them being that of Earl of Mexborough which it still retains. All this is loudly proclaimed on the monument of the first title holder, **John, Earl of Mexborough** who is portrayed in peer's robes. Copies of his peerage grant have been laboriously modelled with the full text upon it, then cast in metal and hung from either end of the tomb chest, a rare conceit at a time when very little metalwork was used on monuments. He looks over the spectator's head and points up to heaven, where, we are to believe, his soul has gone. He died in 1778. The monument is signed and dated 1780 by Joseph Wilton, another prominent London man and one of the three sculptors who were founder members of the Royal Academy.

From the early nineteenth century there is a very interesting wall tablet to **Sarah, Dowager Countess of Mexborough**, in the south-east corner of the chapel, above the Welles' tomb. She died in 1821 aged only 17 and already a dowager; the monument was erected by her sons (plural!!), probably in the 1830s. It is by Sir Richard Westmacott, again, a leading London man, who signed the right-hand corbel on which it rests and left his address on it as a discreet advertisement for his work. The main point of interest is the Biblical relief at the bottom, showing the miracle of the Raising of Lazarus. Religious subject matter, apart from angels, had remained rare on church monuments ever since the Reformation, though it was to become much more common later in the century. Standing allegorical figures flank the inscription panel, Hope on the left with an anchor and Religion on the right with a cross. Between them is a symbol of Eternity, a snake biting its tail, encircling an hourglass.

The series of Savile monuments in the chapel ends with a white marble panel in a tabernacle frame to **John, 2nd Earl of Mexborough** (d. 1830) in the north-west corner. This is provincial work, signed Fisher (of) York, one of the family of sculptors of that name.

Lastly, there is an interesting little memorial in the sanctuary of the church to former Rector of Methley, **Henry Armstrong Hall** who later became Archdeacon of Richmond. It is a bronze tablet with Italian Renaissance-style putti holding a shield, which displays the monogram of the deceased. It is signed and dated 1923 by F.J. Wilcoxson, a good period piece in the academic tradition which Henry Moore was so vigorously rejecting at that time.' (Reproduced by kind permission of Adam White, Curator, Lotherton Hall, 2000).

Modern Wooden Furniture

Much of the wooden furniture in the church has been made not only by the craftsmen of Robert Thompson, the 'mouseman' of Kilburn but by some craftsmen who served their apprenticeship with this firm and others influenced by Robert Thompson and they each use their own unique carved trademark. In the Waterton Chapel there is a small credence table with the carved head of a gnome made by Tom Whitaker who lived and worked at Little Beck near Whitby but is now deceased. Also in the chapel are oak pews carved with a lizard by Derek Slater of Crayke who made the alter rails in St George's Chapel and chairs and table in St George's House, both in Windsor Castle. There is also in the church another oak credence table made by Albert Jeffray, the 'eagle' man of Sessay, near Kilburn, who also made the Bishop's chair and altar of St Thomas's, York.

Memorial Slabs, Effigies and Tablets

In the aisle floor, west of the chapel screen, are two grave covers measuring 6 ft. 2 in. x 3 ft.2 in.; 5 ft.11 in. x 2 ft. 5 in. Prior to 1900 they were in the churchyard being then described as 'two elaborately decorated slabs of limestone ... the inscriptions upon which are no longer legible.' Another slab, quite plain, measures 6 ft.x 2 ft. at the head, tapering to 1 ft.8 in.

Guide To The Stained Glass Windows

(See numbers on plan on page 125)

1 Three lights, St Cecilia, King David and Jubel, son of Lamech, the arms of the Cathedral Church of Ripon and those of the Embleton family. Motto 'Cresco per crucem'. To the Glory of God and in affectionate memory of Henry Cawood Embleton who with his family resident many years at Methley have been generous benefactors of the Church and Parish. He devoted much labour and support to the art of music the welfare of youth and the poor. D.1930. (Glass by Heaton, Butler and Bayne, London).

2 Three lights (Our Lord's Miracles) In memory of John Hollings, who died January 15th 1832, aged 73 years.

3 Three lights (The Triumphal Entry, The Cleansing of the Temple and The Feet Washing): An offering to this Parish Church by Benjamin Burnley, January 22nd 1856.

4 A three light window showing the Ascension of our Lord with apostles and angels, and in the tracery our Lord seated in Majesty surrounded by cherubs, in memory of The Hon. and Rev. Arthur Savile, Rector of Foulmire, Cambridgeshire. This glass was in 1926 placed in the three light east window of the vestry from the east window of the Chancel.

5 East Window of the chancel (five lights) depicts Paradise and the Crucifixion, our Blessed Lord Reigning from the Tree of Life, with attendant angels and St Oswald, the Blessed Virgin Mary, St John and St Paulinus, designed by A K Nicholson of London. This window was erected to the Glory of God and the Adornment of His House by Henry C Embleton of Methley Esquire in the year 1926.

6 All the ancient glass in the church has been re-assembled in the four-light east window of the Waterton Chapel. In the eight tracery lights are angels (chiefly amber) clad in feathers, an exceptional though not unique treatment. Each bears a scroll inscribed 'Sanctus'. Lower are the armorial shields of Waterton and Waterton impaling Fleming, and below, north to south, are SS. Jerome, Ambrose, Margaret, Christopher, John the Evangelist, John the Baptist, Augustine, Gregory. It is chiefly of 15th century date.

7 The south-east window of the Waterton Chapel (four lights), St George, Rachel, St Katherine, St Francis) is In Loving Memory of Rachel Katherine Wallpole, Viscountess Pollington who died June 21st 1854. Her only child caused this window to be erected 1901.

8 Three lights, depicting St Matthew, XIV, 23, 25, 31. Inscribed plate on sill: This window is dedicated to the memory of David Leake of Methley, who died at Glasshoughton September 25th, 1871, aged 72 years.

9 Two lights, depicting 1 Sam.XX, 11, 12: ii 1, 26: In Memory of Hry Alexr Savile, Born 3 Decr 1811, Died 1st March 1851 & Frederick Savile, B. 17th March 1817, Died 2nd April 1851. (Both were sons of John, 3rd Earl of Mexborough, d. 15 Dec. 1860).

10 Two lights: The Nativity and Christ Blessing Children. Philip Hale Savile, Born May 30th, 1843, died Sept. 9, 1843. He was the infant son of the Rector.

11 (a) Our Lord's Baptism. (b) The Raising of the daughter of Jairus. In the trefoil an angelic figure with scroll, One Lord One Faith One Baptism. Below: Mary Leeson born January 22nd, 1779, died February 5, 1849.

12 Tower window, three lights: St Petrus, St Jacobus the Great and St Johannes.

Funerary Helmets and Guantlets in the Waterton Chapel

The items mentioned were carried on the coffin of the deceased at his interment.

Funerary helmet, late 17th century

Of tinned plate, with a soldered seam at either side, the flat top and the one-piece gorget plate soldered on. Six of the original bars remain soldered across the visor. There is a spike for a wooden funereal crest at the top. This helm is typical of helmets made specifically for funerary use from the mid 17th century onwards.

Close helmet, English or Flemish, about 1560

The one-piece skull has a low, roped comb. The visor has a stepped sight and a lifting peg at the right. The upper bevor has a roped upper edge with a recessed border, and a cut-out for the lifting peg. The original gorget plates are missing, and have been replaced by crude, single plates to complete the helmet for funerary use, probably in the 17th century. The tall iron spike for a wooden crest is also an addition for funerary use.

Funerary helmet, late 17th century

The skull is made from a harquebusier's triple bar pot, of the type made in the 1640s and 50s for cavalry. The gorget plates are converted from a pikeman's gorget of the 1630s. The elements joining these, the lower part of the skull, the upper and lower bevors, the visor and the spike for a wooden crest, are all funerary additions of the later 17th century. The long, pointed profile of the upper bevor reflects the shape used by the Royal Workshops at Greenwich in the early 17th century.

Wooden funerary helmet, probably early 18th century

Carved as a pastiche of a close helmet. The scrolling foliage carved in relief on the upper bevor and skull reflects the painted ornament that was commonly put on English funerary helmets. The acanthus scrolls and multi-plate construction is in imitation of classical ornament.

Wooden funerary gauntlets, probably early 18th century

These gauntlets are carved in imitation of multi-plate gauntlets found on some English effigies of the mid 14th century, such as the effigy of Sir Richard Whatton at Whatton in the Vale, Nottinghamshire, of about 1340. The carver has misunderstood some details of the construction; for example, he has continued the finger scales right round inside the fingers, whereas on the originals they would only have covered the outsides of the fingers.
(Reproduced by kind permission of Thom Richardson, Royal Armouries, Leeds)

Heraldry and Hatchments

Hatchments are a familiar sight in many churches, but their origin and meaning are less well-known. The hatchment is the last lingering vestige of the heraldic funeral, a reminder of the days when the knight's shield and crested helm were carried in his funeral procession and then hung over his tomb.

By the seventeenth century, when armour was going out of use, the Dutch started using a diamond-shaped board painted with the arms of the deceased. The fashion spread to Britain, where the board was called a hatchment, a corruption of the word 'achievement' (the technical word for a complete coat-of-arms). The hatchment was usually hung over the deceased's front door for a year before being transferred to the parish church or family chapel. Some were prepared under the instruction of the Heralds, but most were painted in a hurry by local craftsmen, and were often incorrect.

Heraldic funerals went out of fashion by 1700, but hatchments were used until the 1870s; there are a few twentieth century examples.

Hatchments display the deceased's complete coat-of-arms, painted on diamond-shaped wooden or canvas panels anything from two to seven feet square. The condition of the surviving examples varies; in some churches they have decayed and some have been thrown out and destroyed; in others they have been preserved and restored. Hatchments are too valuable to be destroyed, for they are of great interest to heraldists, genealogists and local historians, as the arms show marriages and descents. The backgrounds show whether the deceased was bachelor or spinster, husband or wife, widow or widower. The background behind that part of the arms relating to the deceased is black, that behind the part relating to the survivor being white; a skull instead of a crest shows that the deceased was the last of the line. The family motto is often replaced by a pious sentiment. The full rules regarding hatchments can be found in most heraldic handbooks, and in the standard work on the subject, Hatchments in Britain.

There is one hatchment in the Waterton Chapel and it is that of the Earl of Mexborough.
(Heraldry by kind permission of Russ Fletcher)

Heraldic Basics (Illustrations are numbered)

Tinctures – Colours. Gules – Red; Azure – Blue; Sable – Black; Vert – Green
Metals. Or – Gold (yellow); Argent – Silver (White)
Furs. Ermine – black tails on a white ground, shapes vary (1).
Erminois is a recent variation with black tails on yellow or gold.

Crosses There are hundreds of varieties. Here at Methley we have engrailed which is a scalloped partition line with the points pointing out (2).

Cross moline This represents the centre of a millstone which has a metal piece like this to stop the axle slipping (3). The little square hole is not always shown.

Crosslet A cross with each limb crossed (4).
It can also be fitchy with the bottom limb pointed (5).

Cross forming The end of each limb is spread like a former chisel (6).
It is also known as a cross paty but that term also applies at times to a cross with ends spread into three like an animals paw (7).

Martlets It is a conventional swallow/martin/swift. It was believed they did not come to land and so had no feet (8).

Eagles They are usually shown 'displayed'. They can be shown in other positions (9).

Lions Originally were always rampant (10). It is a fierce beast designed to fill the shield.

A lion that looks at you was originally called a leopard although drawn as a lion (11).

It is now called a lion passant, but a lion's head with no neck looking at you is still called a leopard's face (12). If they are just walking by they are called passant (13). The Welles lion has two tails so it is said to be 'double–queued' meaning two tails.

Fesses and Bars A fess is a broad stripe across the shield (14). If there are more then they are called bars (15).

Gemel (Like Gemini) twins means two or twin – so a bar gemel is a split bar. Two bars gemel, two split bars (16).

1

2

3

4

5

6

7

8

9

10

11

12

13

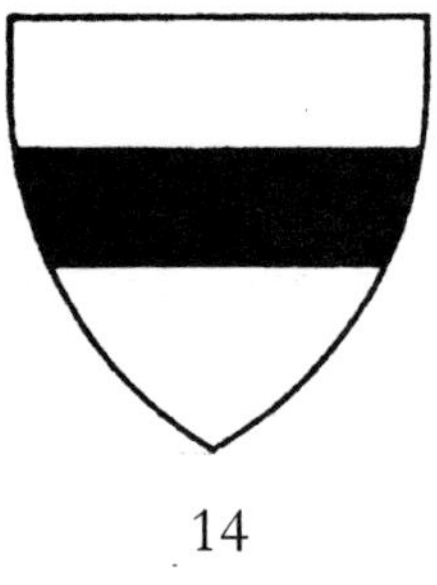

14

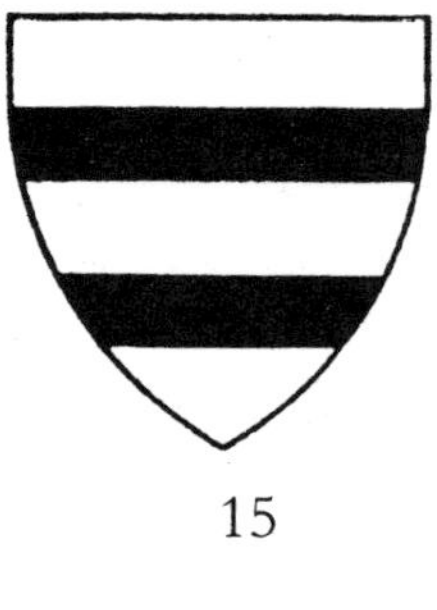

15

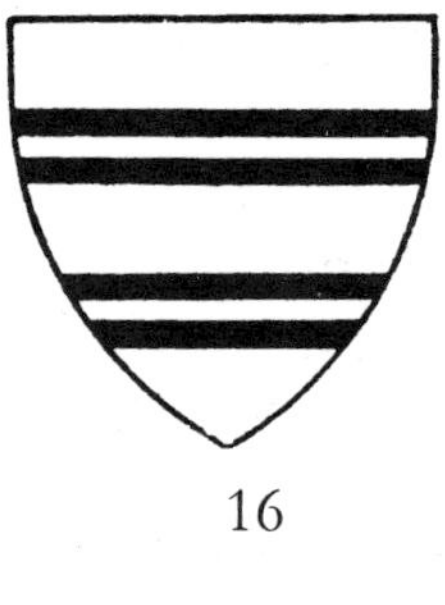

16

Heraldic shields

FLEMING (17) WATERTON (18) WATERTON=FLEMING (19) WELLES (20) WELLES=WATERTON (21) UFFORD (22) BEKE (23) CLIFFORD (24) WILLOUGHBY (26)

From the pedigree it appears WATERTON came to Methley on marriage to FLEMING as father was not of Methley.

FLEMING has arms like Fleming, Bishop of Lincoln (1420-1431), the founder of Lincoln College, Oxford. They form part of the college arms. The small star (a mullet) is the difference mark of a third son and his 'house' or descendants. FLEMING was of Woodhall, Methley.

WATERTON and FLEMING arms are in the chapel east window and on the tomb by the chancel.

The following four shields are painted on the north side of the WELLES tomb starting from the east but leaving out the first shield which has no paint remaining (25) (26) (27) (28) (29).

On the WELLES tomb the central coat is taken by the married arms of WELLES with WILLOUGHBY (27). This must be for Richard (Robert?) son of Lionel who married a prestigious heiress and died before his father (d.v.p.). The arms of WELLES quartering WILLOUGHBY (25) are the arms the child of this son might expect to use. The east and west ends of the tomb repeat the WELLES and WATERTON shields.

Arms round the top of the chapel repeat some of these arms but not WILLOUGHBY. Here also is the contemporary Royal Arms of the Fleur-de-lys and lions passant. The extra coat of arms impaled by WATERTON is for the marriage to Beatrice, daughter of the sixth Baron CLIFFORD by whom he had no children.

FLEMING (17) – Barry (of six) Argent and Azure in chief three lozenges Gules. A mullett Sable for difference.

WATERTON (18) Barry (of six) Ermine and Gules three crescents Sable.

WELLES (20) Or a lion rampant queued Sable (armed and langued Gules).

CLIFFORD (24) Chequy Or and Azure a fess Gules.

WILLOUGHBY (26) uses the arms of Ufford because of marriage to a co-heiress of the Ufford Earls of Suffolk. If the other co-heiress's side die out they could become Earls of Suffolk. They quarter Beck or Beke because they are heirs to Antony BEC the famous Bishop of Durham. These they put higher than their own names.

UFFORD (22) Sable a cross engrailed Or.

BEC (23) Gules a cross moline Argent.

The big monument now on the south side of the nave is for Sir John SAVILE, his son Sir Henry SAVILE the first and last Baronet of Methley and his wife Mary DENT.

Sir John married four times – Jane GARTH, Elizabeth WENTWORTH, Dorothy WENTWORTH and Margery PEATE.

The two big shields of many quarters are for son and father. They are the same except for the red hand of Ulster appropriate to a Baronet at the centre of the son's shield. First – SAVILE. Argent on a bend Sable, three owls Argent (30). Second – GOLCAR. Gules a cross forming Or (31). Third – RYSHWORTH. Argent a bend Sable between in chief an eagle Vert (Azure) and in base a cross crosslet Sable (32). Fourth – ELLAND. Gules two bars between eight martlets in orle Argent (33). Fifth – RUSHDALE/ROCHDALE. Sable on escutcheon within an orle of martlets Argent. Sixth – TANKERSLEY. Argent on a bend Gules, three escallops Or (34). Seventh – THORNHILL. G two bars gemel and a chief Argent. Eighth – COPLEY. Argent a cross moline Sable. Crest. An owl Argent. On east side of tomb SAVILE impaling Dent for Mary DENT of London, wife of Sir Henry SAVILE, Baronet. Sable a fess dancetty Argent in chief three escallops Or (35). On the west side SAVILE impaling GARTH for Jane GARTH first wife of Sir John SAVILE Knight, on two lions passant guardant between three crosses crosslet fitchy Sable (36). SAVILE impaling WENTWORTH. Sir John's second and third wives were Elizabeth and Dorothy WENTWORTH. They had different fathers but probably both used these arms, they had both been widowed. Sable a chevron Or between three leopards' faces Or (37). His fourth wife Margery PEATE was also a widow. Her arms are not shown. She may have been related to the Peates of Sevenoakes, Kent, who bore Argent on a bend engrailed Gules between two escallops Azure three mascles Or (38).

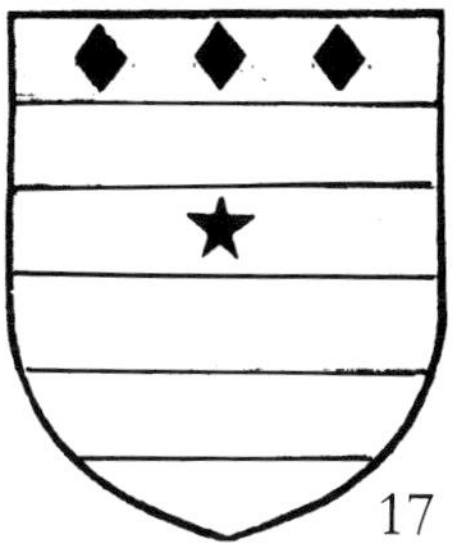
17

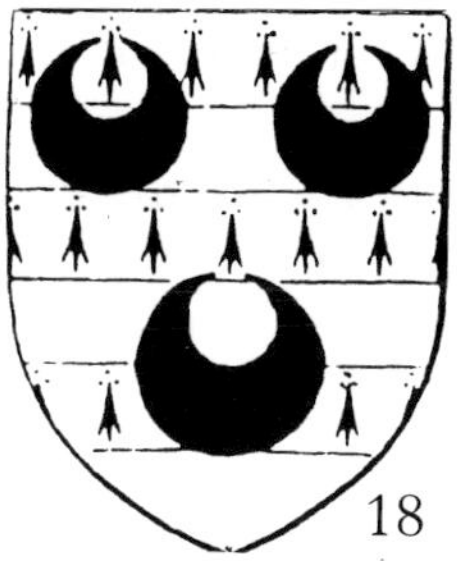
18

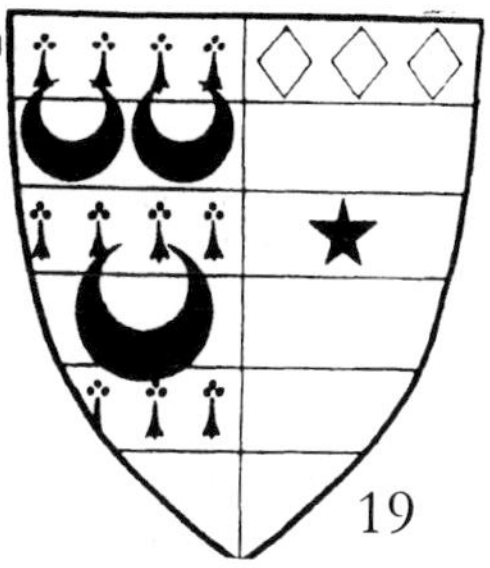
19

20

21

22

23

24

25

26

27

28

29

30

31

32

33

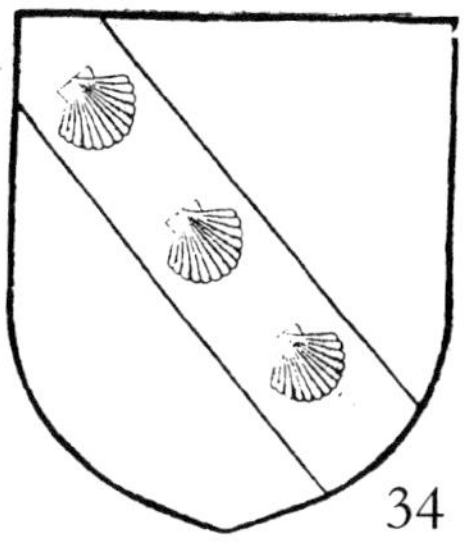
34

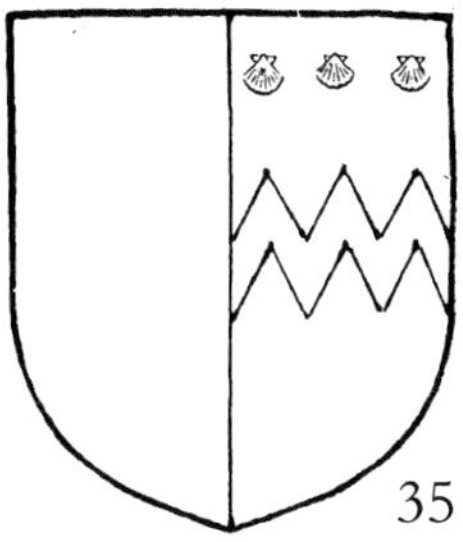
35

36

37

38

Methley Church Choir Fund – Endowments:

William Goulden Legacy

William Goulden was a well-known character in Methley. Son of the corn miller in Mickletown, he was left an orphan and was brought up in Lady Mexborough's household. Afterwards he was butler to Dr. Bickersteth, Bishop of Ripon, and various gentry. He admired church music and by his will left £900 in trust and the income from the trust paid half-yearly for the benefit of the choir and organist of Methley Church.

William Goulden first appears in the 1841 Methley census, living at Pinder Green, aged 14, as a house servant with Edward Dodd and James Lambert, Schoolmasters.

In the 1851 census he is shown as living at the Rectory as servant to the Reverend Philip Yorke Savile. He next appears in the 1881 census, aged 52 years, and is described as an incapacitated butler living at Church Side, the census return shows he was born at Alverthorpe. He died at Methley on 24th April 1918 at the age of 89.

The first copy of choir payments made from the Choir Fund shown on page 136 shows the choirmaster, Mr Farrer, and eight choirmen, no boy choristers are shown, but the next payment dated 27th February 1921 shown on page 136 shows not only eight choirmen but sixteen choirboys, also being paid.

1920 Interest on Fund £15.30. 1994 Interest on Fund £23.00

Bequest of Miss E. M. Embleton

At a Parochial Church Council meeting on 13 March 1929 the Rector stated that Miss E. M. Embleton had left in her will the following bequests:

£6,000 on trust, the income to be used to keep the church of St. Oswald in good and substantial repair.

£800 in trust towards church expenses and each year to provide an excursion or outing for the choir.

The Original Parish Hall

There was no parish hall, as such, at St Oswald's until 19th October 1920 when a wooden building reputedly an ex-Army hospital building of the First World War similar to the one illustrated here was opened. The building, which stood on brick pillars, was a gift from Mr Embleton of the Cedars, Church Side, Methley. The photograph is of a drawing headed 'Proposed Parish Hall, Methley' and is signed Thomas W Embleton but is not dated. T.W. Embleton died in 1921.

Following the purchase of Church Side School by the Parochial Church Council of St Oswald's Church the wooden parish hall was in such poor condition that it was demolished in 1970 and the timber sold for £20.

St Oswald's Church Processional Chant

In July 1987 when I, the author, was Churchwarden of St Oswald's Church I was with Miss Lilian Harrison of this parish to meet an American student, Mrs Jane Frogley, who was particularly interested in the crypt of the church. She had just finished writing a dissertation on a manuscript of medieval music and processional chants and now wished to investigate the origins of the manuscript which were completely unknown. Mrs Frogley was given help and loaned books. The matter there rested until Miss Harrison's death on 29th June 2000 when I was left a quantity of her papers and found a copy of vol. 1 of the dissertation by Mrs Frogley, entitled 'A Processional of the York Use: a Transcription of Bodleian Library MS E Musaeo 126(3612), Description, Dating and History of the Manuscript' dated Michaelmass 1987'.

Received from the Rector & Churchwardens of Methley Parish Church.

1947				
July	20	~~Brought forward~~	~~7 6~~	
		Assistant Organist Mr L Shillito	5 . .	
		Mr L. Shillito	1 3	
		A Pollard	1 3	
		J Idle	1 3	
		J Whittaker	1 3	
		E White	1 3	
		A Green	1 3	
		A Tomlinson	1 3	
		R Lewis	1 3	
		J Beilby	1 3	
		R Eastwood	1 3	
		S. Grecow	17 6	
		P. Walker 7/6 J Norris 8/-	1 1 6	
		K Turner 8/- M Russell 8/-	16	
		J. Shillito 9/- M Bailey 8/-	17	
		M Walker 8/- L Wheeler 7/-	15	
		R Kaye 7/- B Seage 7/-	14	
		J. Foster 2/6 C Riley 2/6	5	
		J. Pollard 2/6	2 6	
		Church Music	1	
		Brought forward from Christmas	7 23 3 6	
		To be carried forward to Christmas	22 7 6	
		withdrawn from Bank.	£ 23 8 0	

Geo. H. Travis }
H. Arundel } Churchwardens

Received from the Rector and Churchwardens of the Methley Parish Church.

Choirmaster	[signature over two pence stamp]	3 10 –
Choirmen:	T Shepherd	1 – –
	E Shillito	1 – –
	Geo. Hopson	1 – –
	J Backhouse	1 – –
	E White	1 – –
	L Shillito	1 – –
	H Shillito	1 – –
	E Shillito	1 – –
Boys.	H Denison 1/5½ C.W. Savory 4/3. H Kaye 5/4. P. Kaye 5/11. H Green. 1/4. J Braime 11d R Braime 3/3. G Wheeler 4/11 D Heath 4/11. A Cheeborn 5/- J. Livesey 5/6. G. Keap 4/7. G.A. Schofield 4/8. E. Harrison 3/10. H. Gillespie 5/6. E. Sawyer 5/11.	3 8 8½
	Balance in hand	– 1 3½
		15 – –

J. E. Stead }
Geo. H. Travis } Churchwardens
27th February 1921

The dissertation stated there were certain clues to the origin of the manuscript – the name of St Oswald, the washing of altars on Maunday Thursday and four altars named St Oswald, the Blessed Virgin Mary, St Katherine of Alexandria and St Nicholas, and that the church had a crypt. Perhaps the most important and significant clue is a colophon at the end of the music manuscript 'orate pro anima Roberti Bawdwyn capellani qui istud processionale fieri fecit'. Walter Howard Frere and Falconer Madan had earlier suggested that the processional chant was probably late 14th century and from a church dedicated to St Oswald in Yorkshire.

Mrs Frogley located twenty churches dedicated to St Oswald within a fifty mile radius of York but St Oswald's, Methley seemed the most promising because it had a crypt located beneath the south aisle of the church with access through the Waterton Chapel which was not built until 1483-4.

Mrs Frogley was informed that at the beginning of the 20th century the last burial took place in the crypt, the burial of an infant of the Mexborough family. Apparently someone who entered the crypt at the time of the funeral contracted a mysterious infection so it was decided that the crypt should be walled up. Another opinion was that the crypt had been walled up because it had collapsed. Some years ago a few of the choirmen got the Rector's permission to raise the slab over the entrance to the crypt and they were able to see a flight of steps descending from east to west with holders for torches or candles fixed to the walls. They could go no further because the vault was sealed off.

Kirk's booklet mentions the altars which were known to exist in Methley Church before the Reformation. The high altar was dedicated to St Oswald, the altar in the Waterton Chapel was dedicated to the Blessed Virgin Mary and there were also altars to St Nicholas and St Margaret. According to Kirk 'of the positions of the lesser altars and the statues of saints abolished at the Reformation it is not easy to be certain', so it was possible that there was an altar dedicated to St Katherine but no record survives.

When Sir Roberton Waterton of Methley died in 1425 he left instructions in his will for the building of a chapel as long as the chancel on the south side to celebrate divine service in the chapel for the souls of himself, his wife, and Kings Richard II and Henry IV. The chapel was not built until 1483-4 perhaps because of the difficult times which came upon the family due to their strong Lancastrian loyalties, but in 1484 the Chantry Chapel of Our Lady in the Parish Church of Methley was founded by Christopher Willoughby and Robert Dymock, Knights and the heirs of Robert Waterton.

At the time of the dissolution of the chantries in 1546 a memorandum reports that 'with goods belonging to the parish, the churchwardens had purchased property in the village, and with the money yielding from this investment funded a priest for the altar of St Margaret in the church'. The memorandum claims that for about two years past the money had been denied and the priest discharged.

There were possibly three or four positions for chantry chaplains in Methley Church at the end of the 15th century, not including the less formal positions for parochial chaplains. Kirk's list of assistant clergy at Methley names John Topclyf 1475, John Watson 1476, Robert Carleton 1485-6 and John Burton 1491-2. There is no mention of a Robert Bawdwyn but various members of a Bawdwyn family in Methley do appear in the Thoresby Society Volume XXXV as early as 1379 and in between the years 1470 and 1530 there are many references to the family in the manor rolls. The search for Robert Bawdwyn was extended and became very involved. Mrs Frogley did not limit her search to Methley and found references to a Robert Bawdwyn in various places but it was in the Borthwick Institute at York that she at last found evidence of what she thought to be the right Robert Bawdwyn. In the archi-episcopal registers for the year 1483 there is a list of men who were ordained accolytes on 13th March, among them was Robert Bawdwyn de Methley. As an accolyte the man's name was given with his home village but for the higher orders of sub-deacon, deacon and finally priest every ordinand needed to have a title guaranteeing a source of maintenance until he found clerical employment. This title was most often provided by a religious house. In the list of those ordained sub-deacon on 1st March 1487 we find 'Robertus Bawdewyn ad titulum priori de northferriby', North Ferriby being situated to the west of Hull. Three weeks later on 22nd March 1487 the same name and title appears in the list of those ordained deacon. Finally on 5th April 1488, 'Robertus Bawdewyn ad titulum priori de northferriby' is ordained priest.

Mrs Frogley believed this to be the same Robert Bawdwyn who caused manuscript E.Mus.126 to be made and there is other evidence in her dissertation to support this supposition. It is possible that he took up his duties as chaplain, either parochial or chantry, in Methley Church immediately after his ordination as an accolyte in 1483.

It is not known when or why Robert Bawdwyn commissioned his processional but a possible occasion was the completion of the Waterton Chapel in 1484, dedicated to the Virgin Mary (and presumably superseding an existing Mary altar elsewhere), thus increasing the scope for processions in the church.

It is not known when Robert Bawdwyn died and there is no evidence of what happened to the processional after his death until it was given by a John Newton to the Bodleian Library on 14th June 1658. Mrs Frogley makes the conjecture that Bawdwyn left the manuscript to a fellow chaplain at Methley and eventually it may have passed to the Shann family and remained in Methley. The Shann family was prominent in Methley from the 15th century to the middle of the 19th century. Robert Shann was chaplain of the Waterton Chantry of the Blessed Virgin Mary at Methley in 1535 and 1546, and three years after the dissolution of the Waterton Chantry on 8th February 1549 he became Rector of High Hoyland. He died in 1561 and was probably buried in the crypt of the church at Methley on 17th June 1561.

It may also be possible that John Newton who matriculated at Brasenose College 1622-3 came to know a young man called Anthony Elcocke from Manchester who matriculated at Brasenose in 1623. Elcocke married a woman from Methley in 1637 and was Rector of Methley from 1653 until his death in 1670 so it is possible that Newton had visited Elcocke at Methley, received information about the manuscript and books of historical interest in the hands of a local family and persuaded them to allow the manuscript and books, etc. to be placed in a scholarly collection by Newton.

The Shann family persistently used the same men's Christian names in each generation and as few dates were shown there was room for confusion as to identity but Thomas Shann (son of Richard Shann born 1561) married Prothasie Hollinge in 1616 and had four sons named Richard, *Augustine, Ambrose and Jerome* and a daughter Agnes.

NOTE: Interestingly the names underlined above are shown in the east window of the Waterton Chapel. Equally there is no record of an altar to St Katherine but there is a stained glass window to St Katherine in the south side of the Waterton Chapel.

The Dominical Procession

In a large church with more than one altar a procession was necessary so that the side altars could be sprinkled. The route that such procession would have taken at Methley is not certain but after studying the ground plan of the church at the end of the 15th century an obvious route suggests itself. This, combined with all the pertinent information available from York Use sources, makes a general reconstruction possible.

E Mus. 126 opens with the following rubric:

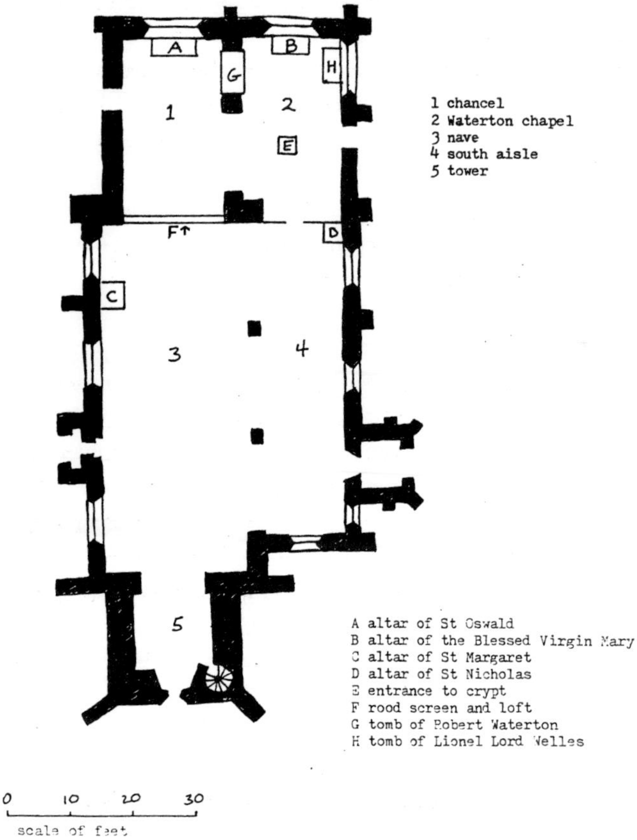

Ground plan of Methley Church at the end of the 15th century

Dominica prima adventus domini ad processionem fiat trina Pulsacio. Denique salis et aque benediccio fiat a sacerdote sacris induto vestibus coram summo altari astantibus turbis et ministris hoc modo sacerdote dicente. 'Adiutorium...'

This tells us that on the first Sunday in Advent (the first day of the liturgical year, used as a paradigm for all ordinary Sundays), the water and salt were blessed at the high altar. After the opening sentences the celebrant pronounced a prayer of exorcism over the salt and then a different one over the water. Thus cleansed, he threw the salt into the water in the form of a cross and mixed them together while saying another prayer. He then intoned the antiphon 'asperges me' and began the sprinkling of the Holy Water. (From Easter Sunday to Trinity Sunday this antiphon would have been replaced with 'Vidi Aquam'.) The sprinkling began at the high altar, then proceeded to any other clergy and assistants. While the celebrant was sprinkling the Holy Water, the choir sang the antiphon 'Asperges me' with its two verses, plus the 'Gloria patri', with the antiphon repeated after each verse. Following other prayers from the high altar the procession began.

At Methley Church it seems most likely that the procession first headed south into the Waterton Chapel, the celebrant sprinkling the altar there and perhaps also the two tomb monuments. The celebrant, presumbly on his own, then went down into the crypt to sprinkle those buried there while the procession was still halted in the Waterton Chapel. The procession would then leave the Waterton Chapel and proceed westward down the south aisle, then eastward up the main aisle. The altars of St Nicholas and St Margaret would have been sprinkled in passing and also any other altars, including that of St Katherine whose position is unknown. The procession then reached the rood screen which separated the chancel from the nave. This screen had a loft, and was decorated with figures of Christ crucified, the Blessed Virgin Mary and St John. According to Kirk it also had an altar associated with it, though the exact location of this altar is not known. At the rood screen (or cross) another versical, response and prayer were said. Having concluded the station at the cross, the procession returned to the choir and mass would then begin.

Often the same material serves for a group of Sundays, such as those between the Sunday after Epiphany and the Purification. Other groups, like the Sundays between the Purification and Septuagesima, have one prayer per Sunday. Obviously the more important the Sunday the more proper items it receives. Certainly the most elaborate and extensive provision is made for Palm Sunday. The rubrics are far from complete, but those which are given, along with the sheer volume of music provided, make it apparent that a splendid Palm Sunday procession took place both inside and outside the church.

Holy Week in general is well provided for in E Mus. 126. Most of the Holy Saturday is given, including the complete 'Exultet' and the prayers for the Blessing of the Font, both with notation. Other major feasts, whether or not on a Sunday, are also well represented.

NOTE: Mrs Frogley's dissertation is printed on 98 A4 sheets, consequently my adaptation of it is very brief. In a letter to Miss Harrison dated 2nd February 1988 Mrs Frogley stated her willingness for an adaptation of her dissertation to be published.

How the Parish of Methley was Formed

The Parish of Methley dates from ancient times, until 8 March 1904 when the Ecclesiastical District of Mickletown was created from the Parish of Methley. The new parish was to consist of that part of the parish of Methley lying to the east of the L.M.S. railway line. Both parishes remained independent until 30 June 1972 when a notice published in the London Gazette by an Order in Council ordered that the parish of Methley and the parish of Mickletown be united to form a new parish which shall be named The Parish of Methley with Mickletown and that the parish church of the parish of Methley shall be the parish church of the new parish.

List of Rectors of Methley

Of earlier rectors of Methley than the following no record has been found.

Date of Institution

1281-1309 WILLIAM DE RADECLYVE, on the presentation of Lady Alesya de Lascy.

1309-1338 THOMAS DE DONCASTRE, on the pres. of Dame Alesia de Lascy.

1338-1358 ROBERT DE IMWORTH, on the pres. of Queen Philippa.

1358-1367 ROBERT DE WALTON, on the pres. of Henry, Duke of Lancaster.

1367-1379 JOHN DE LEDES, pres. by Blanche, Duchess of Lancaster, acting on behalf of her husband, John (of Gaunt), Duke of Lancaster, who was abroad at the time.

1379-1396 WILLIAM DE HAYTON, on the pres. of John (of Gaunt), King of Castell et Legionis.

1396-1400 NICHOLAS DE DAUBENAY, pres. by John (of Gaunt) son of the King of England, Duke of Aquitaine and Lancaster.

1400-1407 WILLIAM DE TURBACKE, pres. by Henry IV, King of England and France, and Lord of Ireland.

1407-1421 JOHN COLNE, pres. by King Henry IV.

1421-1451 ROBERT FLEMYNG. Possibly the son of Robert Flemyng, kt., of Wath and Woodhall, Methley, and brother to Cecily Flemyng, who married Sir Robert Waterton, the founder of the Chantry Chapel.

1451-1452 WILLIAM LYTSTER, pres. by King Henry VI.

1452-1459 THOMAS PASH. pres. by King Henry VI.

1459-1485 JOHN LANCASTER. pres by King Henry VI.

1485-1497 THOMAS BROWNLESS, pres. by Geoffrey Fraunk, esquire of the body (armiger pro corpore) of King Richard III.

1497-1501 THOMAS MEDEFIELD, pres. by King Henry VII.

1501-1538 EDWARD BASSET, pres. by King Henry VII.

1538-1552 HENRY MALLET. No institution record, but his presentation is dated Westminster Palace, March 11, 1537-8. He was apparently the son of a Margaret Dyneley who had married William Mallet of Normanton.

1552-1567 ANTHONY ASKHAM, pres. by King Edward VI.

1567-1591 OTHO HUNT, pres. by Queen Elizabeth I.

1591-1615 TIMOTHY BRIGHT, pres. by Queen Elizabeth I. He was Rector of Barwick-in-Elmet, 1594, holding both livings till his death in 1615. He was the inventor of modern shorthand writing. Buried at St Mary's Church Shrewsbury 8th September 1615.

1615-1618 THOMAS HORNE, pres. by King James I.

1618-1828 HUGO RAMSDEN, pres. by Queen Anne, wife of James I of England.

1628-1649 DANIEL AMBROSE, pres. by King Charles I.

1649-1653 JOHN JOHNSON subscribed, as of Methley, along with many other West Riding Ministers of the Gospel, 6 April 1648, attesting that they were 'patiently awaiting the full establishment of Presbyterial Government in the Church.' He was never Rector, so no institution record of him is found at York, but the minister appointed by Parliament.

1653-1670 ANTHONY ELCOCK, He had married Anne Laburne of Methley 13 July 1637, while Rector of Taxall, Cheshire. Although the Parliament had presented a minister to Methley (John Johnson) who had served against the late King (Charles I) in the war, the parish consisting of loyal subjects, petitioned for leave to choose their own minister, and named Anthony Elcock, who 'left his former living to accept this'.

1670-1686 TOBIAS CONYERS, pres. by King Charles II.

1686-1709 GILBERT ATKINSON, pres. by King James II. The old rectory, commonly known as 'The Parsonage' still standing in Mickletown was built by this rector. Died by the explosion of a gun at Methley.

1709-1750 GEORGE GOODWIN, pres. by Queen Anne.

1750-1780 JOHN SCOTT, pres. by King George II.

1780-1804 JOHN BRIGGS, pres. by King George III.

1805-1841 THE HON. ARCHIBALD HAMILTON CATHCART, pres. by King George III. Also vicar of Kippax 1814-1841. He held the rectory of Methley and the vicarage of Kippax together and resided in Kippax but was buried at Methley.

1841-1898 THE HON. PHILIP YORKE SAVILE, pres. by Queen Victoria. He was the brother of John Charles George 4th Earl of Mexborough.

1898-1921 HENRY ARMSTRONG HALL, pres. by H.M. Queen Victoria. Chaplain in ordinary to King George V.

1921-1934 LUCIUS FREDERICK MOSES BOTTOMLEY SMITH, Bishop Suffragan of Knaresborough, pres. by the Bishop of Ripon and instituted at Methley on 12 August 1921.

1935-1938 PAUL FULCRAND DELACOUR DE LABILLIERE, Bishop Suffragan of Knaresborough, pres. by King George V.

1938-1947 JOHN NORMAN BATEMAN-CHAMPAIN, Bishop Suffragan of Knaresborough, on resig. of the Dean of Westminster (Rt.Rev.P.F.D.de Labilliere) on 2 Feb. 1938. The Bishop collated, the Archdeacon inducted 12 Sept. 1947. The same incumbent was licensed by the Bishop to Mickletown District (and to officiate in the iron church of St.Margaret situate within the limits of the said District), a dispensation having been granted by the Archbishop of Canterbury authorising the Bishop Suffragan of Knaresborough to hold the District of Mickletown in plurality with the benefice of Methley. Pres. by H.M.King George VI in right of his Duchy of Lancaster, on cession of Frederick Northorp, on 17 Mar. 1947.

At some time following the outbreak of war in September 1939 Bishop John must have been seconded for war service because the PCC minutes although they do not refer to the departure of the Bishop are signed by Canon J E Roberts on 23 January 1940. The PCC minutes dated 21 March 1946 refer to the return of the Bishop but Canon Roberts said there was uncertainty about the date. On 25 June 1946 Bishop John signed the PCC minutes of a meeting held on 21 March 1946 and on 30 April 1946 Canon Roberts was in the chair and stated that his last Sunday in charge of the parish would be the 19 May and that Mr Northorp would take services on the following two Sundays and that the Bishop expected to resume duties on Whitsunday. These minutes were signed by Bishop John dated 17 April 1947 but the year must have been 1946. On 25 June 1946 at a PCC meeting Bishop John expressed thanks to Canon John for his work in Methley during his absence and gave an account of his wartime duties. (Canon Roberts on a particular date must have been appointed priest in charge of Methley for the duration of the war).

1952-1957 RALPH EMMERSON, to hold the Rectory of Methley and the District of Mickletown in plurality, by virtue of an Order of the Bishop of the Diocese dated 4 April, 1952 (Pastoral Re-Organisation Measure, 1949), vacant by resig. of the Rt.Rev.John Bateman Champain on 9 Oct. 1948. The Bishop of Ripon instituted and licensed. The Archdeacon of Leeds inducted. The new rector had on 6 Apr. 1949, been licensed as Curate-in-charge of Methley and Mickletown.

1957-1964 CHARLES YOUNG

1964-1970 G. EDWARD EVISON

1970-1979 TERRANCE G MUNROE

1979-1993 MICHAEL WHITTOCK

1993-present GILLIAN R LURIE

Incumbents of Mickletown District

HUBERT STANLEY DARBYSHIRE

FREDERIC NORTHORP

There were a large number of assistant clergy at Methley, the following is a list from 1938.

1938 FRANK LISHMAN
1940 JOHN ERNEST ROBERTS,
1948 RALPH EMMERSON
1950 JOSEPH THORLEY ROE
1954 RICHARD JOHN COOMBS

Coincidences

George Goodwin was Rector of Methley 1709-1750. There is an interesting story connected with Canon Goodwin that is worth relating here. The story is found in the autobiography and correspondence of Mrs Delany, who died in 1788, but whose book was only published in 1861 and consists of six large volumes. The story has since been retold by Mrs A.E. Barr.

"Mrs Delany was acquainted with most of the celebrities of her day, and among her friends was a certain Mrs Vigor, who was the daughter of George Goodwin, Rector of Methley. This lady was first married to Thomas Ward, Consul-General to Russia in 1731, upon whose death she returned to England. Mrs Ward, as she then was, travelled from St. Petersburg by sledge, passing through Livonia and Courland, and at length reached Memel. Here, though in a very delicate state of health, she could only find accommodation in a small inn which at the time was full of soldiers. A gentleman who was staying at the same inn, in whose company Mrs Ward had travelled, went out to transact some business and in course of conversation mentioned her plight. One of those to whom he was speaking said that he knew of some good lodgings and would see to the matter at once. An hour later Mrs Ward received a letter from a Mr Meyer, placing at her disposal such apartments as she required. Having sent her servant for a coach, Mrs Ward proceeded to the house named. Here she found a large mansion in which the best rooms were prepared for her and an excellent supper provided. The next morning, when Mrs Ward was at breakfast, a gentleman appeared, accompanied by a younger man who seemed to be his son. She immediately rose from her seat and told her visitor how grateful she felt for his kindness. Mr Meyer replied, 'All I do is a return: it is in consequence of favours received, so that your debt is cancelled before it is incurred. You must know that I have a great esteem for the English nation in general, but I have obligations to particular members of it which enhance my regard. You see here this young man, who is my son; he was last year upon his travels in England and passing down from the north towards the capital he was taken very ill. His disorder was so violent that he was compelled to take refuge wherever he could find shelter; and this was not easily procured, for his disease was the smallpox, and he was housed in a very dirty inn, where he must have perished for want of care and accommodation. A certain gentleman of the place heard that a stranger was ill and he was so humane as to make him a visit. When he found the nature of his disorder he ordered him to be wrapped up securely and conveyed in his own coach to his own house. To this gentleman's goodness and to the goodness of those about him my son owes his life, and I am indebted for my son. Hence I make it a rule that no person from England shall come to this place without meeting from me every mark of regard I can possibly show.'

'Pray, sir,' asked Mrs Ward, 'whereabouts was it in the north of England that you met with this civility?'

'It was', said he, 'at a place called Methley, near Leeds in Yorkshire.'

'And pray, may I ask what was the gentleman's name?'

'His name, Madam, was Goodwin.'

'Sir,' said Mrs Ward, 'it was my own father!'

Needless to say, father and son were delighted, and Mrs Ward stayed on until her health was fully restored, when she passed back through Hanover to Holland and thence by ship to England."

ST MARGARET'S CHURCH, MICKLETOWN

Late in the 19th century steps were taken to provide Mickletown with a church and an incumbent of its own.

Conveyance, dated 5th December 1882, was made by Philip York Savile, Rector of Methley, to the Ecclesiastical Commissioners for England for a piece of land in Mickletown as a site for an intended new church to be called St. Mary Magdalene Church, Mickletown.

The Ecclesiastical District of Mickletown was separated for church purposes from the ancient parish of Methley by Order in Council dated March 8 1904. The district embraced that portion of the parish lying east of the then Midland Railway line. The Reverend H Stanley Darbyshire was the first incumbent, presented by the Chancellor of the Duchy of Lancaster.

Of the church envisaged in 1882 only the foundations were laid. A report dated January 1902 shows that the foundations of the piers of the nave were found to be defective and would need to be rebuilt since they were resting on light vegetable soil, unsuitable for the foundations.

From 7 January 1900 in the Church Institute, Main Street leased by the Earl of Mexborough to the Rector of Methley, services were held on Sunday evenings on the upper floor, the lower portion being used as a Working Men's Club, later known as the Methley Mine Workers' Welfare Institute presently called Ashlands and used as a nursing home.

In 1905 the church, a galvanised corrugated iron structure lined with wood, was built at a cost of £287. The church was dedicated by the Bishop of Ripon on 3 August 1905 to St. Margaret, it is not clear why the name was changed from St. Mary Magdalene.

On 12 September 1947 the Rector of Methley, John Norman Bateman-Champain, was authorised to hold the district of Mickletown in plurality with the benefice of Methley following the cession of Frederick Northorp as incumbent in Mickletown although both parishes remained independent until 30 June 1972 when the Queen in Council ordered that the parishes of Methley and Mickletown be united to form The Parish of Methley with Mickletown.

In 1980 St. Margaret's Church faced expensive repairs, replacement, or closure and it was decided that the church, but not St. Margaret's Hall, be closed and the land sold. The last service was held on Easter Day 1982 and demolition started on 26 April 1982.

The incumbents of Mickletown lived in the house in Pinfold Lane which was built for the Misses Dennison until 1948 when it became the present Working Men's Club.

Main Street, Mickletown, Methley.

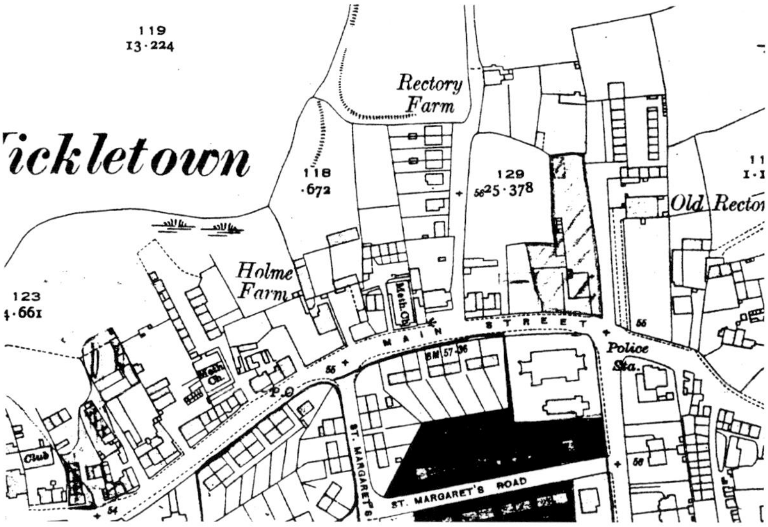

Interior of St. Margaret's Church, Mickletown

St. Margaret's Church, Mickletown

THE METHODIST CHURCHES IN METHLEY

The Methley Society is first mentioned in Leeds Circuit Quarterly Plan of 1821. Plan of travelling and local preachers in Leeds Circuit belonging to Primitive Methodists known also by the name of Ranters.

Originally there were five Methodist churches in Methley, three in Main Street, Mickletown, one at Methley Junction and one at Scholey Hill. Of these churches there were three sects, Primitive, United Free Methodist and Wesleyan.

The Primitive Methodist Chapel, known as the Bethel Chapel built in Main Street, Mickletown at a cost of £600, opened in 1866. It was a large brick built two storey building with a gallery, balcony and large school room. It was closed as a chapel in the late 1940s, became a small clothing workshop and later still became a small electrical workshop. It was demolished in the late 1950s or early 1960s.

The Zion Church of the United Free Methodists was built in 1863 on land in Holmes Yard bought for £100, the men building the church themselves. Prior to this services were held in the slaughterhouse of the local butcher, Mr Joseph Spink, the men washing out the slaughterhouse beforehand. It is reported that in the early years it was necessary to arrive an hour before evening service to secure a seat and over 100 young men and women attended Sunday afternoon bible classes. Following a decline in members it closed 1959/60 and became a building contractor's workshop and later still a car repair workshop.

The Wesleyan Chapel, Main Street is the only survivor of the five Methodist chapels in Methley. It opened June/July 1888 though baptism records date some 30 years earlier. It is reported that the first meetings were held in houses and also in the present Mickletown Post Office. It is a two storey building with gallery and balcony. Because of a dwindling congregation and high cost of heating a false ceiling was built to cut off the upper floor. In 1988 there was a month of celebrations for the centenary of the church.

Methley Junction Primitive Methodist Chapel was built in 1875 to accommodate 200 people and closed during the 1930s. However in my research for this book I noted that there is an entry in Henry Briggs Property Valuation Book dated 1871 showing rent of £83 being received from the chapel at Methley Junction.

Wesleyan Methodist Chapel, Main Street - Centenary June 1988

Scholey Hill United Methodist Church was a single storey building converted from a smithy and certified for worship on 29 November 1876. A Mexborough Estate rent book shows that the Methodist Society paid rent of £1.10.0 in the year 1855. The building was well used and maintained by its members but falling numbers, 16 in 1960, lead to its closure in 1969/70. The building was later demolished.

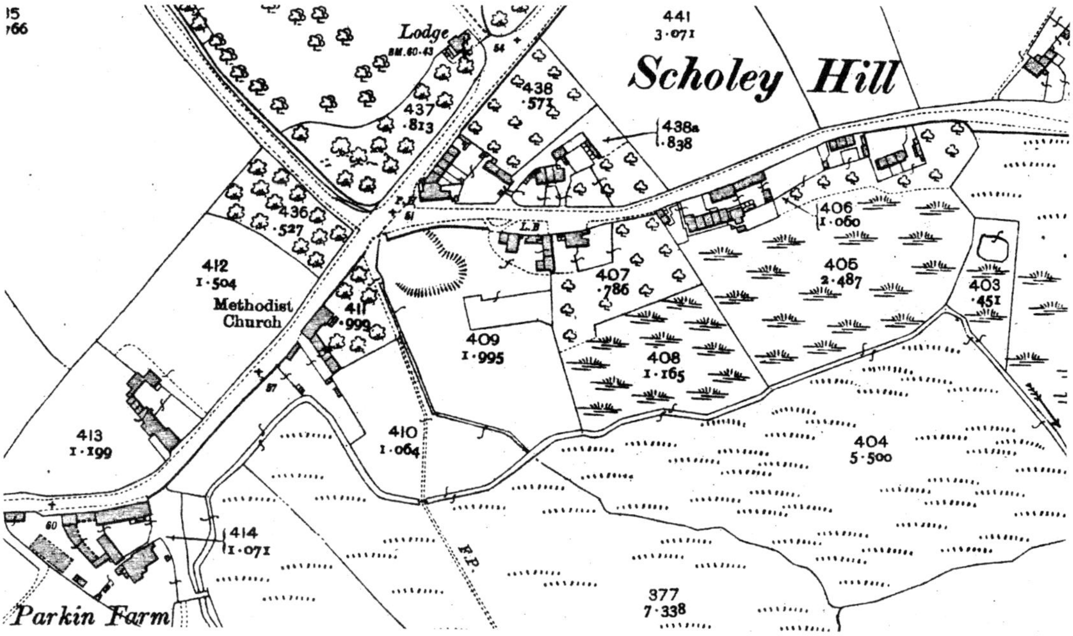

Our Lord he gave us this command
'Go to the world and make your stand.
Take my love to all the world
Let the banner of faith be flown unfurled'.

His followers then to all lands went.
In mission were their days all spent.
The Gospel spread from land to land
By word and deed did the faith expand.

We know not when the faith came here –
The history is most unclear –
But slowly in those early days
Voices were raised in Christian praise.

The town of Methley was no exception
The people knew this was no deception.
Jesus died and rose again,
Methley folk he knew by name.

This new faith was truly great,
It taught to all that love, not hate,
Was to be lived in imitation
Of Jesus, who cared not for men's station.
Rich or poor, free man or slave
For all of them his life he gave.

A king there was in ancient times
Oswald by name, of northern climes.
In battle he was strong and brave
And to our church his name he gave.

King Oswald was a Christian true
Though his soldiers were a motley crew.
To preach the faith, King Oswald sent
For monks to teach just what it meant.

St Aidan came from Lindisfarne,
An Irishman with Gaelic charm.
But he could scarce be understood –
His grasp of English was not good!

Oswald became a good true mate,
For Aidan he would oft translate.
Hark now and learn, if know ye would
How easily things are misunderstood.

SCENE: Oswald and Aidan come to Methley.

O These people, Aidan, are good country folk. Their land is rich. See their sheep.

A I can see no ship. We are far from the sea and it would take long to build a ship and take it to the sea to sail.

O No! Not ship. Sheep – those white woolly things on four legs.

A Oh those. I thought you meant …

O (interrupting) Yes, yes! I know what you thought. But these sheep – do they remind you of Jesus telling Peter that he must feed them?

A You don't expect me to feed all this lot, do you? I thought you wanted me to teach the faith to people.

O Yes, I do. And the people here are hungry for your teaching about Jesus. I want you to feed these people with the word of God.

A Right. Gather round, folks. (A little group gathers)

Now then, you stand on rich ground – the king said so. You have sheep and goats; you have fields and crops. All these were given by God.

PEOPLE: God? We thought it was the Lord of the Manor who let us have them – and for a lot of rent, too. And you try and dig this land – not far down; it's hard, black stone.

A Stone? Stone me!!! (The people start to pick up stones). No, no, put them down. Listen to me – everything you have here is given by God – even this black stone. It's precious as gold.

A This black stone, dear Aidan and dear people, is called coal. It is very valuable. It can be dug up and burned for warmth. King **Arthur** knew all about coal. He knew its value. He said it will build **banks** and no one could **budge** him from that.

A There, what did I tell you. Pure gold, black gold.

NARRATOR: And now you know why we have St Aidan's pit in the village of Methley. Gold, coal – sounds much the same, doesn't it!

The word of God took hold of folk
Who gladly bore their Saviour's yoke.
They built a church to honour their king
To Oswald and Jesus they did sing.

This faith made sense to common folk –
It taught, no matter what the yoke
Of servitude to man on earth
Their freedom came through Jesus' birth.

O'er many years fierce battles raged
As to and fro the wars were waged.
Methley became a royal manor
Given through fighting, lies and clamour.

Though Methley lies in Yorkshire's heart
They fiercely fought the Lancastrian part.
The crown of England was at stake
And Methley men full part did take.
In Wars of Roses, white and red

Some names live on from those dark days
In books and tombs, and Shakespeare's plays.
Waterton and Welles are only two
Of those whose names are known to you.

What of the clergy of yesteryear?
A motley bunch that is quite clear.
Some stayed long, though others short,
But all the faith to Methley taught.

Timothy Bright had a mixed career.
There's quite a tale to his time here.
A medical man, he was given to write,
And of his flock had little sight.

Bright wrote a book on melancholy
And other works about man's folly.
The first shorthand was invented by him
So Pitman's claim could be quite thin.
The fields were strewn with many dead.

But Bright was not a pastor good;
Amongst the folk his name was mud.
He even once was taken to court
For catechism that was not taught.

Many others held the cure
Of souls of Methley, bad and pure.
A royal living, 'twas a plum
And rich incumbents here did come.

We know this was a wealthy place
From what was charged in local rates.
The poll tax levied on Methley village
Was tantamount to rape and pillage!

O no, our Maggie was not the first
To levy such a tax – there's worse
Than her to raise their money
By charging levies that were not funny!

Come onwards now to later days
When other churches sang God's praise.
The Church of England held no sway
With those who travelled another way.

Although ordained in the C of E
The Wesley boys new ways did see.
For John and Charles were very strict
Observers of their Lord's edict.

These men they studied night and day
To learn more of the Lord's true way.
The C of E was rich and lazy
To Wesley; their observance hazy.

A group there formed around these men
Whose ordered prayer and study then
Became known as the method true
And so the group just grew and grew.

To Methley came this Methodism.
The Christian church was now in schism.
The rich to C of E still rode
The poor walked to chapel down the road.

Some were strict, others less so
And other chapels began to grow.
As people more of Jesus knew
Their ways of worship also grew.

In years gone by, it was a sin
If church you entered not within.
Fines were levied, week by week,
On those who Jesus did not seek.

And so our faith became a part
Of every man and woman's heart.
To worship God and keep his laws
Was normal and without a pause.

'Twas late in 1800s here
That slowly it became quite clear
That Mickletown, though there be much land
Had no Church of England near at hand.

Plans were made, foundations laid
For another church that could be made
To save the folk who lived down there
From travelling to St Oswald's fair.

But the best-laid plans of mice and men
Were found to be frustrated then.
The land it simply would not do
For putting on a building new.

But a church was really needed there
Of lighter weight, that the land could bear.
The 'tin hut' of St Margaret's came
And quickly made itself a name.

No pretty sight from outside this –
Yet inside you could find much bliss.
A lovely church, in simple taste,
And many folk to there did haste.

St Margaret's stood for many a year
In worshippers hearts it was most dear
But 20 years or so ago
St Margaret's just had to go.

The cost of keeping in good repair
Had grown beyond what was right or fair.
The church came down, the land was sold.
No longer would the bell be tolled.

In time the chapels too had found
That being together was more sound.
And so today we've just churches two
For worship that is good and true.

In Methley there are names of streets
Commemorating some men's feats.
The name of Savile is well known
For pit and road and fortunes grown.

A Savile was the rector here
By people he was held most dear.
For 50 years he held the post.
In years he served here quite the most.

Robert Hollings in days of yore
Gave money to the local poor.
It is to him we owe the pews
That at St Oswald's we do use.

The Cedars was the home for years
Of Embletons, who, like their peers
Gave of their wealth to needy poor
And those who called at their back door.

St Oswald's to their hearts was dear
Especially in music clear.
An organ and in hymns did raise
Their voice in hymns of gladsome praise.

And so we come to present days
Through years of singing ceaseless praise
To him who died for me and you
And gave the faith for ever true.

For two Millennia he's ruled
And though the love of many's cooled
God's love burns bright in Methley still
In lives of those who do his will.

We hope that this, our little history
Has touched your hearts to bring the mystery
Of God's great love shown down the ages
To men and women, fools and sages.

And should you feel, on Sunday next,
An urge to hear a bible text
Just come and join the worship true
In church or chapel we'll welcome you.

Composed by the Rev. G Lurie, Rector of Methley, 2000.

Methley Millennium celebration, Monday 29th May 2000.